CONTENTS

PREFACE

Of all of the mighty forces in motion upon this blue, jewel-like planet, the sea is perhaps the most awe inspiring, captivating and vital to life. Man's fascination with the sea is as old as his own existence. Since the dawn of time, humans have sustained themselves by means of it, explored its oceans and channels and even sought to master the great watery deep.

Who could not admit to delighting at the sight of a sparkling, sun drenched bay with the happy cries of children playing in its shallow turquoise waters? Likewise, who could deny the allure of the very same water from the vantage point of a cliff top, at the height of a raging gale? The roar of the wind, the stinging rain and the thundering might of the seas crashing upon the dark rocks; the sea in all its moods is something we are drawn to instinctively.

Our love affair with the sea goes hand in hand with our natural fear of it. In my view, anyone who claims not to fear its power and unpredictable nature cannot genuinely claim to know it. Indeed, those who fail to respect the sea put themselves in danger of having their lives claimed by it. Nevertheless, our irresistible desire to pit our abilities against the forces at work on our planet and revel in the business of challenging their ultimate supremacy is just one aspect of what being alive is all about.

Boats in all their forms reflect these fundamental truths and even human nature itself. Boats designed for pleasure, boats designed for the purpose of sustaining and enriching life, boats built to satisfy man's quest to explore the unknown, boats built to conquer other men: whatever the purpose, a vessel's makeup reveals what lies within the heart of those who fashioned it. Through the centuries, as sail was replaced by the tell-tail smokestack and twisting propeller shaft, this transformation was a direct result of man's desire to go faster, develop more efficient means of travel and continue to trade unabated – no matter what the prevailing conditions.

For many, the business of taking on the sea is a matter of necessity. Being a professional offshore mariner means there are occasions where there simply is no choice. For such men, the seas they ply far from land may well have to be challenged, even fought with if the survival of the vessel and its crew are to be gained. For those who choose to risk their own lives for the sake of others, their decision to put to sea in the face of grave danger is likely to have been made long before they don their all-weather gear and step up onto the heaving deck of a lifeboat. For others, like myself, there is a choice and the decision might be dictated by such 'needs' as a pressing itinerary, a desire to 'push the envelope' or even the little white puff from a starting pistol held aloft from the deck of a club tender.

This book is not written with a view to glamorising gung-ho powerboating activities, and neither does it promote risk taking. On the contrary, its aim is to highlight the true strength of the sea, to engender respect for it and to share an unrivalled collection of real life accounts and first hand experiences, as well as theoretical fact and practical know-how. All this against a backdrop of different skill sets, hull designs and sea types.

When lying in bed at night listening to the wild wind shaking the window frames, one's mind might try to imagine the black reality of the storm raging at sea and those who may be battling against it – even fighting for their lives. Whatever the films may show, a full gale or storm at sea rarely generates orderly waves marching in impressive formation across a predictable seascape. On the contrary, truly adverse seastates equal chaos, little or no visibility, deafening noise, disorientation, fatigue and sickness, raw fear and the need for massive effort on the part of a crew to perform even the simplest function. As in the case of other disciplines involving the elements and our environment, good seamanship and the ability to survive will likely be down to good preparation, advance knowledge, an intimate understanding of our vessel and its equipment plus, most importantly, a steel-like determination not to give up.

If this book could be said to possess just one lesson that could be drawn from its pages, I feel it would be this. Don't go looking for trouble unnecessarily. By all means learn how to develop your abilities, raise your threshold and gain a true knowledge of the sea's unique characteristics and of course your boat in relation to these, but in doing so, don't ever take her for granted. The sea may be beautiful but she is also a deadly mistress.

No doubt you have heard of the excelling value of Plan B? This involves always seeking to have an alternative up your sleeve if the unexpected strikes. This is no less crucial for those venturing to sea – whether the motivation is for work or pleasure. Be it a second port of call, the lee of an island, a changing/favourable tide, an EPIRB or a friend at home next to the phone who knows your passage plan, always take care to have that Plan B in reserve. Never let haste or the excitements of putting to sea rob you of the opportunity to think through what you might do if things go wrong. The latter is dependant upon your experience as well as your ability to estimate genuine risk. But only the fool puts to sea ill-prepared or with a spirit of 'it won't happen to me' overriding his thoughts and actions. Having a realistic approach to powerboating involves not only recognising a duty of care to yourself, but also to the lives and welfare of those in our care; our crew, our family and those who might need to come to the rescue if things go awry.

The sea sustains and enriches us, it fills us with wonder and, thanks to modern technology, many more people can now appreciate it for all that it truly is. Well-found powered craft, of the type described in this book, no matter how advanced, follow in the tradition of all the best vessels before them. The skill sets needed to gain the most from them may be different from those needed for the designs of the past (and this also applies to sail) but the rewards and challenges to be enjoyed are no less substantial.

In conclusion: to those who have contributed so generously to the compiling of this book I give my unreserved thanks. To all readers of Heavy Weather Powerboating, may this book serve you well and add to your safekeeping and enjoyment of your times on the water. May a fair wind and a following sea be yours to enjoy!

Hugo Montgomery-Swan

THE HUMAN FACTOR

HEROES OF THE GREAT STORM

BY IAN SKIDMORE

In this first chapter we reflect on the early forms of powered craft as employed by the RNLI. This account not only highlights the skill and courage of the coxwain concerned, but also sheds light on the ancestry of modern powered craft.

It drives on with a courage, which is stronger than the storm.
It drives on with a mercy, which does not quail in the presence of death.
It drives on as a truth, a symbol and a testimony that man has been created in the image of God and that valour and virtue have not perished.

Winston Churchill, speaking at the RNLI's centenary celebrations in 1924

The advancements in marine technology over the last 50 years have been significant. Major developments in electronics and computerisation, not to mention modern materials and construction methods, have revolutionised many aspects of powerboating and lifesaving. Elsewhere we look in depth at the effect these advancements are having on the leisure and professional craft of today, but first, let us remind ourselves of just how far powered-craft technology has come since the early post war years.

The UK's Royal National Lifeboat Institution has been a very great contributor to the science of designing boats for use in extreme sea states. In fact, from the early double-ended pulling boats of the 19th century to the technological wizardry of the RNLI's very latest Tamar Class (a design of lifeboat we feature elsewhere in the book), the Institution has consistently sought to push the boundaries of powered excellence. Of course, no matter how able a vessel may ultimately be, its ability to succeed in the face of severe conditions remains largely dependent upon the abilities and good judgement of the person standing at its helm. Indeed, this factor is no better illustrated than in the following account involving the crew of the Moelfre lifeboat and their heroic coxswain, Dick Evans. Here, the author Ian Skidmore affords us the opportunity to read a key extract from his book *Lifeboat VC*, a documented and alluring account of the life and times of this renowned RNLI Gold Medal lifeboat cox.

'In the Anglesey fishing village of Moelfre, where houses gather like a frown on a headland overlooking Liverpool Bay, the people are used to wild weather.

Over a hundred and fifty years ago, on 25 October 1859, when the fiercest gales in living memory had lashed the coasts of Britain, Moelfre had been hit by the worst of them. The first shipping to be caught had been the sailing ships of the Channel fleet at exercise off the Eddystone. Gusts of over 100mph sent them sliding into the troughs of mountainous waves. That was at 3pm. At 8pm the storm, which by this time had torn away coastal embankments and chewed up railway lines in Devon and Cornwall, reached Anglesey.

Outside Holyhead harbour the iron paddle steamer *Great Eastern* was soon in danger; inside, ships sank at their moorings or were smashed into a flotsam of broken spars. The next day an even wilder storm hit Liverpool Bay. Ships dragged their anchors and were hurled on to rocks; at Flint a factory was levelled when its chimney was blown down. Liverpool Observatory recorded the highest-ever wind force – 28lb to the square foot – and the sea level rose 4ft. The Meteorological Office recorded the gale as 'a complete horizontal hurricane'; but, at Moelfre, Charles Dickens was one of many reporters who described the events in more harrowing terms. For it was there that the worst disaster of those terrible two days occurred. In a force 12 gale, when the winds gusted at over 100mph, the auxiliary steam clipper *Royal Charter* in passage from the Australian goldfields, was drawn onto the rocks outside the village, within sight of her home port of Liverpool. The vessel had brought her passengers, mostly miners returning home with their gold, halfway round the world when she sank with the loss of 450 lives.

During the storm 133 ships were sunk and 90 damaged; 800 lives were lost – twice as many as had been lost at sea during the whole of the previous year. The storm has always been known to seamen as the Royal Charter gale; every year, a service of remembrance is held in Llanallgo Church, where those bodies which were recovered from the wreck are buried.

Among the congregation on 26 October 1959 were the men of Moelfre lifeboat, led by their 54-year-old coxswain Richard (Dick) M Evans. As they left the church after the service and walked down the path between the graves, Dick turned to his wife, Nansi, a farmer's daughter who was always upset by this commemoration of tragedy at sea. 'Don't worry,' he comforted her, 'We'll never have to launch the lifeboat in seas like that.'

He was to be proved wrong within a mere 24 hours, for the wind had been blowing hard all night and by the morning it was a full gale.

Donald Murley Francis, an engineering fitter who was second coxswain of the lifeboat, had been worried since he left his cottage on 27 October. A seaman all his life, he reacted to weather like a scientific instrument. A tiny, darkly Celtic man, with eyebrows like angle-irons, he moved like a ship's cat. At 10.30am, an 80mph gale was blowing and he came to a decision; leaving the factory, he turned his steps towards the village. He knew he would be needed.

Burly Evan Owen, greying and merry-eyed, was at work at the lifeboat station from early in the morning. He had been the station mechanic since 1946, and, apart from Dick Evans, was the only member of the crew employed full-time by the Royal National

The **Edmund and Mary Robinson** *underway.* © ***RNLI/Graham Farr archives***

Lifeboat Institution. He was usually to be found in the minute engine-room of the lifeboat, polishing, inspecting, testing his engines. A wartime RAF mechanic, he knew instinctively that lives depended on his skill.

Hugh Owen, the bowman, had been with Dick Evans since they both pulled an oar on the sailing lifeboat. Although never a deep-sea man, he was an expert in a small boat. A stone mason by trade, he had been obliged by lack of work to take a job as a road foreman with Anglesey council. Almost at the moment Murley Francis walked out of the factory gates that morning, Hugh Owen said goodbye to his council road gang and walked the two miles to the village. At his side was another council employee, Hugh Jones, who had never been a member of the crew.

Dick Evans, Murley Francis, Evan Owen and Hugh Owen made a formidable team bonding their individual strengths with reciprocal respect. Dick Evans would often say that if Murley, Evan and Hugh were with him he would take the lifeboat to hell and back. He was shortly to get the chance.

Dick Evans was the archetypal seafaring man. With a healthy complexion, clear blue eyes, broad shoulders, a 44in chest and hands like crane grabs, he stood 5ft 9in tall and had the quick rolling walk taught by a lifetime on wet decks. That morning he was helping Nansi lay the places for lunch in the kitchen of their semi-detached home on the outskirts of Moelfre. From time to time he glanced out of the window as the gale worsened. He knew that the lifeboat was certain to be called out and the thought worried him.

To a coxswain his boat is a personal possession – a passion even. Over the years he learns how she will react to every turn of the weather or malice of tide. He needs to know whether she will take a beam sea and how she would run before a gale. The best cox is the one who eliminates as many risks as he can and then faces bravely those which remain. But, only the day before, the 42ft, Watson-class *Watkin Williams* – the boat Dick had commanded for three years – had gone for servicing to the boatyard at Beaumaris, several miles round the coast. His only experience at sea with the reserve lifeboat, *Edmund and Mary Robinson*, was moored, and all the way he had been nagged by what Commander Dutton, the RNLI Chief Inspector, had told him on the telephone. 'She's given a great deal of trouble during the service. Do your best with her and telephone me the moment you reach Beaumaris, whatever time of day or night.'

They had cast off from Pwllheli at 7am into Bardsey Sound. Almost at once the 6-knot tide turned against them and, despite two 45hp engines, the boat barely managed to creep through the next stretch of water between Bardsey Island and the mainland. At Caernarfon, Dick decided to wait for the tide to drop before tackling the 'Swellies', a stretch of rock-strewn channel in the Menai Strait which extends for a mile between the Britannia Tubular Bridge in the west and the Menai Suspension Bridge in the east. It was 8pm before they moored the lifeboat on a buoy at Beaumaris.

The passage had taken 13 hours but Dick still knew very little about the new boat except that in her handling she was totally different from the *Watkin Williams*. Twenty three years older, the *Edmund and Mary Robinson* had none of the then 'modern' navigational aids of his usual boat. Dick would be uneasy until he had the feel of her.

At 11.50am on the morning of 27 October, the telephone rang and Dick went into the hall to answer it. It was Captain Owen Roberts, a retired ship's master who was volunteer duty coastguard at Moelfre watchtower. 'There's a ship dragging her cable in the bay,' he said. 'It doesn't look good. She was sheltering from last night's south-wester but the wind is veering rapidly to the north and she's been caught. She's being blown on to the rocks. All the other ships that were in the bay last night have managed to get out to sea, but she's trapped. She's the *Hindlea* out of Cardiff, 506-tonner. In ballast from Manchester to Newport.'

Essential information exchanged, Dick put the phone down and went back into the kitchen. 'Got a service,' Dick told Nansi briefly. 'Have to go.'

Nansi was a handsome, happy woman with a captivating laugh, but there was no trace of it as she watched Dick walk away. The moment he closed the front door Dick knew that he faced the most difficult service of his career. In forty years at sea he had never known such a wind. It was a full gale from the north; 90mph, he judged, and still increasing. Blowing from the sea to the shore, it gave the worst possible conditions for a launch, Dick thought, as he struggled, leaning on the wind, to the boat-house. Slates torn from the roofs smashed at his feet; they had the cutting edge of an axe and often he had to dodge as one hurtled towards him. From village barns, balls of hay bowled down the street like tumble-weed whilst tentacles of seaweed torn from the rocks whirled over his head like airborne octopuses to land in the guttering of houses.

From Dick's house the road drops gently as it curves round the bay; then it climbs the headland to run through the upper village. There a path leaves it and follows the line of the cliff top to the lifeboat station with its slipway to the sea. When he left the shelter of the cottages on the eastern face of the headland the full force of the gale struck him and for the only time that day he was grateful it was blowing on-shore – from any other quarter it would have swept him from the cliff top on to the rocks 30ft below.

The sea was frightening. As far as the horizon it had become a moving mountain range of grey water. Waves bigger than he had ever seen, some higher than houses, scrambled white crested over each others' backs. He began the slow struggle along the cliff top to the lifeboat station, dragging himself hand over hand along the iron railing at the edge.

Captain Roberts was waiting for him, sheltering under a wall. He looked anxious.

'I hate having to send you out in this, Dick,' he said. 'But that ship will soon be driven on to the rocks and once she gets into the breakers you won't be able to get near her.'

Murley, Evans, Owen and Jones were already in the boathouse. As Dick pushed open the door, the roar of the wind was muffled by the sound of the lifeboat engines. There was little hope of rounding up a full crew; telephone wires were down all over the island, and maroons would be useless in this weather. His glance fell on Hugh Jones. He had never been to sea in a lifeboat, even on exercise, but Dick needed every hand he could muster.

'Will you volunteer?'

The reply was equally brief. 'Of course,' Hugh Jones said and reached out for a life-jacket.

Each man knew that to take a small lifeboat totally unfamiliar to them into such seas was dangerous in the extreme. A man caught in a wild storm at sea has two choices; he can be brave or he can be cowardly. A special sort of courage is needed, however, to leave a safe home, walk down a village street and step deliberately into a situation of grave danger. These five men had taken that step and they would not turn back.

Dick clambered up the ladder on to the deck of the lifeboat and lashed himself to the wheel, which was corded to give a surer grip.

'Let's go boys,' he said. One by one the crew followed him aboard.

'Check each other's life-jackets,' he ordered. 'Make sure they are properly fastened.'

He watched them tying the holding tapes; the jackets would be of little use in the seas they were going to meet, but there was reassurance in the familiar routine. By now the gale was gusting to 104mph. An identical wind had driven the *Royal Charter* on to the rocks a century earlier. That wreck, below low water mark, was half a mile along the cliffs from the lifeboat station where Dick and his skeleton crew of four were about to put to sea.

Even in calm weather the ride down the slipway is heart-stopping. As the *Edmund and Mary Robinson* raced through the open doors the waves reached up to drag at her. She hit the water like a bomb, submerging her bow completely in the boiling sea.

Instantly she righted herself and the crew scrambled about the deck, hauling up the radio mast.

The propellers bit into the water and the first cloud of spray, like shattered glass, was flung into Dick's face. He stood behind the inadequate protection of a low screen, bracing himself against the padded back-rest. As always in the first moment of service, Dick prayed. Unless some power outside himself came to his aid, he and his crew were dead men. He had learned his seamanship from his grandfather, who had passed on the accumulated sea lore of centuries, but not even he had told him how to cope with 40ft waves coming from every point of the compass. When he prayed, Dick felt strength flowing into his arms and he was to need it. The words of the prayer, like all the commands in the boat, were Welsh: 'O Arglwydd Arwain Fi...Please God Guide Me.'

Dick was not afraid of the lifeboat sinking, but when they left the shelter of land he watched the slow run of each wave growing bigger with every yard and towering above sullen deeps and he knew it was in real danger of capsizing or being completely overwhelmed. Modern lifeboats, it is claimed, will right themselves in seven seconds in any seas. Older boats, like the *Robinson*, are good sea boats but not self-righting. Beam seas slammed on to her iron ribs, half turning her over. The radio mast touched the water and the men under the canopy were thrown into a tangled heap of sea boots and oilskins.

One moment the lifeboat would be climbing almost vertically up a 30ft wave, briefly seesawing on the crest, and the next she plunged into a trough. Each mountainous wave rose to an upward curl that threatened to engulf them. The impact of a second wave could send the *Robinson* somersaulting. Dick ordered acceleration to full revs on each crest, hoping the momentum would carry the boat to the peak of the next. Up and down she went, like a switchback car. Each time the prow of the boat buried itself in a trough, the men feared they would never resurface, but somehow they always did. Her deck canting, water thundering on the iron canopy, the lifeboat ploughed on through the maelstrom. To Dick, lashed to the wheel, drenched to the skin and blinded by foam and scud whenever he raised his head above the windscreen, it seemed they would never reach the coaster.

The *Hindlea* was less than half a mile from the slipway but it was an hour before they saw her. Dulas Bay, a sand-and-shell-bottom anchorage, was safe in southerly gales, but the gale blowing from the north was forcing the coaster inexorably into the breakers. She was lying to her starboard anchor in 8 fathoms of water. Every attempt by the crew to get to the fo'c's'le to put out the forward anchor had been defeated by the heavy seas crashing over her decks. She was heeling sharply and her engines were straining the single-anchor cable to breaking point. As the lifeboat crew watched, the 100-fathom cable whipped clear of the rough seas and the coaster was propelled towards the jagged plateau of rocks. The lifeboatmen could do nothing until the *Hindlea* skipper, Roland Chipchase, a 54-year-old Tynesider, ordered his crew of seven to abandon ship.

As they waited they played a violent game of pat-a-cake to bring life back into their frozen hands and Dick beat his palms against the corded wheel. With the tide setting to the south-south-east, it was a constant battle to keep the *Robinson* head to sea on the starboard beam of the coaster. At last, at 1.55pm, an hour and a half after the lifeboat had taken up her station; the order was given to abandon ship. By now she was inside the 5-fathom line within 200 yards of the rocks and huge seas were breaking over her decks. The crew edged along the port side of the poop deck, clear of the round of the coaster's stern.

Edging towards the *Hindlea*, Dick wished he could have put out a drogue; but there was too little sea-room astern. The drogue, a conical sea anchor on a 10-fathom cable, would have kept the *Robinson* head on to the breaking sea and taken some of the crippling strain from his arms as he fought with the wheel. His strength alone could not hold them stable. He ordered maximum revs, for as soon as speed was reduced his boat

The wreck of the Hindlea *following the day of the Great Storm.* © *RNLI*

was thrown back by the seas. Now he put her on the lee of the *Hindlea*, but the coaster was tossing so wildly that he found himself coming up on the weather side.

Suddenly, through the white cloud of spray, he saw a glint of metal and felt his heart somersault. The violent pitching of the coaster had lifted her stern clear of the sea and her propellers, 9ft from tip to tip, were cutting through the air only 10ft above the bow of the lifeboat. In that same moment a snarling escarpment of water hit the *Robinson*. Dick felt the turbulence of air from the propellers as the blade came within inches of his head. Then the *Robinson* was sent rolling on her beam-ends, her mast disappearing under the water. Using every scrap of skill to bring the lifeboat under control, Dick fought with the wheel, an insistent voice bursting in his head; 'It's the end. She's capsizing.'

Incredibly the *Robinson* did not capsize. Engines screaming at full revs, fighting the pull of the sea, she answered to the helm. A second wave, smaller than the first, righted her and, her deck shuddering, she slammed against the steel plates of the *Hindlea*. One of the crew, bolder than the rest, jumped from her poop and landed with a crash of sea boots on the lifeboat. Ignoring the dangerous pitching of the deck which every moment threatened to catapult him into the sea, Hugh Owen dashed out from the canopy and dragged the seaman to safety.

As the sea carried the *Robinson* clear of the ship, Dick realized that the only way they could hope to rescue the crew was to repeat the dangerous manoeuvre. He would have to bring the boat back under the propellers and hold her by the ship's side long enough to give the men on board an opportunity to drop into the lifeboat.

The second approach almost ended in disaster. On her run in, the *Robinson* was caught by the gale and suspended in mid-air, level with the deck of the *Hindlea*. Dick could have reached out and touched the white, frightened faces of her crew as the *Robinson* raced past, before crashing into a trough. The next attempt would have to be made when the *Hindlea* once more heeled to port and the lifeboat could take advantage of the meagre shelter of her poop.

Ten times the *Robinson* went alongside. On three occasions, she came away empty handed, but on the other approaches men jumped to the lifeboat and were grabbed to safety from the wave-washed deck.

There was only one member of the crew left aboard the *Hindlea*. Twelve men were now on the lifeboat. Dick had stretched his luck to breaking point and the *Robinson* had taken heavy punishment. Sturdy though she was, there was a limit to the pounding she could take from the seas and the constant crashing against the steel hull of the *Hindlea*. Even if she held together, could she make the passage back to Moelfre? Would it not be wise to avoid the risk of further damage to the lifeboat? But as he weighed the alternatives Dick knew there was only one answer. He could not sail away leaving the last man to his fate. He turned the wheel and made his final run in.

The eighth man was over the coaster's side, hanging desperately from the rail. As Dick watched, a figure in oilskins emerged from the lifeboat's canopy. He could not see who it was, but he took his hand from the wheel to give a brief encouraging wave. They came round the *Hindlea*'s stern, passing under the madly spinning propellers. In the engine room, Evan Owen responded instantly to every command for 'revving', and with surges of power, now forward, now aft, the *Robinson* edged towards the poop. Behind him Dick could hear the dry whine of the prop-shaft.

There was an explosion of light and spray. Over his head Dick saw the steel wall of the *Hindlea* rearing away. The propellers seemed to be cackling with malicious laughter as Dick felt the lifeboat lifting under his feet and the wind under the keel. The sudden shift of the *Hindlea* had again exposed the rescuers to the worst of the weather and a steam-rollering wave hurled them out of the water. They were flying.

Dick braced himself for the crash that would come when the *Robinson* dropped back in the sea; his hands were ready on the wheel to turn the boat in an instant out beyond the reach of those propellers. But the impact was so violent that the wheel was wrenched from his grasp. He was flung, winded, against his metal back-rest. Choking for breath he managed to grab the wheel and haul himself upright. He was uninjured but, as he looked round, he was stunned by what he saw. The lifeboat had landed on the deck of the *Hindlea*.

There was no way out now. The next wave would tip them, like rubbish from a bin, over the side bow-first into the sea. Dick threw a despairing glance towards the canopy and the men with whose lives he had gambled and lost. He had a split-second picture of the families of his crew – grouped wives, mothers and children on the headland at Moelfre, straining for a sight of the returning lifeboat. He had known them all their lives. He thought of his own wife, who could never join the group on the headland, for she had always to stay within earshot of the phone. She would be sitting there with his two younger sons, listening fearfully to news bulletins on the radio, waiting, dreading the sound of the telephone ringing. A great wave of love for his family flooded over him. In that moment he loved them more than he had ever loved them in his life. He did not want to die, lashed to a lifeboat wheel, his body ripped by rocks. What right had he to take his crew to their deaths in an attempt to save the lives of eight men he did not even know?

The deck shifted violently under his feet and for a moment he thought that the *Hindlea* was breaking up under him. It was the second wave. He felt the *Robinson* once again lifting and surging forward, while behind and below him he heard the rush of water. Miraculously the wave, which by any reckoning should have swamped them, had lifted the boat clear of the deck. As she was swept back over the side, he saw Hugh Owen and Hugh Jones struggling to hold the last survivor. They had plucked him to safety as the wave carried them past.

It was 2.11pm by the time all the men were off the *Hindlea*; there was only one injury, a broken ankle. There were no casualties among the lifeboat crew and despite the hammering she had received, the *Robinson* had sustained no irreparable damage.

Steering her away from the *Hindlea*, Dick realized that their mission still had a perilous course to run. The boat was on a lee-shore within 100 yards of some of the most dangerous rocks on that coast – a toy in a breaking sea. The survivors were in a bad way and his own men were beginning to show the effects of their ordeal. Dick's waist was raw and bleeding where the ropes tying him to the wheel had chafed at the skin. He had been soaked by the first burst of spray when the boat was launched and the salt had caked on the fresh cuts so that every movement he made was a burning agony. His sea boots, brimming with water, encased his lower legs and feet which felt as if they were fashioned from clumsily modelled clay, and there was no response from his toes when he braced himself against sudden movement. The muscles in his legs were taut and knotted like wet bed sheets. His face was white and his eyelids gummed into narrow slits by the sea salt which crumbled like an Arctic landscape at every movement of his head. His hands were frozen to the wheel and he had long since lost any feeling in them. His numbed fingers could never unfasten the rope which secured him. If the boat capsized, he would be dragged over the rocks that came ever nearer.

The early Watson Class lifeboat. © *RNLI/Graham Farr archives*

The presence of eight survivors caused congestion on the lifeboat. She rode lower in the water and the breakers round the *Hindlea* threatened to engulf them. There was little room to manoeuvre between the coaster, which was already beginning to break up, and the rocks on the shoreline. More than ever Dick needed the aid of a drogue, but to order one of the crew to set it would be too dangerous. The passage to the comparative safety of the open sea was long and tricky; he had to nurse the boat every yard of the way.

He had to get the *Robinson* back to Moelfre. There would be a fire in the chapel vestry where the good women of the village would be waiting with hot food and drink and dry clothing. The prospect encouraged him; he screwed up his face to clear the salt from his eyes and set course for home.

Each breaker had to be met head on; the quiet water beyond provided the opportunity to go abeam until a second wave reared its head of tangled spume and sea-wrack. Deserted by gulls, the waters on the far side of the breakers resembled the crusted surface of an empty planet. Each swell encircled a shallow crater of water and beyond there were wave crests like crumbling cliffs.

The logical way back was on the weather side of Moelfre Island, a dangerously rocky outcrop beyond the headland which protected the village beaches. The inner channel, while giving some shelter from the hurricane, was treacherous and in that sea there was little chance of navigating it safely. They would have to take the outer course, where they would be at the mercy of the worst of the weather.

In the event a single wave that must have been over 30ft high lifted the *Robinson* on to its cowled crest and carried her, planing helplessly half out of the water, past the length of the island before dropping her in quieter water beyond the tide-rip. Dick has no memory of the ensuing minutes. Somehow he brought the lifeboat on to the moorings; the crew and the passengers were taken ashore and he found himself blinking in the bright light of the chapel vestry. His next conscious recollection is of walking across the fields behind the chapel to the lifeboat station. Blood from cuts on his face, where he had rubbed it clear of his vision, mixed with salt and ran into his mouth to lie, bitter-sweet, on his tongue. He stomped, rather than walked, like a toy bear in oilskins, his legs rigid, his arms stiff at his sides.

Dick recalls:

'I sat on the slipway utterly exhausted. Suddenly I realized that tears were streaming down my face. They were tears of joy. My crew and I had saved eight men from a certain death and I felt very happy about it. By now everyone knew about the rescue; the ships were all talking about it. My own son David was chief officer on a tanker, the *Pass of Balmaha*, hove to in the Bristol Channel. The captain had told him when he went up to relieve him that a lifeboat was out somewhere off the British coast on a lee-shore in a 104mph hurricane. My son, who had been out in the boat with me on several occasions, said to the captain, 'Surely there's no lifeboat out on a lee-shore in this wind expecting to save lives?'

'That's what all the ships are saying,' the captain said.

My son was pacing backwards and forwards in the wheel-house. He heard one ship say, 'I'm sorry for those lifeboatmen, they'll never get out of that.' Then he heard another ship. 'My God, that lifeboat's got the crew off. It was the Moelfre lifeboat.'

David leaped down to the captain's cabin three steps at a time. He cried, 'Captain, Captain, it's my old man that's out in that lifeboat.'

Back in Moelfre, Dick reported to RNLI headquarters. 'The boat's badly damaged, but her engines are all right and she's still seaworthy.'

'Belay that,' he was told. 'Don't you dare take that boat out again until she's had a thorough inspection by your district-inspector.'

Twenty five minutes later, however, the Moelfre lifeboat was launched again.

'Breaking the rules,' Dick says, recalling what happened. 'I was continually breaking the rules, but what else could we do? The *Essari*, formerly the *Pass of Lennie*, sister ship to my son's, was lying three miles off the slipway. Her engine room was flooded and she was dragging her anchor. Besides I wasn't worried. The sea was totally different by then. We were able to get a line aboard her and only had to wait 20 yards off her stern in case we were needed. Anyway, we knew that the Beaumaris lifeboat had been launched to relieve us. A terrible passage those lads had too, coming from the Sound in Beaumaris into a northerly hurricane. But they arrived, bless them, and we were able to return to station.'

But not, even then, to rest.

'I sent the crew home,' Dick goes on, 'and then the mechanic Evan Owen and I stayed up all night in the boathouse trying to patch the boat up. Six o'clock the next morning I received a call to go out again to relieve the Beaumaris boat. I fired the maroon and to my amazement those same four lads came pounding down the path again. Y'know lifeboatmen do have tremendous guts. You've got to be with them to realize the kind of men they are.' It was 5pm on 28 October when, at last, the lifeboat returned to the slipway.

For this truly remarkable feat of seamanship and his outstanding courage in one of the most daring sea rescues of the century, Cox'n Evans was awarded the RNLI gold medal – the first to be presented for ten years – known to the world's seamen as 'The Lifeboat VC'. Motor-mechanic Evan Owen was awarded the silver medal; Donald Murley Francis, Hugh Owen and Hugh Jones each received bronze medals for their part in the rescue. The medals were presented by HRH Princess Marina, Duchess of Kent, then president of the RNLI. Two years later, in 1961, at a ceremony at Buckingham Palace, Her Majesty the Queen presented the five life-boatmen with the Silver Medal for Gallantry at Sea.

One other tribute remained to be paid. In 1964 the *Watkin Williams* again went in for her five-yearly refit. When her replacement chugged into Moelfre Bay the cliffs were lined with the seamen and their families who make up most of the population of the village. As she approached the slipway, elderly sea captains raised their trilbies and fishermen their stocking caps, while a ragged cheer broke out.

After serving at every lifeboat station from Land's End to the north of Scotland, the *Edmund and Mary Robinson* had come back to the lee-shore of her legend.'

From *Lifeboat VC: The Story of Coxswain Dick Evans, B.E.M. and His Many Rescues* (David and Charles, 1979, by kind permission of the publishers).

CONCLUSION

It is clear from this account that the heavy displacement hull of the reserve lifeboat, the *Edmund and Mary Robinson*, proved highly capable in these dangerous shallow waters. The steepness of the seas would likely have proved even more of a challenge for a modern planing vessel because of the speed these hulls require in order to perform to their optimum. Indeed, this old lifeboat's slow but dependable gait came into its own in these horrific conditions. Furthermore, her low central point of gravity played a huge part in keeping this open cockpit-styled lifeboat from capsizing, as did her forward weight in preventing her from flying her nose too greatly. Notably, despite Dick Evans' considerable skill and good judgement, there were, nonetheless, occasions when he and his crew could do little more than simply trust their fate to the abilities of the boat. This is where sound design and good construction methods really come to the fore. There are times, whether when negotiating a 'rogue' sea or perhaps when passing through a vicious overfall, that a wave or series of waves may be so unpredictable or severe that there is little more one can do than to keep the power on and shut your eyes! That split second of reflex-induced blindness is the moment when you trust your life to your craft. If its design or make-up is wanting, then the moment you emerge could be the moment you experience disaster. As Dick Evans testified, knowing your craft's strengths and limitations is a big factor in coping with extreme sea states. This acquired knowledge should also be the deciding factor in determining whether venturing out into a particular sea state or weather condition is even possible.

Hugo Montgomery-Swan

LIFEBOATING
AND THE
HUMAN ELEMENT

BY PAUL STEVENSON

Leading investigative journalist Paul Stevenson
explores the relationship between man and machine,
and how the advancement of technology is affecting
the role of RNLI lifeboatmen.

It stands to reason that those who venture out into adverse sea states can learn much from the experience of those who do so with the noble intention of saving life at sea. The nature of this lifesaving work demands that such men and women put to sea in all weathers; theirs is not 'the luxury of choice' based upon a favourable weather forecast. The RNLI (Royal National Lifeboat Institution) has one of the greatest records of experience in this field: from the selfless men of the Institute who handled the pulling-and-sailing lifeboats that saved countless lives between the years of 1843 and 1932, to their successors, the motor lifeboat crews, who have served with such skill and commitment ever since.

The range of powered craft the RNLI have employed since the 1930s has been very varied, with each type demanding the use of particular skills and degrees of understanding peculiar to that craft. Take, for example, the different helming techniques needed in the operation of the purely inflatable D and C Class inflatables compared to those techniques required to helm the current Atlantic 75 and 21 Class rigid inflatable boats. Not to mention, of course, the huge skill set differences required to helm these smaller craft and the Institute's most recent addition, the mighty Tamar Class. That said, though the skill sets may be different, the need for excellence on the part of the operator remains the same throughout the RNLI fleet, especially when it comes to navigating safely in heavy weather.

The significance of the human element in modern lifeboating should not, therefore, be minimised. Despite all the high-tech advancements that have been witnessed in lifeboat design over the years, the most significant contributing factor involved in the process of saving life at sea remains the people responsible for the lifeboat's operation.

Lifeboat coxswains and helmsmen have to know how to make life-and-death decisions in the same amount of time it might take you or I to utter the word 'um'. To illustrate: when a lifeboat is making for a stricken yacht in extreme weather conditions on a lee shore, close to unyielding cliffs (an environment where so much happens so quickly), this is a time when its coxswain will need to call upon all his professional ability to make clear, rapid decisions. No computer system yet devised is able to replace or replicate the instant decision-making and action needed to know how to respond to such a fast-moving event. Decisions, it has to be said, that no doubt will likely be forged upon the balancing of such complex and diverse thought processes as 'estimated risk' and the human quality of 'compassion'.

Of course, a good skipper should always consider his crew and welcome their contribution to the overall running of the vessel. No more so is this the case than in foul weather when each member of the crew depends upon the abilities and functions of his fellows to such a large degree. Nonetheless, the role of the coxswain or skipper is ultimately to be the chief decision maker. So, after having gleaned all he can from the combined experience of his crew, the skipper's word must then be final, and good discipline among his crew will ensure they carry out his instructions promptly. But let us not overlook the fact that on modern lifeboats, besides the key information brought to the skipper's attention via his crew, the coxswain is also the one processing or driving the supply of data from such items as the radar, the chart plotter, the RDF, the sounder,

An Atlantic Class RIB being driven hard over the crest of a sea. Props are likely to cavitate upon landing. © *Rick Tomlinson*

the weatherfax, the VHF, even the rudder and engine displays. That's a lot of information to disseminate and it's perhaps not unknown for this to result in 'data overload'.

Modern lifeboating, therefore, places many demands upon personnel in comparison to yesteryear when, before the big advancements in technology and the subsequent integration of it into the marine environment, the function of a lifeboat coxswain was less complex. The difficulty that the chiefs and naval architects of such organisations as the RNLI therefore have is to ensure that modern technology serves to genuinely complement the attributes of the people using it. How detrimental it is when technological advancement oversteps that sometimes 'fuzzy' but all-important demarcation line where exists the superior ability and resourcefulness unique to people.

RESCUE BY *SPIRIT OF PADSTOW*

The significance of the human factor working alongside technology is well illustrated by the events that took place in the waters off the north Cornwall coastal town of Padstow on 25 June 2007.

The 40ft wooden yacht *Cawesande* was nearing the end of its passage, sailing from the Scillies to Padstow up this spectacular but challenging stretch of Atlantic coast. Skipper Tony Burris, with his wife on board as crew, was aware that bad weather was forecast for the region, but he was sure from his calculations that they would make it safely to harbour before the storm broke. However, when the yacht reached position 50° 37 N 005° 01 W, north of Trevose Head, the storm suddenly developed enormous power, screaming in from the open Atlantic to catch *Cawesande* just 4 or 5 miles short of safety in Padstow's harbour, blowing out the foresail, leaving her drifting at about 3 knots and taking on water off the lee shore. Even Alan Tarby, coxswain of the *Spirit of Padstow*, who signed on as a fisherman straight from school and understands the local sea conditions as well as anybody, was surprised at how rapidly and ferociously the weather had deteriorated.

At 1108hrs Falmouth Coastguard paged Padstow Deputy Launching Authority Nick Billings to request a launch of ON1283, the *Spirit of Padstow*, to go to the aid of the yacht. She is an all-weather Tamar Class lifeboat, 'the pride of the fleet' you might say, built in 2006 and powered by twin Caterpillar C18 1000hp diesels. Look up Trevose Head on Google Earth and you will see the size of the challenge they faced, but imagine what the Head looked like that morning, with the wind, which had been increasing ominously all day, now gusting in from the north-west, building from force 8 to 9, with high water predicted to be at 1418hrs. Nick Billings agreed the request and the crew were paged immediately. This would be a major test of courage, skill and discipline on a day that none of them would ever forget.

Teamwork is also essential when launching a modern lifeboat, because there is more to it than simply getting the vessel down the slipway and into the water. The crew on duty must start 'prepping' the boat ready for launch as soon as the call comes in, so that it is ready to launch by the time the rest of the crew arrive. First, all the hatches and waterproof doors must be closed, then the shed doors must be opened, the winch engine started, the on-board computer booted up (this latter requirement takes some two and a half minutes in all); the computer then opens all the sea valves, seacocks, fuel valves, cooling valves, sterntube cooling valves, and principal electric systems.

Padstow lifeboat is crewed by 24 men and women plus the coxswain and mechanic. All 24 are volunteers from varied walks of life: hotelier, fishermen, restaurant owner, boatbuilder, painter and decorator, sales representative, digger driver, to name but a few. Some have over 30 years' experience as RNLI volunteers, others a lot less, and one prospective crewmember was waiting to join on his 17th birthday.

'There is an excellent internal communication system on this boat, using VHF,' Coxswain Alan Tarby explains. 'The computer knows what we need to do and does it all in a set sequence, producing a list of any items it couldn't open. For instance, if you don't get the sterntube cooling valves opened it's pretty catastrophic, because the shaft seizes up in the tubes. It's also very important to make sure that everything is as the computer tells you, so Michael England, our mechanic, goes down and physically checks it all anyway. If the computer didn't boot up, you could do it all manually, so it wouldn't be the end of the world; you could still go, but it does affect your judgement. If all your electronics are telling you one thing and your instincts are telling you something else, you do have to make a decision. I consult my colleagues, because I can learn from all of them. Round here, in water I know well, I trust the electronics, but I also follow my instincts when making decisions.'

The next check is to ensure that all the electronics are speaking the same language. 'We cross-reference the radar with the chart systems every time we launch, by picking a known spot of land and referencing it with the radar and comparing that with the chart. On a shout like the *Cawesande* we could see, and were working on, our landmarks, so we wouldn't be worrying about the chart system particularly. Just get the bearings of an op and, if visibility is reasonably good and we are running back into a place we know quite well, simply get on with it.'

Michael England, Padstow station mechanic, telephoned Falmouth Coastguard and was told that the yacht was 40ft long with two people on board. He informed Falmouth that he was waiting for the crew to arrive and would be launching in approximately ten minutes. The Coastguard said that the yacht might not have ten minutes, although they both knew the reality is that, however great the emergency, it takes time to assemble a crew of volunteers from their normal work, however hard and fast they work and drive. On this service, for example, one crewmember drove his lorry in so fast that he scattered roof joists and planks on every bend of the winding road to the station; such was the urgency, he left them where they were until the service ended. In the meantime, the duty team put on their heavy-weather gear and went out into the storm to make sure the lifeboat and slipway were ready for an immediate launch.

They launched at 1120hrs. On board were: Coxswain Alan Tarby, Mechanic Michael England (also a former fisherman and son of Trevor England MBE, himself a renowned former coxswain of the Padstow lifeboat), Second Mechanic Chris Murphy, and Crewmembers Neil Simpson, Steve Nicholas, Luke Chown, Ian Kitto, David Flide and Tom Norfolk. The boat was ready for them when they arrived. Such was the speed of their arrival that Coxswain Alan Tarby did not at first realise that he had too many crew on

The state of the art Tamar Class Padstow lifeboat performing at its best in heavy seas off the north Cornish coast. © RNLI/Nigel Millard

board; he considered dropping two off at the slipway, but the sea conditions had deteriorated quite quickly and the stricken yacht was in a perilous situation, so he decided to keep heading out towards the endangered yacht at full speed. Two of the crew, Neil Simpson and Luke Chown, went below to the forward cabin and strapped themselves in. Everyone else was strapped into their seats within the wheelhouse, for they all knew that, as they rounded Trevose Head on their way towards the casualty, the *Spirit of Padstow* would meet the full force of the seas and weather, likely slowing them from the design speed of 25 to 15 knots 'overground' at best.

For the first mile offshore they were also fighting through the tide race which, in terms of vicious tide-ripped seas, was arguably the most difficult part of the passage to negotiate. Beyond this boiling zone of troublesome overfalls there is the deeper Atlantic coastal water, where seas of some 4 metres high were mounting up in steady succession that day. Each time the lifeboat lifted its bow to the crest of a big sea, the throttles had to be eased back in corresponding fashion to prevent the vessel from flying its head too wildly. With such modern equipment as suspension seats protecting the crew from the hull's shock loadings, it's feasible to drive a boat of this type much harder than one might otherwise in sea states of this ferocity. In real terms, though, whilst this may mean far greater speeds can be achieved without necessarily endangering the crew, the negatives obviously include the increased forces and strain imposed upon the vessel's structure and its key components. This is where the vital importance of adequate engineering and advanced build technologies truly come to the fore.

But back to the job in hand: to complicate matters further, the crew of the *Spirit of Padstow* were now to experience the first few evidences of a heavy 10-metre groundswell running in from the west. Official RNLI instructions state that in a rescue situation, when circumstances change to this degree, the crew should remove the lifeboat to a position of safety, and for a rebriefing of the crew to be undertaken. But on a lee shore such as this, where could Coxswain Tarby go to rebrief his crew? That 'position of safety' would have necessitated a 10–12 hour passage around Land's End and into Newlyn Harbour, or alternatively a two to three hour 'hellslide' journey east, all the way out to the wreck-littered waters of Lundy Island. 'Removing to a position of safety' simply was not an option, for clearly such a place did not exist!

Coxswain Tarby wryly observed: 'There are two kinds of calls from yachtsmen: the ones who tell you they are just about to sink, and when you get there, there is absolutely nothing wrong with them; and the ones who tell you that nothing is wrong with them, but when you get there they *are* close to sinking! What we do in either case is try to get somebody aboard to assess the situation, which includes determining how much water the vessel has taken on and then finding a way of establishing a means of proper communication with the lifeboat.'

At 1142hrs they arrived at the casualty, which was lying towards the west with the wind approximately 45° off her starboard bow. The blown-out foresail was flapping in the wind and she was rolling heavily in the massive seas. The yacht's crew were both in the cockpit where they apparently felt safer, only venturing below when they needed to talk on the VHF, which was still working; then it was a case of 'straight back up to the cockpit'. Coxswain Tarby noticed with some relief that the female crew was wearing a lifejacket and that the male skipper was wearing what appeared to be a floatation jacket; they duly told Tarby that they were not injured or unwell, but they could not sail due to the shredded jib, that they had water just above the cabin sole, and that the pump had stopped working.

Coxswain Alan Tarby next discussed the options, as he saw them, with his crew, namely: a tow down to Newlyn some 60 miles away, after having got the *Cawesande*'s crew airlifted off (subject to the rescue helicopter captain's view on its feasibility), or alternatively put two lifeboatmen on board the yacht to assist with the evacuation of the yacht's stricken crew to the lifeboat, before beginning the long tow back to Padstow. Luke Chown and Chris Murphy volunteered to transfer to the yacht to clear the pump, get the water out, and be available to help rescue the crew if the decision was to call in the rescue helicopter. Coxswain Tarby explained to the yacht's crew via VHF radio what he was planning to do; they were happy with the proposal.

'It's very difficult getting alongside a yacht in these conditions with a boat as substantial and high-powered as a Tamar Class,' explained Tarby. 'Because the *Spirit of Padstow* was so much bigger and her decks so much higher than *Cawesande*'s, there was a real danger of coming down on top of the yacht. Normally you'd board by putting the lap of the bow in against the boat and then jumping but, because this lifeboat was so much higher than the deck of the yacht, we had a 2 foot drop from our deck down to hers. You've really got to time it just right in order to avoid doing damage to the casualty in these instances. As it was clearly not that low in the water, and it didn't appear from the way it was rolling that the yacht was at risk of sinking, we allowed ourselves a little extra sea time to do some planning.

'The consensus was that we should just lay there for a while to see what was happening, so, as skipper, I decided to agree to the views of my crew. After this 'pause for thought' I gingerly dodged up, allowing for the delay on the gearbox of the Tamar (something that takes a bit of getting used to), and aimed to lay 2 or 3 feet off, waiting for the moment when the two boats would come within jumping range of each other. Despite the gale that was blowing, I managed to manoeuvre alongside the damaged yacht after 17 attempts, finally placing the starboard shoulder alongside the yacht's port chain plates. Chris Murphy jumped down to the yacht and we then backed away, hard astern. We repeated the manoeuvre and on the second attempt Luke Chown also jumped aboard.

'Chris reported to me that both of the yacht's crew, in their sixties, were looking quite weary, and in his view they would be better off in the lifeboat; that was good enough for me. Sometimes people are reluctant to leave their boat and take a bit of persuading, and I can understand that, because a boat can come to mean a lot to you; but that was not a problem with skipper Burris, so I decided it would be best to attempt the transfer from the cockpit. We normally position ourselves along the starboard deck of the lifeboat and, when the yacht crew signal that they are ready, I bring the lifeboat back alongside, jiggling the throttle all the time, just dodging, placing the starboard shoulder as close to the yacht's cockpit as I dare, at about 45°. Then the crew just grab the occupants, pulling them up off the yacht and aboard the deck of the lifeboat. But on this occasion we soon discovered that the height difference was going to be a problem; skipper Burris and his wife really tried, and we admired them for that but, because I guess they were understandably feeling a little old and weary by that time, they simply couldn't manage the leap. Having a big boat like the Tamar, despite all its astonishing abilities, is not always the advantage you might think.'

Could he not have towed the yacht back to harbour at Padstow with the crew on board? Coxswain Tarby shook his head. 'The Doom Bar is the big problem: if you get wind against tide it's always a nasty place, with rocks on one side, a sandbank on the other, and a very narrow channel to navigate through. Plus, towing a boat in a following sea is extremely difficult anyway, because it tends to broach or overrun the tow rope. In this case, it was impossible even to consider as long as the crew of the yacht remained aboard her. We would have put them in even greater danger than they would have been out there in the huge swells of the open sea.'

Another option was to get them airlifted off, but Tarby wasn't sure whether that was feasible as the screaming wind was showing no signs of abating and, furthermore, was clearly driving them ever closer to the deadly granite cliffs. In any event, an airlift would still mean towing the yacht out to sea. This is because it's easier for a helicopter to get a crew off when a yacht or similar-sized vessel is under tow at 2 or 3 knots.

By 1213hrs Tarby had run out of any other options, so he informed Falmouth Coastguard of the situation and asked for a helicopter. Meantime, *Cawesande* was drifting to leeward at approximately 3 knots and was now only 2.5 miles from the lee shore of Trevose Head. The VHF was then used to contact the two lifeboatmen on the yacht.

'I had to make sure the boys on the boat had made the tow rope fast; they had, so I knew that was secure,' Coxswain Tarby explained. 'In the half-hour it took the helicopter to arrive, we were holding off to give ourselves more sea room, just dodging, feathering up a big wave, then easing down, and up again on minimal throttle. Dodging like that gave me time to think of more options if the helicopter rescue didn't work.'

Communication is all in such situations. Chris Murphy briefed the yacht's crew on the procedure for a hi-line helicopter transfer and ensured that they would be happy to co-operate. *Rescue Helicopter 193* from RNAS *Culdrose* arrived on scene at 1245hrs and radio contact was made. Coxswain Tarby realized that it would be easier for *Rescue 193* to lift all four off the yacht, rather than have him attempt to go back alongside in those conditions to pick up his crew; he would never do anything that would put the *Spirit of Padstow* at risk. This was agreed with the pilot, who confirmed that the yacht had to be under way at about 2 to 3 knots to facilitate the airlift. Tarby altered course to 020° to place the wind 30° off his port bow and continued the tow at that speed. The helicopter duly positioned herself over the casualty yacht and used a hi-line to lower a winchman down onto its heaving deck. Tarby then went into the cockpit to clarify the situation with the lifeboat crew. The female crew casualty was lifted first, then the yacht skipper, followed by Luke Chown, Chris Murphy and finally the winchman. The 10-metre swell made the lifts 'very difficult', a fact that was noted on the official report of the incident. This was shown too by the fact that Luke Chown was unceremoniously dunked in the sea on his way up to the helicopter. 'He came up to the surface spitting water, looked up at the helicopter and shouted "You bastards!" We all laughed at that,' Alan Tarby recalled.

Rescue 193 departed at 1308hrs taking the survivors and lifeboat crew to the Padstow playing fields, where they were met by the local Coastguard auxiliaries. Coxswain Tarby altered course for Padstow with the yacht in tow and, with the crew safely lifted up, eased the engines up to 1000rpm, increasing their speed to 4—5 knots. He reported that the *Cawesande* towed very well because of her traditional design and long keel whereas, according to him, 'some modern yachts skitter about under tow like yearling foals!'

They arrived at the Doom Bar at 1420hrs, three hours after they had left port, right on the high water of the neap tide. As his long experience had led him to expect,

This all-weather vessel is dependant upon a fully enclosed cabin to maintain its integrity in such short, steep and violent seas. © *Safehaven Marine*

A Severn Class lifeboat underway. The vessel's semi-displacement hull is capable of excellent head to sea performance. © **RIB International Magazine**

monstrous waves were crashing right across the Bar, so much so that for much of the time the yacht's hull was not even visible behind the breaking seas. However, despite the horrendous conditions, the lifeboat crew managed to spot another yacht, anchored approximately 400 metres south of Stepper Point in a shallow area where local fishermen kept their store pots. They knew that this was a poor choice of anchorage given that, with the wind now more in the north and with the tide about to ebb, the area was going to become very rough indeed, and the pots posed a risk of fouling the yacht's propeller, so they agreed with the coxswain that they would check on the anchored yacht on their return to station.

At 1435hrs they were clear of the Doom Bar, so they could afford to shorten the towline. Tarby contacted Padstow harbourmaster to request assistance with berthing the yacht because, although there was now no sea running, the wind was still a very strong force 6 to 7 and blowing straight across the open expanse of the Camel Estuary. The lifeboat would normally enter with an alongside tow, but at Padstow the gap between the harbour quays is too small, and with swinging room in the inner harbour very restricted, he asked Assistant Harbourmaster and Duty DLA Nick Billings to launch the harbour RIB, which attached a stern tow to the casualty yacht; this allowed Coxswain Tarby to enter the inner harbour where the yacht was placed alongside another vessel. Crewmember Murphy, fresh from his helicopter flight, had opted to come back to the harbour to help with the mooring of the casualty yacht. She was secured at 1445hrs. The lifeboat was then taken to the outer harbour, and the decks and towline were secured while waiting for Crewman Simpson to come back on board.

Five minutes later the harbour RIB brought Crewman Simpson back to the lifeboat, and Assistant Harbourmaster and Duty DLA Nick Billings requested Coxswain Tarby to check on the yacht anchored south of Stepper Point and ask what his intentions were; the assistant harbour master had been trying to contact the yacht for some time, but had been unable to raise him. The weather was such that, in the interests of safety, the coxswain made sure all crew were down below and strapped in. When this process was completed the *Spirit of Padstow* proceeded at best speed but, as the tide was now ebbing, he knew that the Bar would be treacherous. At approximately 1500hrs the lifeboat crossed the Bar, which Tarby described as 'a mass of breaking, dumping waves'. At 1515hrs the lifeboat approached the yacht *Fly*, a modern 30ft sloop which was facing north-west with the tide running slightly against the wind. The wind was still north gale force 8, with 1.5-metre waves breaking about 10 metres in front of the yacht. This gave Coxswain Tarby a difficult choice to make: he knew it would be far too dangerous to tow a boat across the Bar in these conditions, but neither could the yachtsman be left where he was with the situation worsening rapidly because, as the tide dropped, the force of the ebb increased and the yacht was starting to slew, making her motion unpredictable. He decided the only viable option would be to take the yachtsman off and leave the boat where it was.

Secured by their safety harnesses, Crewmen Simpson and Nicholas made their way to the foredeck of the lifeboat to talk to the skipper, who was standing on his own foredeck. Coxswain Tarby positioned *Spirit of Padstow* so that her port shoulder was a couple of feet off the yacht's port shoulder. The lifeboat crew checked the yacht for damage and found that the yacht's anchor was fouled, as they had feared. The skipper did not believe that his engine was powerful enough to work the yacht clear of the shore.

Although the boats were rolling, a transfer at this time did seem feasible, so Crewman Simpson suggested to the yachtsman that he leave immediately. Tarby placed the lifeboat in the ideal position for this, but for some reason the yachtsman went back into the cockpit, 'possibly to retrieve his camera'. While he was below, the *Spirit of Padstow* was blown away from the yacht and Coxswain Tarby had to back away and reposition her in difficult conditions, surrounded by a lot of broken water, at a depth of approximately only 2.5 metres. Tarby stated that he 'found it very difficult to manoeuvre in such a shallow and confined area of sea. In fact, this depth of water is not sufficient for several of the vessel's key systems to function properly at all.' Furthermore, the lifeboat's motion must have rendered the bow thrusters pretty ineffective, not to mention the force of the wind, which would have been making it very difficult for the helm to bring the bow round to the weather.

At 1540hrs the yachtsman had made his way back to the yacht's port rigging. He was wearing a lifejacket and safety harness, attached to the yacht's jackstay. Coxswain Tarby knew that, because of the underwater profile of the Tamar Class lifeboat, he needed to be going ahead to get water flow on the rudders before he could engage astern. He placed the starboard engine ahead, gave a burst of power, and then applied astern on the port engine. She started to turn into the wind and it appeared that she would go alongside nicely but, as so often happens at sea, it was not to be as simple as that, because as the manoeuvre was half completed, 'a wave broke against the starboard side of the yacht pushing it down towards the lifeboat'. Coxswain Tarby applied astern power, but the unpredictable movement of the yacht, the shallow water and confined space made the situation treacherous, and the lifeboat's stem hit the yacht's port amidships. The combined result of the roll of the yacht and the sudden impact from the lifeboat caused the yachtsman to lose his footing and he fell overboard. His lifejacket did not inflate.

Coxswain Tarby immediately backed away and Crewman Nicholas threw a rescue line to the yachtsman, who was still attached to his yacht by his safety line. He passed the line through the 'D' ring on his lifejacket and attempted to tie a bowline to himself. However, the motion of the yacht kept forcing him under the water, making the lifeboat crew very concerned for his safety. The yachtsman did manage to tie a bowline onto himself, and the lifeboat crew threaded the 'Perry Buoy' onto the rescue line and sent it down to the yachtsman to give him more support. After two minutes or so, with the knot secured, the yachtsman managed to undo his safety harness and was hauled to the lifeboat's starboard well deck where Crewmen Simpson and Nicholas hauled him on board. Coxswain Tarby then took the lifeboat to deeper water while the yachtsman's condition was assessed. After a couple of minutes he said he was unhurt but shaken, so Crewmen Kitto and Nicholas assisted him back to the wheelhouse where he was wrapped in a thermal blanket and given oxygen therapy. Within just 30 minutes of his being taken on board the lifeboat, his yacht had broken free and dragged across the Bar to be washed ashore later at Daymer Bay.

It was too rough to attempt to cross the Bar, so at 1600hrs Falmouth Coastguard were contacted and asked for helicopter assistance to transfer the yachtsman. *Rescue 193* was working with a casualty at St Ives and gave an ETA of 40 minutes. Oxygen therapy was continued while *Spirit of Padstow* made her way towards the boathouse to check conditions at the slipway.

At 1615hrs the lifeboat was passing Gulland Rock when *Rescue 193* made radio contact giving a revised ETA of 15 minutes. In fact, it did arrive at 1630hrs, and rendezvoused with the lifeboat, preparing to lower a hi-line. The yachtsman was now showing signs of agitation and said that he did not want to be lifted as he had hurt his back on his trip back from the Azores. Coxswain Tarby knew that he would not be able to cross the Bar until at least 2130hrs due to lack of water and the sea conditions (a further five hours sea time) and he was concerned that the yachtsman may have ingested water and therefore needed to be seen by a doctor, so the helicopter winchman suggested that the casualty could only be lifted in a vacuum stretcher, which was duly lowered to the lifeboat with the winchman himself. At 1630hrs the yachtsman was lifted from the lifeboat and taken to the Royal Cornwall Hospital (Treliske).

The *Spirit of Padstow* now made her way back to the mooring, as conditions at the slipway were too severe to rehouse safely. At 1652hrs, just as they were attempting to pick up the mooring, Falmouth Coastguard called them again: there had been reports of a yacht going aground inside the estuary, at Daymer Bay. For the third time that day, the crew made their way below and strapped in to make passage back to the Bar. At

1705hrs the crew of the lifeboat could see the yacht high and dry and Alan Tarby reported to the Coastguard that it was probably the yacht *Fly*, but the Coastguard would need to climb down the rocks to confirm. He stood off until it was confirmed, then headed back towards the boathouse, picking the mooring up at 1720hrs.

CONCLUSION

Coxswain Tarby's leadership and management skills were tested to the full that June day. His crew were briefed at all stages and, although they are a strong team, nonetheless the value of their training and commitment had been thoroughly challenged. The crew had acted throughout on Coxswain Tarby's instructions and he has commented on what a superb job they did: 'To ask a crewman to transfer to another vessel in the conditions present on the day of the yacht *Cawasande*'s rescue is a difficult thing to do. Crewmen Chown and Murphy showed considerable courage by undertaking this task in what were life-threatening seas,' stated Tarby following this memorable service.

The north Cornwall coast is so dangerous, and its weather so unpredictable, that when the RNLI is called out it is usually to go to the aid of capable yachtsmen who are passing Padstow on passage between Wales and the Scilly Isles. 'You've got to be "well found" to play around on this coast, but with 40 or 50 yachts in the harbour you can expect one or two to get into trouble: mechanical breakdown, fouled propellers; most of it, though, is down to genuine bad luck,' says Tarby. 'The big lesson here is that you never put yourself in a position where your only refuge is on a lee shore; when things go wrong, you need to get out of there as fast as you can. I know some yachtsmen find that a bit daunting; they want to get ashore and get out of it, but the north coast of Cornwall is one of those places where there are no safe harbours; it's pretty unforgiving if you get it wrong.'

This comment was made in recognition of the challenges that face yachtsmen but is just as valid for motorboat cruisers. Having the right boat, the right crew and the correct equipment for the job in hand is essential when it comes to the prevention of critical problems at sea. These same 'ingredients' apply, of course, to coping successfully when things do go wrong.

But it becomes clear from this record of events that even modern lifeboats have their flaws. No designer or naval architect yet has ever built the perfect vessel; indeed, it's fair to say that one perceived design advantage can so often create a corresponding disadvantage elsewhere in the boat's anatomy or performance. The old saying 'boat design and construction equals compromise' continues to be true even in the 21st century. But most importantly, as the likes of Coxswain Tarby prove, to this day, the most important and influential element of any vessel, especially a lifeboat, is the man at its controls.

Hugo Montgomery-Swan

SEASICKNESS

BY HUGO MONTGOMERY-SWAN AND PAUL GLATZEL

Seasickness and a worsening sea state can represent a life-threatening combination. Paul Glatzel and Hugo Montgomery-Swan analyse the causes of seasickness and what can be done.

Why is it that some people can spend hours bobbing around in a boat without a care in the world while for others even the sight of an outboard brings them out in a cold sweat and a rapid descent into seasickness? Contrary to popular opinion anyone can succumb to seasickness and even the most experienced boater is likely to fall foul of this debilitating condition at some stage.

CAUSES

What causes seasickness or mal de mer? Seasickness is motion sickness and arises from the brain's attempt to take in all the varied data that it is being fed from the various sensors around our body. On one level, the inner ears transmit data about balance and the position of the body and our eyes feed in data giving the brain an idea of where the body is relative to its surroundings, whilst pressure sensors pick up on the forces acting on our feet and other parts of our body due to gravity. Finally, our muscles send data about what they are doing, whether they are working or are stationary, and what directions they are moving in.

It is hardly surprising, then, that our brain ends up being overloaded by these conflicting messages, as much of the data seems to contradict other elements of it. For example, as you focus on some close work – a chartplotter or a chart, for example – the page or screen is not moving, yet your other sensors are telling your brain that you are bouncing around all over the place. If an engine fails or needs attention, for example, the likelihood of seasickness striking as the crewmember attends to the problem is high. The combination of rough seas, strength-sapping gear, mechanical problems and debilitating sea sickness is a common reality, and can test the resolve of even the hardiest seaman.

THE WARNING SIGNS

As a skipper you need to know what to look out for in case you or one of your crew is about to succumb, and what to do once they have.

Mention seasickness and we all imagine hanging over the side getting the chance to reacquaint ourselves with our breakfast. Before this occurs, though, you are likely to feel lethargic and slightly drowsy, and this rapidly develops into a nauseous feeling and a cold sweat. These symptoms get worse, and any attempt to focus on close work, like reading, often worsens the situation. As the nauseous feeling grows, so the onset of violent vomiting is almost inevitable.

PREVENTION

What can you do to prevent seasickness? Rule one is to stay off big, rich breakfasts prior to making a passage! Acidic foods, even some fruits, can be problematic too. Bread is always good at calming the stomach, as are dry crackers, and you can't go wrong with cool, fresh water either. So, plain food and drink, both before a passage and during, is sensible. Champagne is supposed to be good – if you can afford it! But seriously, try fizzy water, as it's often the gas that can help.

As with any ailment there are a mixture of remedies, from the medicinal through to 'old wives' tales'. If you or your crew are likely to succumb to seasickness, it is best to take seasickness tablets before you go afloat. Some swear by wristbands while for others ginger capsules are the answer. Whatever works for you, just make sure that you apply the remedy early, as once you have your head over the side it's far too late!

Don't overlook mental attitude either. As some people can become seasick just by looking at a moored boat, this rather implies that psychology plays a part. So if you approach your boating feeling that you are likely to get sick, you are far more likely to do so. Think positive and concentrate your mind on something else. Get talking and keep your mind active. Seasickness will cause people to go into decline to the point where they can become so lethargic that even in dangerous conditions they may simply 'switch off'. Remember at all times that you are also dealing with a mental problem – so the sufferer needs to fight this element as well as dealing with the physical symptoms.

TREATMENT

As an observant skipper you will hopefully have picked up on the signs of the onset of seasickness before your crewmember starts to vomit. If you do, there are a few things that you can do that may prevent them vomiting. Firstly, get them into the fresh air and give them the task of steering the vessel. Asking them to steer helps them focus on the horizon and gives them the chance to anticipate the movement of the craft. Alternatively, lie them down on the deck and get them to shut their eyes, which helps to reduce the number of 'inputs' their brain is receiving.

At the vomiting stage there is not much you can do for the victim beyond making sure that they are comfortable and safe. Ensure that another crewmember is with them as they lean over the side, just to make sure they don't fall overboard. Once they have

Over the bar, then safely home. But this last stretch could be the most demanding.
Seasickness and fatigue must not gain the better of the helmsman at this
critical time. © **RIB International Magazine**

stopped vomiting, if there is a place where they can rest, get them there. Bear in mind that they are losing fluids every time they are sick, so make sure, just as you would when ashore, that you replace liquids and salts when you can.

Retching endlessly will cause a person to sweat and not only lose body fluid but also become cold as the body cools and clothing next to the skin gets damp. So make sure that your sufferer is not in danger of succumbing to hypothermia. Also avoid overheating as this will encourage the onset of sickness. Therefore, getting your clothing right prior to departure is essential and, with the forms of modern clothing now available, this should be achievable. Tight neck seals aren't helpful so it may be wise to get your upper body out of the suit and into the fresh air.

If you have suffered from extreme sickness, you'll know that at the time you really will feel that you have never felt worse than at that moment, so ensure your crewmember gets plenty of sympathy and try to get them ashore as soon as possible. In serious situations, don't hesitate to contact the Coastguard, as talking to them will ensure that you are doing the right things for your casualty.

CONCLUSION

In summary, as a skipper try to prevent seasickness by ensuring crew take medication, keep a look out for the symptoms and, if you spot them, be proactive and try to prevent the situation worsening. Try to get the casualty lying down if at all possible. Ensure you have plenty of water on board as well as rehydration sachets to replace lost salts. If your route allows it, and if the situation continues to be serious, amend your passage in order to get the crewmember ashore.

FACING THE ELEMENTS

ROGUE SEAS AND FREAK WAVES

MICHEL OLAGNON & EDWARD PITT

Leading international oceanologists Michel Olagnon and Edward Pitt discuss the 'science' surrounding the destructive nature of rogue seas and freak waves in the light of the actual experiences of those operating powered vessels in offshore waters.

For many years now, the *Jeanne d'Arc* has been the name given to the ship used by the French Naval Academy for providing their young midshipmen with the invaluable opportunity of gaining first-hand offshore experience through their round-the-world training cruises. The current *Jeanne d'Arc* is the third vessel to bear this illustrious name and was originally the helicopter carrier, *La Résolue*.

The *Jeanne d'Arc* that sailed round the world in 1962–63 was the second ship to bear the name, and being rather 'long in the tooth' she was only one year away from her last voyage. Built in 1930, she had been in service continually for some 30 years. With a displacement of 9,200 tons she could motor fully laden at a top speed of 25 knots – a considerable achievement for a boat of her age and tonnage. This *Jeanne d'Arc* was also armed with four double 155mm turrets, and four 75mm, six 40mm and twenty 20mm guns. She could accommodate 156 cadets in addition to 28 regular officers and a crew of 620.

In December 1962, on the way from Balboa to Callao, her port propeller shaft broke from fatigue and the propeller was lost. After returning to Balboa and inspection of the damage in dry dock, Paris ordered that she avoid the hurricane season of the South Pacific and sail via California, Hawaii and Japan to Hong Kong, where the propeller would be replaced.

Even at only 30° north, winter can be rough in the North Pacific. On the morning of 4 February 1963 Captain André Storelli had been sitting most of the night on the bridge, in his nightclothes, in order to keep the *Jeanne d'Arc* hove-to, two points from the waves on the port tack. This was in an effort to optimise the effect of the remaining propeller in the strong westerly seas that were by now running 6 to 7 metres in height.

At 0947 a group of large breaking waves was sighted about half a nautical mile dead ahead and appeared to be travelling towards the ship at an angle to the main wave direction, just beyond an area of relatively calm water (4 to 5 metres wave height). The captain ordered an immediate turn of 25° to port to enable the ship to face the waves on a better heading and to protect the problem propeller.

The *Jeanne d'Arc* succeeded in paying off by about 15° before she met the first wave 2 points on the port bow. The height of that wave was estimated at around 15 metres. It heaved the ship with terrific force, causing her to fall into the trough with a significant trim (about 15°); leaning greatly to starboard (the heel has been estimated at 30°), she continued paying off for about 20°. To counter this, the captain ordered, 'Helm amidships!' and then '25 to starboard!'

Between the first and second wave (a distance of about 100 metres) the *Jeanne* had time to return more or less to her waterline, but she was soon heeled over to starboard by the second wave, to an angle of about 35° (the safety HQ's inclinometer 'hit the stops' at 30° while the ship was still continuing her rolling motion). As the ship was riding these two waves, the freeboard deck and the quarterdeck were submerged in turn, and the sea covered the catwalks of the first deck, with water reaching the top of the bulkheads when the ship was at maximum heel. The man on watch at the SILAS buoys, which were fixed at the height of the second deck, could see the buoys actually floating; one of the floats of the port buoy, in fact, was torn away. The third rogue wave was cleared in much the same way, although it was not as big or quite as powerful. It took 30 seconds at the most to clear all three waves.

Captain Storelli named the event 'The Glorious Three' after the notorious 'Days of July' of French history. (The use of the term 'freak' to qualify waves did not appear until the seminal article, *'Freak' Ocean Waves* by Laurence Draper, was published in *Oceanus* 18 months later.) On arrival in Tokyo, Captain Storelli simply said, 'Nobody knows what saved the *Jeanne*, but it would have been made widely known who lost her.'

An explanation of the event in a note from the executive officer to the crew is the first well-documented report of rogue waves that we know of, and the several decades of scientific studies that have passed since have confirmed the captain's foresight and the note's interpretation of the events.

The note states that the phenomenon was characterised by five abnormal features:

1 The exceptional height of the waves (crest to trough height at between 15 and 20 metres) and their remarkably vertical front.
2 The shortness of the gap between two consecutive waves (about 100 metres).
3 The travelling direction of the wave group that came at an angle of 20° to 30° from the main swell.
4 The high velocity of the wave group (about 20 knots).
5 The shape of the waves, showing a short crest front (600m to 800m) with a steep decrease at both ends.

The limited extent of the waves is illustrated by the observation made of the occurrence by the vessel *Victor Schoelcher*. This ship was hove-to abaft the beam, at about 2nm distance, but did not experience these rogue waves at all. Nonetheless, those on its bridge saw the *Jeanne d'Arc* disappear on three occasions into the troughs of these huge waves that appeared to come out of nowhere.

A suggested explanation in the officer's note is that the wave train arose from a resonance between either the swell and the wind or, more probably, between two wave systems: one resulting from the prevailing wind ahead of the path of the cold front, the other about 60° from the first, created by the wind blowing after it.

WHAT IS A ROGUE WAVE?

A rogue wave is a wave of unexpected height and severity in relation to the prevailing sea state at the time it occurs. For a long time, reports of rogue waves were discounted on the grounds that sailors were prone to exaggeration, or that rogue waves were convenient excuses for poor seamanship. However, the more widespread use of measurements began to provide abundant evidence that some waves were well beyond normal expectation.

The topic caught the attention of researchers who investigated two main issues:

1 Are there more high waves 'appearing from nowhere' than can be accounted for by conventional theories or, with so many people going to sea, are they just the extremes that are bound to be encountered at some time?

2 Can one formulate a theory to explain how monster waves could develop from normal sea conditions?

A third issue also arose: are there some characteristics in the sea state or the meteorological conditions that would make the occurrence of a rogue wave more likely?

Before going any further, it may be useful to recall some of the properties of ordinary-wind waves.

GENERATION

When the wind blows over the sea surface its dragging force creates wavelets, as some water particles are pushed up over others before gravity brings them back down. The wavelets merge to build small waves at first, and then the continuation of the wind effect, and of further merging, enlarges them, while at the same time they increase in height. It is worth noting that waves travel at speeds in proportion to their length, the longest ones being the fastest. Waves are thus the combination of many elementary wave components, and since those components have different velocities, the combinations are ever changing.

Due to the random nature of the relative phases of the components, waves are modulated, resulting in large waves when crests are of a fairly even height, and smaller waves when crests and troughs balance each other more evenly. Given their random nature, large waves are statistically bound to develop from time to time. Typical figures show that, on average, a wave twice the prevailing significant height occurs slightly more frequently than once every day, with this figure rising to a ratio of 2.5 (about once per month) and peaking at a ratio of 3 (about once every 50 years.) Fortunately, it is extremely unlikely that the significant wave height would be very high at the precise time that those increased ratios are reached.

However, the combination might be more complex than that, and interactions between large components might create waves greater than the sum of their individual elements. A typical model for such interactions is the non-linear Schrödinger equation that represents a theory explaining how energy can travel in packets, or groups of waves, with the same amount of energy sometimes spread over half a dozen waves, and sometimes gathered into a single wave. That theory enables the construction of extreme waves with the look and feel of actual measured rogue waves, yet the scarcity of measurement data prevents us from knowing precisely how often these would occur in nature, or even if they occur at all.

Opposing currents have a focusing effect in addition to the effect of steepening a wave's gradient: the crests bend around the middle of the flow, where the current is at its strongest. Waves always propagate perpendicularly to the crests, and they are thus focused towards a single point, where they rise in a pyramidal breaker. Directional factors can also, on some occasions, explain the explosive combination of wave trains and high waves created by the mere superimposition of a high wave from each train.

A dangerous sea breaks in isolation three waves astern of the pilot vessel. Waves of this type travel at considerable speed, and keeping a sharp lookout in following seas is essential.
© **Safehaven Marine**

DURATION AND SPEED

Someone watching a wave may feel that it travels unchanged from its point of origin to the shore, where it eventually breaks and disappears. However, individual waves are much more short-lived. They propagate as wave trains – large areas of agitated water within which waves are forever appearing, growing up, melting down and disappearing; the elementary components are recombining all the time because of their different speeds. The life duration of an identifiable individual wave is thus in the order of a few minutes, during which time the wave travels a number of miles.

In the open sea, a wave lasting 16 seconds has a length of 400 metres. The 8 seconds while the ship surfs down the back of the previous wave and sees the overhanging front may seem an awfully long time to a seaman, and the changes in the incoming wave while it covers the 200 metres to the trough may appear to him as if in slow motion, but reconstructions show that swift changes in the shape of the wave add to its severity. For instance, in the case of the 'New Year Wave' at the Draupner platform, the wave front extended from -10 to +10 metres 20 seconds before the crest hit the platform, from -14 to +10 metres 10 seconds before the hit, and from -6 to +18 metres at its peak. Within a few seconds a 'hole in the sea' had opened, and if any ship had stuck its bow into the hole, the crest of that 24-metre wave would have seemed to have risen 32 metres, from -14 to +18!

WHERE AND WHEN: THE 100-FATHOM DEPTH LINE

As a master on a small reefer (refrigerated cargo vessel) crossing the Bay of Biscay in a very rough sea in 1961, Captain Wilson Cameron's Spanish third mate reported that they were on the 100 fathom (200m) line and that 'very dangerous seas are often found around there'. His father and grandfather had frequently warned him about the area. Captain Cameron altered course accordingly and the sea conditions improved.

Several years later he was sailing as chief officer on a 156,000 ton ore carrier on the same voyage and noticed that the course had been set right on the 100 fathom line off the coast of Portugal and Spain. When he advised his master, the latter said that he did not believe yarns from third mates and maintained course.

A few days later, off the coast of Spain, the wind was north-west force 6 to 7, and the carrier was spraying and occasionally shipping water, but the weather was not troubling her to any great extent. The sky was partly cloudy with a full moon in the west. At 0520 the moon was blotted out and all turned dark. Cameron turned to port to see what kind of cloud could obscure the moon so completely and was amazed, horrified in fact, to discover it was no cloud but an immense wave approaching on their port beam. It stretched far north and south, had no crest, nor white streaks, and as it approached at speed he could see its front was nearly vertical. About 80 to 100 yards away the wave started to break, and in another few seconds it reached the ship and struck her fair abeam. Fortunately, the vessel rolled away just before the impact and survived. Some of the damage was quite extraordinary, for instance the forecastle deck was set down about 3 inches.

Captain Cameron later tried, with little success, to draw attention to the dangers of the 100 fathom line. Having read his account in the 1993 *Mariner's Weather Log*, I discussed the point with many scientists and sailors, but none of them seemed to have

Breaking seas of extraordinary size and ferocity in the Mealista Channel, Outer Hebrides. © Murray Macleod

heard of the tale. Yet on the night of 20–21 May 2006 the *Pont-Aven* ferry, with more than 1,000 passengers on board, was hit by a wave more than 17 metres high when sailing out of the English Channel near Ushant. 150 cabins were flooded, and the vessel had to turn back to Roscoff for repair and medical assistance for the injured. Then, two days later, a grey-haired French sailor came to our institute, asking to talk to a scientist, and told me about the 'unknown dangers of the 100 fathom line'. (It should be noted, however, that the *Pont-Aven* was not on the 100 fathom line but had headed straight into the heart of a storm when the crew had thought that they would pass behind it. The unexpected high wave added to a sea state *already* more severe than anticipated.)

From a scientific point of view, the 100 fathom line is the point where the longest deepwater waves begin to become affected by the sea bottom and steepen, as they would over a shoal. There may also be reflections on the sloping edge of the continental shelf, which can usually be found at such depths, that amplify the waves. It is thus no wonder that unusual sea events occur around it. Additionally, it is not unusual at such depths to find reflections on the sloping edge of the continental shelf that increase wave size.

THE AGULHAS CURRENT

The east coast of South Africa, especially between Durban and Port Elizabeth, has long been recognised as an area where high waves occur and ships sink. These waves even have a name of their own: 'Cape Rollers'.

In July 1909 the luxury steamer *Waratah*, sometimes referred to as 'Australia's Titanic', en route from Durban to Cape Town, disappeared with 211 passengers, and to this day no trace of the ship has ever been found. Since then, there has been a long record of wave-related disasters in the area, such as the *World Glory*, broken in two by a single wave in 1968. A rogue wave is therefore the most likely cause for the loss of the *Waratah*.

It has long been known that opposing currents make waves higher, steeper and therefore more dangerous. Yet the Agulhas Current exhibits a number of features that may have lulled many a shipmaster into a poor route choice. First, the current comes out to the south-west of the Indian Ocean rather swiftly, and adding up to 5 knots to the ship's speed, while saving a significant amount of fuel by sailing on its back, is often an incentive hard to resist. At the same time, when the weather is clear and the sea looks calm and glassy, it may be difficult to imagine how a low-pressure weather system, sitting a few hundred miles to the south a few days before, could send high waves to the north-east which will in turn grow even higher on meeting the current. Moreover, the shear at the edge of the current flow has a focusing effect as it 'bends' the wave crest. So even though shipmasters may, in order to keep safe, try to avoid the 100 fathom line or the shelf break where that edge is supposed to lie, they may forget that, on some occasions, current changes which bring that limit as far as a hundred miles or more offshore can propagate slowly down the current.

Returning to the definition of a rogue wave as a wave of unexpected height, the Agulhas Current shows that sometimes the problem is simply that expectations are not realistic, due to an unawareness or ignorance of hidden factors. Over the last decade, the South African authorities have sent out warnings when the conditions are ripe for high waves, and the number of accidents has dramatically decreased. However, in other areas of the world, such as the Kuroshio Current in the north-western Pacific Ocean, wave-current interaction is also possible but less predictable because the current does not follow such a stable course as the Agulhas system.

THE COLD FRONT AND CONVOLUTED STORMS

Most eyewitness accounts report that rogue waves approach at an angle to the prevailing wave direction. This would suggest that a new wave train could be arriving from another wave generation area close by.

Meteorological conditions most prone to creating such generation areas are cold fronts, Polar lows and other quasi-cyclonic squalls, or low pressures with convoluted courses where the centre turns back over its track.

The famous 'Hallowe'en Storm' – the 'Perfect Storm' – of 1991 that caused the loss of the *Andrea Gail* with her crew of six, had a track in the shape of a figure of eight. A ship close to the track faces waves from many different directions, as the storm moves about her. When those wave trains superimpose they raise high waves, often pyramidal, where the crests cross.

It is worth noting that in the *Pont-Aven* incident the same storm had been around for at least 48 hours. Her previous crossing of the Bay of Biscay, in very rough conditions, had been extremely difficult for both passengers and crew.

THE RUNNING FETCH

On some occasions the storm and its wave generation area can travel at the same speed and in the same direction as the waves themselves. This is called a 'running fetch', as the

***Looking forward in heavy seas during a big roll aboard** Jeanne d'Arc.*
© ***Monsieur Dujardin***

fetch – the area where the wind generates waves – runs with the storm. The most active wave generation then occurs at the place where the waves are already at their highest, while some distance ahead the biggest waves have not yet arrived, and the significant wave height looks rather low, especially in relation to the meteorological forecast.

HOW SHIPS CAN BE SUNK BY WAVES

In simple terms, the three most common ways for a wave to sink a ship are: breaking it, rolling it or filling it.

BREAKING

Any wave begins with a trough, and the higher the wave, the more water it sucks back before pouring it over the foredeck. In February 1986 Captain Andy Chase was standing by the engineer who was taking a photograph of a rogue wave off Cape Hatteras before it hit the *SS Spray*. The wave bent the foremast back about 20°, tore the forward firefighting station off the deck (rails, monitor, platform and all), threw it against the face of the deckhouse and bent all the catwalks back severely. Captain Chase recalls: 'We were diving down off the face of the second of a set of three waves, so the ship just kept falling into the trough, which kept opening up under us. We were on the wing of the bridge, with a height of eye of 56 feet, and this wave broke clean over our heads!'

The scenario is very simple: the weight of the ship accelerates her down the back slope of the previous wave, the bow sticks into the lower part of the front of the giant incoming wave, and thousands of tons of green water fall onto the fore part of the ship. What happens next depends on the structure of the vessel.

Jack Williams was a pilot on the *USS Bennington* aircraft carrier in June 1945. In an interview about his wartime experiences he recalled the following incident: 'I was on the *Bennington* in the typhoon off Okinawa. You gotta understand that the vessel's flight deck is 70 feet above the water. We were taking green water over the flight deck, not white water. Green water, 70 feet of it! This thing was riding up 70 feet and down 70 feet. And I stood on the catwalk, and I can still remember seeing us do that. Man, it was hair-raisin' stuff... Entire battle cruisers were actually disappearing in these troughs... Planes were flying off the deck; it was a mess! The water coming up hit the flight deck and just snapped it like candy. The *Bennington* ended up with about 12 or 15 feet of its flight deck overhang hanging down.'

On a ship with an exposed bridge or control rooms in the forecastle, such as a passenger ship, the water is likely to smash the windows of the bridge and flood the electrical equipment located there. The Semester at Sea education programme is meant to give students 'hands-on' experience of nature. On 1 February 2005 their ship, *Explorer*, limped into Honolulu Harbour after heavy seas disabled three of her four engines. The 591 foot *Explorer*, with 990 people aboard – 681 students, 113 faculty and staff, and 196 crewmembers – was about 650 miles south of Adak, Alaska, when a giant wave tossed the ship around in heavy seas, damaging engines and injuring two people. At 1130 the night before the incident, the crew were warned by the bridge of high-velocity winds. At 1225 the chief engineer's window blew out, allowing a large amount of water to rush in and damage the console and equipment on the bridge, causing everything to go out. They said the 55 foot wave was a vertical wall coming right at them.

On many occasions the sudden load increase on the fore part of a ship, due to the weight of the green water, creates an abnormal bending of the hull girder that is sufficient to induce global buckling on the deck or bottom. In the 'best' cases, the ship shows a bent profile, with the bow either down in the water, as with the *Bencruachan* in 1973, or raised up. In the worst cases, the ship breaks in two, as happened to the *World Glory* in the Agulhas Current in 1968.

Bottom buckling of the hull girder might also happen when the ship 'rides over a wave', although thanks to the increased thickness of bottom plates designed to withstand water pressure, the hull girder is less likely to be damaged than the deck.

The hatch covers of the fore holds may also not be able to withstand the blow. The breaking of those hatch covers, together with water ingress through ventilation holes and the subsequent flooding of the holds, is one of the hypotheses put forward to explain the loss of the *Derbyshire* during Typhoon Orchid in 1980.

ROLLING

On the morning of Saturday 4 November 2000 the 56ft research vessel *RN Ballena* capsized in a rogue wave south of Point Arguello, California. The research vessel was

This flybridge cruiser is advancing towards increasingly threatening seas. Note the dangerous trough and curling crest three seas ahead, which could represent the 'rogue' in the pack. © *Safehaven Marine*

engaged in a routine side scan sonar survey of the seabed for the US Geological Survey, along the 30ft depth contour approximately a quarter of a nautical mile from the shore. The weather was good, with clear skies and glassy swells. The forecast swell was 7 feet and the actual swell appeared to be 5–7 feet. At approximately 1130 the crew observed a 15ft swell beginning to break 100 feet from the vessel. The wave crested and broke above the *Ballena*, caught her broadside and quickly overturned her. All crewmembers were able to escape the overturned vessel and deploy the liferaft. The crew attempted to paddle to the shore but realised the chances of navigating the raft there were low, due to strong nearshore currents. The crew safely abandoned the liferaft approximately 150 feet from shore and successfully swam to safety. They climbed the rocky cliffs along the shore and walked about 2 miles before they encountered a vehicle from Vandenberg Air Force Base, which immediately called the emergency services.

The *Ballena* incident is unfortunately not unique. Many fishing vessel losses show the same characteristics: the weather may seem settled and the crew fully occupied in their work, so that if an abnormal wave is sighted it is too late to take any action. The breaking wave takes the boat beam-on, and whereas a sailboat could keep its balance

An isolated breaking sea offshore, which needs to be avoided at all costs. Note the length of the breaking crest and the degree of expended energy.
© **RIB International Magazine**

thanks to the high rotation inertia brought by the mast and keel, a motorboat is easily rolled over. On some occasions the rolling motion goes a full 360°, but while a sailboat could survive if the crew wasn't washed away in the maelstrom, on a motorboat all windows of the wheelhouse are likely to get smashed and electrical control systems flooded, so that a few normal waves are then sufficient to sink the disabled ship.

FILLING

High waves can also catch a boat from behind and flood the ship if openings are not secured. This could occur either because of carelessness or simply because of ongoing work requiring them to be open, as with the doors of the fish hold in fishing operations. On 16 December 1990, while returning in heavy weather from fishing grounds in the Gulf of St Lawrence, the *Nadine*, a 37m fishing vessel, listed to port and sank by the stern. A search-and-rescue operation was immediately undertaken to locate the ten people aboard. Two crewmembers were rescued and the bodies of six victims were recovered. The other two crewmembers were never found.

The enquiry board determined that the *Nadine* sank because the openings on the afterdeck and the transverse bulkheads were not secured. Water was thus able to enter the vessel and eventually flood the lazaret, the fish holds and the engine room. This ingress gradually reduced the vessel's stability until all reserve buoyancy was lost and the vessel sank. Poor weather, darkness, lack of training and the suddenness of the sinking hindered the crew as they abandoned ship, and all these factors contributed to the loss of life.

CONCLUSION

In the *Jeanne d'Arc* incident, thanks to their extraordinary shape and exceptional height, the waves stood out against the already existing rough sea and could be detected just in time to change the ship's heading to an appropriate course. The action taken prevented the ship meeting the waves head-on, which would have increased the risk of serious damage to the bridge and upper decks, and also of submitting the hull to very high stresses, especially if the ship had come to 'ride over' the crest of one of the waves. As it was, the ship rode her way over each of the obstacles, gliding into the troughs and never pounding or ramming. As a consequence, both equipment and crew suffered only minor damage. It is worth noting that all access to the decks had been prohibited for more than 24 hours, and as a result there were no major casualties.

Those who were on board did not share the late Admiral Storelli's self-effacing summary of events, quoted earlier. The ship was saved by his appropriate action, firstly by recognising the danger on sighting the waves, however unexpected they might have been at a time when the weather was clearing up at last, and secondly by quickly assessing the nature of the risks for his ship and taking action to counter them. It is clear, then, that here a powered craft has the advantage over a sailboat of being able to respond quickly, unlike a sailing vessel, which may simply have to face up to the sea and wait.

Ocean waves seem to follow each other at regular intervals, and sailors tend to call a wave 'abnormal', 'rogue' or 'freak' when its height or steepness departs too wildly from a similar regularity. Nevertheless, experience, statistics and scientific models recognise the existence of such extremes, however unexpected they might be to the seaman. The odds are such that, in an entire life at sea, you have as much chance of never encountering a 'rogue' wave as you have of being hit at least once. Yet, what is going to sea all about if it is not about preparing oneself to meet the unexpected?

WEATHER FORECASTING FOR POWERBOATS

BY CHRIS TIBBS

Leading maritime weatherman and meteorologist Chris Tibbs explores the issues relating to weather and accurate forecasting from the perspective of the global powerboater.

Heavy weather means different things to different people depending, among other factors, on their experience and the size of their boat. What may be heavy weather for, say, a sports fishing boat will hardly upset the champagne on a modern large superyacht. Where we are and what the boat is designed for will also shape our feelings as to what are acceptable conditions, and what are extreme. What is considered a storm in the Channel Islands may be just an everyday occurrence in Shetland.

Whilst wind strength is important in its own right, it is the waves that the wind generates that create a dangerous sea state. Wind in itself may make it difficult to manoeuvre and may cause damage in a marina, but it is the destructive power of the waves that brings about most of the devastation and loss of life at sea. Closer to home shores we have tides and shallows that will affect the sea state as well as the land affecting the force of the wind.

Weather routeing is a service that provides comprehensive expert weather forecasts and advice on optimum routes throughout a ship's passage, and with the advent of bigger and better computers and the use of more accurate weather models, formal weather routeing has become increasingly common. Communications are continually improving, making the distribution of information easier. For ship routeing, it is often wave models that are used to route shipping away from the areas of extreme waves, rather than pure wind strength, as it has long been recognised that these waves can cripple ships. Although some view weather routeing as primarily a means of saving fuel costs and keeping ships on schedule, the role it plays in reducing damage to ships and cargo is of greater significance.

We have been routeing informally for many years. Pilot (routeing) charts, showing average meteorological conditions, have been around for a long time, and *Ocean*

Passages for the World, a publication originally for sailing ships, is still going strong for both small and large ships. It gives recommended routes to follow, at different times of the year, for crossing the oceans of the world and avoiding areas with the worst meteorological conditions.

WEATHER ON A GLOBAL SCALE

Temperate latitudes are generally in a band of depressions that cross the oceans from west to east, bringing unsettled weather with rain and wind. This is typical of the weather of western Europe and the west coast of the US, but is also typical of regions extending from about 40° to 60° both north and south of the Equator. On the eastern side of large land masses there are areas where depressions deepen or form, and although the weather is different, depressions and storms are prevalent.

Closer to the Equator (typically between 5° and 20° north and south) we enter a band where tropical cyclones are likely to occur. These tropical cyclones have various names depending on the area. They are known as hurricanes in the Atlantic basin and in the eastern Pacific, and typhoons in the western Pacific, while in the Indian Ocean they are known as cyclones.

Whatever the name, they are intense storms with in excess of 63 knots of wind and often cause widespread loss of life and damage. After the publicity of Hurricane Katrina hitting New Orleans in 2005, nobody should underestimate the power of these storms. The areas that are affected by tropical cyclones appear to be expanding, and in 2004 Brazil, an area that was previously thought not to be affected, was hit by a tropical storm. Not quite powerful enough to be classified as a hurricane, the surprise was its location. It is uncertain whether this is due to global warming, or just because we have better satellite coverage. However, the signature shape of a tropical storm has also been seen in the Mediterranean Sea. With rising sea surface temperatures we may see more of these storms outside of their 'usual' locations.

The area between 20° and 40° is an area of more variable wind, where semi-permanent subtropical high-pressure systems generally sit over the oceans. These highs are given names: the Azores or Bermuda High sits in the North Atlantic, and the St Helena High sits over the South Atlantic, to name just two. The air around high pressure systems moves in a clockwise direction in the northern hemisphere, and anticlockwise in the southern. On the eastern and Equator sides of the highs there are the steady winds of the Trade winds. This is generally an area of light wind, and the highs move north and south with the seasons. On the western sides of the highs is an area of light and variable wind, sometimes called the Horse Latitudes. Large depressions will displace the highs, and sometimes a low gets stuck on the Equator side of the high where it becomes 'cut off' from the flow of westerly winds high in the atmosphere. The low may then hang around for a number of days, with little movement before it finally dissipates.

In high latitudes very strong depressions bring storm force winds, and a weather chart of the North Atlantic will often show depressions near Iceland or southern Greenland. However, further north, near the Pole, high pressure is in control, and although the Poles can be windy, precipitation is low. Antarctica is actually classified as a desert, and although in pictures it looks as if it is snowing, this is in fact wind-blown ice particles.

This just leaves Equatorial regions where, over the oceans, The Doldrums – more scientifically called the ITCZ (Intertropical Convergence Zone) – are to be found. This is an area of lower pressure and is characterised by light wind and heavy squalls.

So we can split the world up into different areas, defined by the likely weather to be found, and although bad weather can occur anywhere, our location determines the likelihood of it taking place, as well as its form.

In addition to the large systems mentioned, there are smaller mesoscale phenomena to watch for. These may be generated by the land and are usually thermal in nature. Near mountains, particularly those covered by snow and ice, strong katabatic winds can hurtle down from the mountain peaks, bringing cold gale force winds. As well as being very strong they hit the water at an angle, sometimes causing vessels to heel excessively. Thunderstorms, waterspouts and line squalls can bring intense weather conditions and strong wind.

THE BEAUFORT SCALE
Long before anemometers were used, Admiral Francis Beaufort published the first Beaufort Scale in 1808. By combining wind strengths and wave heights we can get an indication of what waves we can expect for any given wind speed. This is expected wave height away from shallow coastal waters and the shelter of land. It cannot include the influence of waves coming from a long way off generated by another system or a significant change in the wind direction.

The table on pages 210 and 211 links wind speed, wave heights and probable effects on a powerboat. The force has a name allocated to it, and although some forecasts are given in Beaufort force, others are quoted in knots, mph, kph, or metres per second (mps). In general, the description of the wind strength will be kept to the Beaufort description.

WHAT GENERATES THE WEATHER?
The sun heats the Earth (land or sea) which in turn heats the air above it, and this is one of the fundamentals in understanding the weather. The Earth is heated unequally, with the majority of heat energy being absorbed by the Equatorial regions and the tropics. The weather then helps to redistribute the heat more evenly, moving heat and moisture from the Equator to the Poles. Moisture in the atmosphere is important, with the absorption and release of latent heat. Ocean currents also help with this redistribution of heat, and this is why the Gulf Stream and other ocean currents are so important. Global circulation generates the areas or bands of weather described above.

Depressions, also called 'lows', or 'storms' on American weather charts, concern us the most, as they bring bad weather with strong wind, heavy seas and considerable rain. We will concentrate more on these systems as they have such an effect on life in mid latitudes.

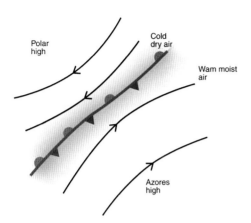

1 *The polar front in equilibrium. Although in the diagram it is marked as the Azores High this depends on the ocean and can be any semi-permanent sub tropical high.*

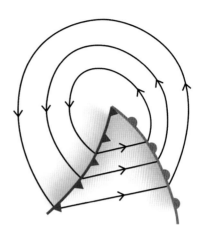

2 *A disturbance along the polar front starts to form a wave. As a tongue of warm air moves into the colder air the surface pressure lowers and the depression starts to get its own circulation.*

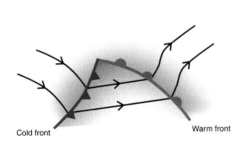

3 *The depression becomes fully formed. The arrowheads show the general direction of the wind around the depression. The surface wind will cross the isobars pointing in towards the centre by about 15°.*

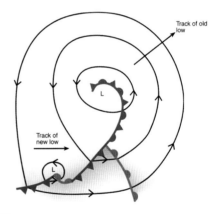

4 *This is the mature stage, as the depression declines in intensity. The fronts become occluded. However, a secondary low may form along the trailing cold front and in this way a family of depressions can form.*

No two depressions are ever quite the same, and descriptions of the development of depressions are a generalisation. Many depressions form along the Polar front, an area where warm, moist air from the tropics meets cold, dry air from the north. Higher in the atmosphere, above the Polar front, the jet stream will also be found where there is a strong temperature contrast in the air between 'blocks' of air of differing characteristics.

If we look at the diagrams 1–4, we can see the development of a low and where a possible secondary low may develop. Secondary lows will often form at the triple point where the occluded front, warm front, and cold front meet. On satellite pictures this may appear as cloud with a distinct comma shape; soon we see circulation forming around this cloud, which is the development of a new low. It can rapidly deepen, making a significant difference to the weather. Whereas we may have been expecting to pass well to the south of a depression, we suddenly find a new low intensifying close to our position. At other times, when a mature depression has a cold front running close to parallel to the isobars, what is termed a 'wave depression' may form on the front. A first sign on the weather charts will be a widening of the isobars along a cold front and a change in symbols along the front to warm-front symbols. Soon this will become a depression in its own right as it forms as one of a family of depressions. The members of this family will be linked by a front, and there may be four or five depressions in the family before the system dies away completely.

WEATHER CHARTS

Weather is shown on charts that look a little like ordnance survey maps, with lines going around the centres of high or low pressure like the contours showing hills and valleys. The lines on weather charts are isobars and connect places of equal pressure. The charts that are most useful to mariners are the surface charts that show the surface air pressure; think of it as the weight of all the air above your head. When predicting the wind, the closer together the isobars are on the weather chart, the stronger the wind. This is similar to the contour lines on a land map, where the closer together the contours are, the steeper the hill. On a weather chart this is called the pressure gradient. In the northern hemisphere the air closely follows the isobars in an anticlockwise direction around low pressure, while around high pressure it flows in a clockwise direction. This is reversed in the southern hemisphere.

Around low pressure the isobars are usually the closest together on the western side of the depression after the cold front has passed through. What makes this considerably worse is that in the warm sector of the depression we will have had a strong, steady mainly south-westerly wind. This will build up a large sea from the south-west. As the wind swings to the north-west after the passage of the cold front, the wind strength increases. This in turn generates a cross-sea that can become dangerous. Waves are a function of wind strength, fetch (the amount of uninterrupted ocean that the wind is blowing over) and time, and the greater the wind strength, time and fetch, the greater the size of the waves. This is important, as there is such a close correlation between wind speed and wave height.

FRONTS

The charts also show fronts, which are the borders between air of different characteristics, and they define the air following behind the front. So a warm front is the leading edge of a block of warm air (the warm sector). Their different characteristics, and where they have spent much of the recent past, is called air mass theory and goes some way to explain the temperature and humidity within an air mass. For example, air that has spent a long period of time around the Azores High becoming warm and moist is known as tropical maritime air, having come from the tropics and over the ocean. As it moves northwards towards the UK it will be travelling over a cooling sea, so the air above will become cooler. This air is quite stable because as it cools it resists any attempt at upwards motion. Clouds form in low bands, and mist or fog is likely.

Behind a cold front, however, is cold, dry air coming from the north or north-west, having spent its time over Canada or Greenland. As it arrives we get a change of air and a noticeable drop in temperature. This cold, dry air is moving over the warm sea, and the lowest levels of the air get warmed. This warm air rises, so after the cold front we will get big squalls and maybe thunderstorms, along with strong gusts of wind.

One of the most dangerous aspects of the passage of the cold front is the change in wind direction. This can be an abrupt change from a mainly south-westerly direction to a north-westerly one. For a large depression, with close to gale force winds or stronger, this causes a big sea to form, initially from the south-west. As the wind changes so do the waves, and a cross-sea develops; this can become dangerous, with breaking waves and swell from two distinct directions at 90° apart.

Depressions that deepen and move across the oceans are usually well forecast, and with modern communications we should get some warning of these storms. However, secondary lows can develop and deepen rapidly, generating strong wind away from the primary low. As a rough guide, secondary lows are more likely to deepen and become stronger than the parent low if the secondary low forms more than 600nm away from the primary low. This is often to the south of the initial low and may be further south than is usual for storms to develop.

When we look at weather maps of our area, we get used to the wind associated with the isobar spacing of the area. The wind around systems is directly related to the distance between isobars and, rather importantly, the latitude. So the expected wind for a given isobar spacing at, say, 60°N near Shetland is considerably less than

THE WIND CHILL FACTOR

Well known to mountaineers, wind chill is the ability of strong winds and low temperatures to cool people (or all warm-blooded animals for that matter). Low temperatures and a strong wind will quickly put the equivalent temperature to below zero. We are all thankful of a cooling breeze in the summer months, but during the winter this can cause an early onset of hypothermia. Good clothing makes a difference; however, once wet, even though not overboard, hypothermia can quickly become a problem. On fast boats the speed of the vessel should be taken into account, as 30 knots may be the wind speed felt, whether it is the true wind speed, the speed of the boat through the water, or most likely a combination of wind speed and forward motion.

THE BEAUFORT SCALE

Force	Wind speed (knots)	Description	Sea State
0	<1	Calm	Like a mirror.
1	1 to 3	Light air	Ripples.
2	4 to 6	Light breeze	Small wavelets.
3	7 to 10	Gentle breeze	Large wavelets with occasional white horses.
4	11 to 16	Moderate breeze	Formed waves with fairly frequent white horses.
5	17 to 21	Fresh breeze	Moderate waves, many white horses.
6	22 to 27	Strong breeze	Larger waves begin to form, many white horses and the possibility of some spray.
7	28 to 33	Near gale	Sea heaps, foam from breaking waves blown in streaks by the wind.
8	34 to 40	Gale	Moderately high waves increasing in length, spindrift and foam blown in lanes.
9	41 to 47	Severe gale	High waves with failing crests. Spray may affect visibility.
10	48 to 55	Storm	Very high breaking waves, visibility affected by spray and blown foam. Surface generally white
11	56 to 63	Violent storm	Exceptionally high sea with continual breaking waves. Foam and spray seriously affect visibility.
12	>64	Hurricane	Exceptionally high sea with continual breaking waves. Visibilty very seriously affected by blown spray.

Typical power conditions and action to be taken, depending on the size of craft

Perfect planing conditions.

Good planing conditions.

Ideal racing conditions with mini-waves aerating hull for maximum performance.

Fast planing, lightweight boats begin to jump over larger waves at speed.

Possibly marginal planing conditions if wind over tide. Skipper to ensure all crew are secure, correctly attired and move with care on deck while underway.

Reduced power, essential use of engine trim and working of throttles for smaller craft.

Reduced power; testing conditions for 7m craft and under. Essential for all ancillary gear to be secured. Loose items to be stowed to maximise effective weight distribution.

Reduced power; displacement mode necessary at times, becoming dangerous for smaller craft. Personal safety and integrity of vessel are now key considerations.

Displacement mode with reduced power at crest tops. Increased working of throttles. Keen lookout required for rogue seas. Gear failure of ancillary items likely. Use of fuel – critical.

Slow speed but maximum use of power to dodge or negotiate dangerous waves. Survival conditions for all but the most seaworthy offshore craft. Ensure all emergency and lifesaving equipment is to hand and ready for deployment.

Survival tactics. Headway likely no longer possible. Tactic of dodging to be considered. Lives of those aboard at risk. If not already contacted, contact with Coast Guard etc. essential.

Survival tactics. Potential survival of craft and crew largely dependent upon strength and size of vessel.

Survival tactics. Survival unlikely for any powered vessel other than well-found ship.

Amidst failing light and worsening weather, a 10m open vessel makes its run for cover. © Paul Lemmer

the wind for the same spacing at, say, 30°N, the latitude of Madeira. If, for example, there were 100nm between isobars at 4mb spacing at 60°N, we could expect 26 knots of wind, whilst for the same 100nm spacing at 30°N we would expect 46 knots of wind. This suggests that although we recognise what is going to be bad weather near where we normally sail, we need to take special care when moving to different areas of the globe. It happened to me many years ago between Gibraltar and the Canary Islands: a fairly innocuous-looking low produced gale to storm force winds and a heavy sea. It was there on the weather charts to see, but because it was further south than our usual area, the severity of the forecast was not appreciated on board.

EXTREME STORMS

EXPLOSIVE CYCLOGENESIS

Since most depressions are well forecast, pleasure boats should be able to reach shelter ahead of a storm. Commercial shipping and fishing boats, trying to earn a living or meet a schedule, may get caught out as sea conditions worsen, and get overwhelmed. Sometimes depressions deepen quickly, and secondary lows form rapidly. In some places in the world these are called 'bombs', although this term is generally going out of fashion, and the more accurate name 'explosive cyclogenesis' is becoming more widely used. This is where surface pressure falls by more than about 24 millibars in a day. Because of the rapid development it is not easy to forecast; the weather models may pick it up, but until it can be seen in the clouds from satellite pictures, and surface observations reflect the development, there remains some uncertainty as to when or where it may develop, if it does at all. These rapidly evolving depressions are most common in winter months in mid latitudes; however, a well-documented tropical low did develop between Fiji and Vanuatu in the South Pacific. Moving south out of the tropics towards New Zealand, the low rapidly deepened, and three lives and seven boats were lost. It was named the 'Queen's Birthday Storm'.

Cut-off lows can also cause problems. These generally occur further south (in the northern hemisphere) than where we usually expect lows to be. They are cut off from the driving force of the jet stream and usually develop to the south of the subtropical high. They can generate much stronger wind than is normal for the area, and as there is no jet stream driving them, they are often slow moving and may drift to the west against what is the usual pattern of lows moving from west to east. They regularly occur between Gibraltar and the Canary Islands, and boats will often report that the strongest winds of a transatlantic passage are in this area. The depressions may not look particularly deep, but at this latitude small changes in surface pressure will generate strong winds.

TROPICAL CYCLONES

Hurricanes, cyclones and typhoons are relatively small but intense storms that form within the tropics. Their 'normal' breeding ground is 5–20° from the Equator, although this does vary between the oceans. They are particularly nasty due to the extreme wind and sea state that they produce. Because of the potential for loss of life and property they are well monitored, and if a storm does develop, a great deal of effort is put into monitoring and forecasting it. The forecasting is good, although it is still very hard to make a precise prediction as to exactly where a storm will make landfall. An additional hazard, when near the coast, is the storm surge that accompanies the tropical cyclone. This may be 6 metres or more and may cause damage to moored vessels, as well as producing widespread flooding.

The hurricane seasons are well known, although we do sometimes get storms outside of them. Tropical disturbances become tropical storms and, if they develop further, will become tropical cyclones. They are given names to help distinguish between different storms. There is sometimes more than one storm at any one time, and it is much clearer to use a name rather than a position of latitude and longitude. It is also easier, when referring back to a storm, to use a name instead of a date or year. The names of tropical cyclones are set in advance, and generally, if a storm causes loss of life and widespread damage, the name will be withdrawn from the list and not used again. The various ocean regions take differing approaches towards the naming of storms.

Although tropical cyclones contain very strong winds, they move relatively slowly, allowing time to escape their path, which usually means getting away to the Equator side of the track of the cyclone. This may be easier said than done without perfect knowledge of the exact track of the cyclone and your position relative to it. It would take a very brave person to cross the track of a hurricane. In the US a 1-2-3 rule is used for avoiding hurricanes: the danger area is determined by adding 100 nautical miles to the tropical storm force radius (the radius of expected wind greater than 34 knots) at 24 hours forecast, 200nm at the 48 hours forecast position, and 300nm at 72 hours. This gives an area outside of which you are unlikely to be severely affected. The 34 knot wind field is used as it is considered to be a critical level. At this stage, sea state development approaches critical levels, resulting in rapidly decreasing vessel manoeuvrability. Below this level, however, course and speed will also be severely restricted.

Positions and forecasts obviously need updating as often as possible and give the areas most likely at risk. Although there is a diurnal swing to the barometric pressure in the tropics, it is usually stable and there is not likely to be any rapid change. If, when in the tropics, the barometer does start to fall rapidly, it is an early signal that a tropical depression or low is forming. Depressions, hurricanes and storms are reasonably well forecast, so they should not catch us out unless we are trying to cut corners and try to beat a storm to a home port or shelter before it builds to an unpleasant or dangerous size. In many cases it is attempting to keep to a schedule that makes us take a risk – small delays soon accumulate into large ones.

Having been caught in a hurricane, the most overpowering sensation is one of noise from the wind and the sea. Outside on deck it is impossible to communicate unless shouting directly into someone's ear. We were lucky and survived, with the most dangerous time probably being after the wind had eased a little, when the waves had built to an extreme size, and we needed power to avoid getting caught beam-on.

SMALLER-SCALE DISTURBANCES

It is not just big depressions and hurricanes that can cause problems. The weather is driven by heat and the unequal heating of the Earth. Not only does the Earth heat to a greater extent near the Equator, but there is a big difference in the heating characteristics between the land and the sea. Over the land there is a much greater difference between day and night temperatures, whereas over the open ocean the difference is minimal. Countries and states near the coast, and island communities, have a much milder climate than areas in the centre of continents. This has led to the terms 'maritime climate', which describes the weather of coastal areas, and 'continental climate', where the biggest extremes between maximum and minimum temperatures will be found, not only on a daily time scale but also on a seasonal one.

REGIONAL WINDS

The vast majority of boating is conducted near the coast, and although this is in a maritime climate, the different heating characteristics of the land and the sea are important. On a daily scale this can be seen with the summer regime of sea breezes developing in the afternoon, only for the wind to drop away at night. On a longer timescale we see low pressure developing over the land during the summer months and this becomes semi-permanent. We see these heat (or thermal) lows over Spain, California and India and all land masses during the summer months. They control the wind and weather to such an extent that they become well known, and are given names such as the Monsoon of India and the Meltemi of the eastern Mediterranean.

The heating and cooling of the land therefore plays a big part in our weather, but so too does the shape and height of the land. This is a more mechanical effect; when voyaging along a coastline in light winds we often find a big increase near the headlands, or when entering and leaving a river entrance. One of the best known

Fury on the weather side. A well-found semi-displacement vessel takes a wave 'broadside'. Conditions generated by a severe low off the Irish coast are delivering winds well in excess of force 8. © *Safehaven Marine*

examples where the wind is bent and funnelled by the land is through the Straits of Gibraltar. The high lands of Spain and Africa force the air through the Straits; this is sometimes referred to as an example of a 'gap wind'. When entering or leaving the Mediterranean the wind will nearly always be blowing from the west or the east. What may be a light to moderate wind quickly increases to gale force in the Straits, with large breaking seas.

The Mediterranean is a complex place to forecast for, as winds are very localised, being modified by the changes in temperature as well as the topography. Looking at a map of the area, it is obvious that the sea is almost completely surrounded by mountains. There are a number of winds that can become dangerous in a short period of time, the best known being the Mistral. This wind can suddenly blow gale or storm force from a blue sky, turning a haven for holidaymakers into an exercise in storm avoidance. The Mistral is usually forecast and is caused by a depression passing to the north. As the cold front sweeps south the mountains act like a dam to the wind, and all of a sudden the wind 'bursts' around the sides and rushes with storm force down the Rhône Valley and out into the Gulf of Lyon. Even in the summer the Mistral can reach 50 or 60 knots and is worst opposite valleys. Similar, but not as well known, is the Bora, a wind of the Adriatic that has been reported as being so strong as to derail trains as it rushes down the mountainside. Again it bursts onto the coastal waters with gale force ferocity.

The Bora and Mistral are examples of local winds that can be dangerous even in places where the climate is generally described as being ideal. The term 'Mediterranean climate' is not only used for lands close to the Mediterranean, but for areas with a similarly good climate around the world.

In high mountain areas we will also find katabatic or downslope winds. These are driven by the air cooling in mountains, and the cooler, denser air 'falling' down valleys from the mountains to the sea. Often worse at night, these winds are localised. However, they can be strong, turning a supposedly sheltered anchorage into a dangerously windy bay. Also, when approaching a high coast at night we may not get the shelter we expected.

In some areas of the world, coastal jets form that run parallel to the coast. These are strong bands of wind blowing along the coast and may exceed 35 knots (gale force 8) when the rest of the area is experiencing considerably lighter winds. Ideal conditions for this to happen are when the strongest pressure gradient is close to the coast, when coastal hills or mountains help to orientate the flow, where the sea surface temperature is lower than the land, and if there is a low-level inversion caused by high pressure.

In these situations the actual wind can be double that which you would expect from the isobar spacing. Research in the UK and America shows that there are areas where this is quite common. One of them is in the English Channel, when there is high pressure to the north and an easterly or north-easterly through the Channel. The jets are fiercest when triggered by headlands, with the strongest wind downwind of the headland. Beachy Head and St Catherine's Point (Isle of Wight) will generate strong bands, and on the French side the Cherbourg Peninsula may also trigger a strong band of wind. One night, crossing the English Channel, we found 40 knots of wind to the west of St Catherine's, when expecting less than half that. When the tide turned against the wind the sea state was uncomfortable. This is just one example; coastal jets have been observed in many places around the world when the right conditions prevail.

In a similar way, near Cape Finisterre in an easterly or north-easterly wind, there is a large acceleration zone, often to gale force near the headland, extending for a considerable distance downwind (more than 100 miles at times). The extent of these

Running back into port following this KNRM lifeboat's service in the rough waters of the North Sea. © KNRM/RIB International archives

HIGH PRESSURE

Little has been said about high pressure, as most of the time this will give us reasonably calm seas and light winds. However, since it is the pressure gradient that generates the wind, it is important to see where any low pressure is close to the high, as there will be a tightening of the isobars and a strong wind. These areas can be termed 'squeeze zones' and are often found in places around the edge of the high, usually between the high and a transient area of low pressure. As highs are generally slow moving the wind direction is steady, blowing for a long time and generating bigger waves than one might expect just from the wind strength.

acceleration zones is not always well forecast when the areas of forecast are large and giving the general conditions likely to be met, rather than the local conditions around headlands and near mountains.

TIDES AND CURRENTS

In tidal waters we are familiar with tidal rips and overfalls; with shallow water and in any wind above a force 3 to 4 there will be places, particularly around headlands, where steep breaking waves will be found. This is when the wind is against the tide, although the faster the boat, the less of an effect the tide has on our performance (a 3-knot tide reduces speed over the ground by 50% if motoring along at 6 knots, but only 10% at 30 knots). Overfalls and tidal rips are marked on charts, and with careful planning and timing there is generally no need to pass through the area. However, places like the Portland Bill Race still catch people out.

Of greater concern are areas where there is a strong ocean current; the best examples of these are the western boundary currents found on the western side of the ocean basins. The best known are the Gulf Stream and the Agulhas Current. These are large-scale movements of warm water away from the Equator and tropics. In both cases the stream exceeds 4 knots at times. This has the effect of shortening the wavelength and thus steepening the wave when the current is opposite to the wind direction. This makes it a dangerous place to be... One of my first crossings of the Gulf Stream was on a small cargo ship. A cold front swept down from the US, and we had about 40 knots of northerly wind against the current. Conditions quickly became dangerous, and we were lucky to do only minor damage, as the wavelength was so short there was no time to rise over the waves, and they continually swept the vessel.

In addition to problems created by wind against the current, a lot of energy, in the form of heat, is brought north, and depressions quickly develop or deepen near the Gulf Stream. The area near Cape Hatteras has a fearsome reputation. The north wall (boundary) of the Gulf Stream may be marked by thunderstorms generated by the mixing of the warm, moist air brought north by the Gulf Stream, and the cold, drier air to the north. Some experienced skippers say that the wind in this area can be twice that expected, with a sea state to match.

THUNDERSTORMS, SQUALLS AND WATERSPOUTS

On a small scale, thunderstorms and squalls can give gust fronts of well over gale force. As the gust and the rain arrive together they can cause difficulties, and the reduced visibility from the heavy rainfall (or hail) makes navigation hard. Waterspouts are the marine equivalent to tornadoes, but thankfully at a reduced intensity. They can be found almost anywhere, although shallow, warm water is where they are most likely to occur. As they are slow moving it should be possible to avoid them; if not, they are short-lived but will swing your boat around, and control is difficult or impossible.

WEATHER FORECASTING TODAY

Weather forecasts vary around the world in the information that they give. They usually begin with severe weather warnings, then follow with a general synopsis of large-scale systems. This will then be refined for smaller, more useful areas and will tell us of the different relevant variables. Wind speed will be given in one of the following: the Beaufort Scale, knots, metres per second and, if a land forecast, in mph or kph. Thankfully, forecasts for a particular area tend to be in the same units. The forecast will continue with a description of the weather that includes visibility and may give a forecast for the sea state. However, forecasts are still for a relatively large geographical area and will not cover every headland or bay, and this is where we need experience to tell us where there may be areas of concern or danger.

Over recent years there has been an explosion of forecasts available from the Internet. This is a great source of weather charts and model output from the supercomputers of met services around the world. Most of the model output available is purely generated by computer and does not have any human forecaster input, so it is still important to get professionally produced forecasts.

On the Internet it is also possible to get wave forecasts that are very useful if planning long passages. These forecasts will usually split the sea state into wind, waves and swell directions; they will also give wave heights and duration, giving a good indication as to conditions likely to be met. As the models cover large areas, the resolution is generally too coarse to take tides and areas of shallow water into account. The edge of the continental shelf is also an area where waves are likely to be higher than forecast.

Wave heights given are the 'significant wave height', which is the average of the highest third of the waves. We can expect individual waves to be close to double the significant wave height. However, as previously mentioned, the most dangerous time is usually after a marked change in the wind direction, typically after the passage of a cold front where two significantly different wave trains meet.

With the advances made in forecasting, and with improved communications, the chance of getting 'caught out' on short passages by large-scale storms or a hurricane is thankfully small. Local conditions (in meteorological terms) may, however, give rise to problems, with the wind and waves increasing more than expected. They may be mechanical in nature, as with winds funnelling through gaps (eg the Straits of Gibraltar) and around headlands, or thermal, with the unequal heating of the land and sea, or often a combination of both.

***Even after a gale, a big swell will remain and its effects will be felt over many miles of sea for a long time.* © RIB International Magazine**

Weather forecasting is not an exact science, and conditions only a few miles apart can vary significantly; one vessel may be hit by a large thunderstorm, whilst another misses it completely. Forecasts are therefore unlikely to give exact conditions but they will give a very good indication, to those putting to sea in powered craft, of the type of conditions that can be expected; after that it's down to experience and knowledge to provide the rest.

BLACK HOLES AND DISAPPEARANCES

BY HUGO MONTGOMERY-SWAN
PAUL LEMMER, MURRAY MACLEOD
AND ALAN PRIDDY

Hugo Montgomery-Swan, Paul Lemmer, Murray Macleod and Alan Priddy relate their experiences of surviving rogue troughs, the phenomenon commonly known as 'black holes'. As this chapter shows, these seas can be encountered both offshore and inshore and can be the cause of major damage to a vessel – even its loss.

In this chapter we will focus specifically on the real-life accounts of offshore RIBs, with an LOA no greater than 10 metres, being swamped whilst underway. The phenomenon commonly known as 'stuffing' envelops the boat in the foot of the wave it is advancing upon. This is generally the result of a surfing motion which creates a nose-down/transom-up attitude at the very moment the bow needs to be raised to meet the sea ahead. In the case of a steep following sea of short trough length, issues such as loss of steerage can further complicate an already dangerous scenario.

RIBs by nature are particularly resilient in this type of incident. A hard boat, particularly of the planing type, is less likely to be either as forgiving or as robust as a sponsoned craft, but any planing craft travelling at speeds greater than the following seas in which it is being driven is a likely candidate and, of course, the greater the speed the more likelihood of damage to both craft and personnel. Furthermore, at very high speeds of the type described by Neil Holmes in chapter 17, it is clear such accidents need not just be limited to following sea states alone. Alan Priddy's round-the-world expedition experience is particularly noteworthy in my view, for it highlights the very principles of survival: seconds count, and the need for preparation and emergency rehearsal is vital. The demise of *Spirit* in the mid Atlantic makes sobering reading, for the speed at which the sea can gain mastery over even a well-found vessel can be truly breathtaking.

IN SUNSHINE AND IN GALES (Hugo Montgomery-Swan)
The accounts that follow look at cruising craft travelling at speeds of no more than 40 knots: vessels of the type in which I recall making one particular solo Channel crossing some seven years ago – a 4.8m, 50hp RIB; a craft aboard which, only the year before,

I had successfully circumnavigated the British Isles. The striking white-crested blue seas frequenting the English Channel on this fine, fresh summer day were being driven along as big rollers from the direction of the south-west. Mid channel, 35 miles offshore, I experienced the sudden misfortune of the entire boat literally vanishing beneath the sea's surface. As it buried itself without the slightest warning into the foot of the sea ahead I can clearly remember looking up and seeing the top of the helm console beneath the water, the sun shining down through its surface, and instinctively holding my breath until the moment of resurfacing! To my surprise the little boat came up like a cork with its engine running, and it was a simple job to open the scuppers, drain the decks and get on my way again.

Another instance involved running before a gale in a 7.5m RIB off Cape Wrath. The skies were dark, the conditions threatening. In order to prevent the boat surfing at too great a speed down into the deep troughs of the following seas, I adopted the unconventional tactic of putting the throttle hard astern in an attempt to brake the RIB's descent. This worked well for some time but, upon negotiating one particularly large sea, nothing, it seemed, was able to prevent us from a catastrophic slide or surf down the wave's face, with the result that the boat was well and truly buried in the trough below. The vessel was duly brought to an abrupt standstill, and with its tubes filled brim to brim, the small, sports-boat-sized scuppers proved quite hopeless at allowing the water to escape quickly. Further to this, the stern console had also become awash, resulting in the batteries shorting out, causing all the metalwork on the boat to become live. Virtually everything we touched gave us a painful 'belt' of electricity. Having bailed the boat out amidst the breaking seas, we played Russian roulette: having to choose either to greatly drop our speed and therefore stand little chance of being able to outrun the storm or, alternatively, to push on faster to avoid the storm, with the gamble that we might suffer yet another, perhaps even more serious 'stuffing'. I opted for the former, sitting on the back of the big seas until we clawed our way around Cape Wrath just in the nick of time before the full force of the southerly gale hit. In fact, the following account involves the very same sea area. Professional RIB operator Murray Macleod describes an incident he experienced off one of the Scottish Isles' most tide-troubled headlands, the Butt of Lewis.

INCIDENT OFF THE BUTT OF LEWIS, OUTER HEBRIDES (Murray Macleod)

On this particular day we were on passage from Scrabster, on the north coast of Scotland, to my home base on the western side of the Isle of Lewis in the Outer Hebrides. The RIB in question was designed as a 10m offshore vessel, fitted with twin 270hp diesels, built for a discerning owner whose cruising area was the north coast of Scotland, encompassing the Outer Hebrides.

Engaged as a professional delivery skipper, I had already taken this very able and extensively equipped boat to Scrabster the previous week from Uig on the Isle of Lewis, part of the Outer Hebrides of Scotland: a journey of about 120 miles under normal conditions, but which had on this occasion turned into a 200-mile escapade. My foolishly leaving an important piece of equipment behind in Lewis required me

Time to hold your breath! This boat is about to be immersed in a deep trough where drysuits and a free-draining deck are just two factors involved in both crew and vessel emerging unharmed. © **RIB International Magazine**

to have to 'turn tail' mid voyage in order to collect the forgotten item; infuriating!

However, after spending a few relaxing days around Orkney and the neighbouring Scottish north coast, and following the completion of some essential work to her engines, I duly set about preparing for the west-bound return trip to Uig. The June weather, a great deal better than the rest of the British Isles was enjoying at the time, looked favourable, with just a moderate north-easterly wind of about force 4 blowing from the east. This promised to be good, if indeed it held, as the seas would comfortably be on our tail pretty much all the way. With a reasonable sheer to her prow and a good offshore hull, the boat was well suited to this type of sea state; in fact, I anticipated the going to be quite pleasant.

I should mention, however, that on the outbound journey, I confess to feeling that perhaps the boat felt a little bow heavy, but simply put this down to too much ground tackle in the bow area: there was a large Danforth anchor up in the forepeak locker, plus a considerable amount of chain and a heavy-duty electric anchor winch system to make the task of anchoring less arduous.

We enjoyed lovely weather in Scrabster Harbour as we went about the routine job of thoroughly checking the boat over prior to departure in order to ensure everything was well secured and stowed in its proper place. Then, it was a quick visit to see the harbourmaster to pay our dues and thank him for his help before we cast off.

We 'ambled' out of the harbour at tickover so as to let the engines get up to running temperature before gently nudging her up onto the plane and proceeding at about 15 knots or so out towards the mouth of the bay. Visibility was good, and even The Old Man of Hoy, Orkney's famous 450ft sea stack, could just be made out, standing proud on the far side of the mouth of the Pentland Firth.

Since we were in no hurry we stopped several times to investigate the sea caves and beaches along the way, but caution had to be exercised as an offshore moderate northerly swell was running. The stretch of coast from Dunnet Head along to Cape Wrath is breathtaking in its rugged beauty, with craggy headlands, isolated coves, high cliffs and sea lochs adorning its entire 60-mile length. At our cruising speed of 28 knots it took a little under three hours before we sighted Cape Wrath, home to some of the most troubled and respected waters found anywhere around the British coast. Here, my crewmember Hannah and I decided to heave-to in order to take pictures of the scenery about us. Then, after ten minutes or so of picture taking, we repacked the camera before carefully loading our next waypoint into the GPS: the Butt of Lewis. Located some 40 miles west of Cape Wrath at the northern end of The Minch, the seas off the Butt of Lewis are likewise to be negotiated with caution. Some marine almanacs recommend that if mariners can see white water off the Butt they should stand off from the headland by at least 5 miles.

Nearing Lewis we had a call from my friend Calum back at Uig, asking how we were getting on. I explained to him that the conditions were reasonable, but that the RIB's tendency to dip her nose into the deepening troughs was increasing. Hannah and I had already received several soakings in the process, and I could see that we would have to helm the RIB with all due care and attention if the sea conditions were to become any more testing.

As we got closer to the Lewis cliff line, I had to start working the throttles and steering across the seas to avoid thumping into the back of the bigger waves. This avoidance measure was being necessitated largely by the wind over tide conditions we were experiencing, and the nearer we got to the lighthouse at the Butt, the worse it got; no longer able to maintain our cruising speed of 24 knots, we were now having to back off at times to as little as 10 knots amidst the heavy seas.

Within a 1-mile radius of our position, we could see standing, white-topped seas, curling and surfing in regimented style all about us. These were certainly exciting conditions, but, in reality, nothing a well-found RIB couldn't handle, so we pushed on, adapting our speed as we went in order to ride on the back of the waves wherever possible. This technique took plenty of active throttle use, but our 540 horsepower diesel engines responded well, giving us plenty of positive thrust when it was needed and, in turn, helping us keep pace with the breaking seas surrounding us. This tactic of riding on the back of the following seas was employed, of course, with the intention of preventing the craft from sliding down the angry face of a sea, nose first, into its equally aggressive trough.

Because Hannah had relatively little experience of such seas I kept her abreast of what I was doing and why. This degree of communication seemed to reassure her and helped to maintain a positive focus. When the sea we were riding on dissipated, we powered on up onto the back of the next and so forth, repeating this exercise until eventually, after about a mile of heavy going, we considered ourselves to be through the worst of it.

The wind was still behind us and the sea state continued to be testing, even though by now we were about half a mile south-west of the lighthouse. But then, without any apparent warning, the sea literally seemed to disappear from beneath us. The chasm that now appeared in front of us was, in reality, an exceptionally deep trough into which we were tipped by the steep face of the sea we had just breached. There was no time to take evasive action; we were in free fall and only the boat could save us. I gasped, then instinctively held my breath.

Hurled into the 'hole' with breathtaking efficiency, thanks to our vessel's extreme angle, we plunged into the green morass, its freezing water enveloping the RIB's crumpling bow tube. A sensation of events unfolding in slow motion is the lasting impression I have as the water came rushing up the deck to overwhelm us.

The impact would have been sufficient to have torn the helm console off its fixings completely on a lesser boat, or at the very least smash its screen. Also, if it hadn't been for the design of the seats with their high back supports and the deck foot straps through which our feet were firmly pushed, the force of water would have carried us clean out of the boat. I was grateful, too, for the sturdy wheel, of course, which I gripped with all my might.

As the buoyancy of the tubes came into play, the boat seemed to haul itself free, almost with a groan, as sea water flooded off her in all directions, though when I looked astern I was concerned, but not surprised, to see the entire rear deck was full to the brim. The weight of shipped water was immense, but what relief I felt when I saw Hannah still astride the portside navigator's seat; a little shaken, yes, but still composed and safe. (Undertaking an MOB manoeuvre in these conditions, even if the engines remained running through the swamping, would have been the stuff of nightmares.)

Full credit must go to the RIB's stability and the speed at which the water emptied out through the large-diameter transom scuppers. As the next wave lifted the boat back on its 'haunches', tonnes more water streamed out of the vessel but, with each snarling wave rearing up astern of us, we were at risk of being swamped yet again. Even with the power of the twin Cummins 270hp diesel engines, the RIB was painfully lethargic, but to their credit and the integrity of the engine housing, we managed to maintain headway, albeit at minimal displacement speed.

While I got Hannah to check the 'elephant trunk' transom scuppers to ensure they were free of any ropes or lines (rope and debris will quickly be drawn into these ports as the water surges through their outlets, with the likelihood of them becoming fouled around the propeller), I sought to trim the nose of the RIB down to its fullest extent and get the engine RPM increased as quickly as humanly possible, as forward motion was critical in order to get the water moving out through the scuppers. In order to assist, Hannah had to stand or kneel in about 3 feet of water, but it had to be done and this inspection then reassured us that we could continue to power up without something fouling the propeller.

Murray Macleod, aboard the 10m RIB, rises to the crest of a very large swell off Cape Wrath. Power is essential in climbing such big seas. © Paul Lemmer

All the time spent in Scrabster stowing our kit, including the dinghy, had been to no avail, as everything had come adrift in the stuffing. Despite every pump on the boat working flat out, I wasn't in a position to know whether water had got into the engine housing and hence whether the diesels would keep running. As it transpired, the engine housing had, in fact, maintained its watertight integrity and kept the engines dry. Engine housings can be the Achilles heel of an inboard-powered craft, which is why, so often, outboard engines can be more suited to offshore use. The latter are tough, less vulnerable than their inboard counterparts and, in some respects, more simple in terms of their associated engineering. No matter how good its technology or performance, a diesel inboard, either poorly installed or housed within an inferior unit, is a major breakdown waiting to happen.

Next, upon trying to open the locker hatch on the rear seat, we found that it could not be released. Evidently, the watertight integrity of this unit was less than that of the engine compartment and so, upon filling with water, the automatic lifejackets stowed inside had all inflated at once. The pressure of these inflated 'bags' was such that they squeezed up hard against the hatch and its handle, preventing movement. A common fault on open-deck craft, such as RIBs, is that their lockers are often less-than-dry. In my view, other than perhaps the anchor locker, every locker on an open boat should be watertight; anything less is unacceptable.

As the revs increased, so did our speed, and amongst the breaking seas the shipped water quickly ran free, allowing the boat to become fully operational once again. From here onwards, we picked our way gingerly along, the rest of the journey being uneventful. When finally we got into Miavaig, a check over the boat proved that she had sustained no damage.

CONCLUSION AND LESSONS LEARNT

The main learning points from the experience are: always carry spare clothes and stow them within a dry bag; if you have them, change into dry clothes as soon as possible to prevent hypothermia (it would have been good practice for us to have been wearing drysuits on a passage of this type) In the case of a diesel installation, a watertight engine housing, with its air intakes set well above the flood line, is essential, as indeed is the overall design and integrity of the latter. Vessels such as the RNLI Atlantic Class, which feature an open transom/rearward sloping deck combination, have no need of transom scuppers, of course, but a fully transomed craft designed for offshore use must have large-diameter scuppers. Bilge pumps are obviously essential too, but can be knocked out if the electrics are lost in a swamping. Hand bailers should be carried, and items such as flares and spare hand-held radio should all be kept within a watertight container that's both secure and accessible.

What seemed like a relatively easy passage for the RIB turned into an eventful afternoon, thanks to one 'black hole', or rogue trough, catching the boat and ourselves off guard. The lesson here is never to assume that the unexpected can't or won't happen at sea.

Looking back on this event, in reality there is not much we would have done differently. The weather conditions were not bad enough to warrant taking a very wide berth of the area, but it was the tidal conditions that created a far bigger hole in the water than might have been expected, and greater caution on my part would have caused me to give the Butt of Lewis a wider berth than we did. It just goes to show the wisdom of preparing a boat for the worst, and of paying attention to such detail as the proper stowing of loose ropes and fenders.

A plan of immediate action should include first getting rid of the water by the most effective means; next, assessing the situation – crew first, boat after; then, running through the boat's key systems to ensure electrics and engines are still in working order. Try to get the vessel up on the plane as quickly as possible and ensure all scuppers/elephant trunks are open. Steer towards more sheltered water or run downwind in order to assist the boat's engines to gently increase their RPM. Keep a strict watch ahead and astern for dangerous waves and proceed with due caution. Check communication systems and radio the Coastguard to inform them of your current situation and course.

INCIDENT IN THE LITTLE RUSSEL CHANNEL, CHANNEL ISLANDS (Paul Lemmer)

We had checked the weather forecast to ensure there would be no unexpected surprises and set off from the Solent on a sunny Friday morning for a camping weekend on the small Channel Island of Herm. Our vessel was an unusual Trident 8m trimaran RIB, fitted with the then latest Evinrude 225hp Ficht outboard motor. The voyage was to be something of a glorified offshore sea trial/shakedown for this unique yet practical craft. The trip across was fast and trouble-free and we enjoyed a pleasant couple of days on Herm with friends, who had travelled by means of another Trident RIB from Jersey, and my wife, who had flown into Guernsey from the mainland.

Despite a brisk force 7 doing its best to lift the tents from their moorings and send them skywards towards the Cherbourg peninsula we enjoyed our time on Herm, sampling its fare and taking in the beauties of the low-lying isle.

On the day of our return the wind had moved into the north-east and was still blowing a steady force 5, sometimes gusting force 6, though the sea was no longer the boiling mass of white foam it had been the day before. Despite the apparently calmer seas my crewmate decided, in his wisdom, to take the easy option of flying home at several thousand feet and not at the probable 8 to 10 feet altitude that the RIB would undoubtedly be reaching. So, as they headed for the airport, I headed for the island of Alderney, which was on my intended course back to the Solent. I was now concerned about what might lie in store for me in the notorious overfalls that surround the tiny British island, especially as the tide had now turned against the wind and was beginning to build up an angry-looking sea. For the first few miles the conditions were easily managed by the trimaran hull, which seemed to favour being driven at speed into the wind, cresting the seas in the process and dancing sweetly over the nasty chop with uncanny ease. However, as I approached the Little Russel channel, looking out toward the direction of Alderney, I could see a mass of white water that appeared to stretch as far as the eye could see.

I duly pulled back the throttles to a little above planing speed and, as the perimeter of the boiling sea was encountered, it occurred to me that my small vessel was the only craft out in these conditions and that I was entirely on my own in what were increasingly ominous-looking waters.

Despite the steep breaking seas, the Trident handled the conditions surprisingly well, although I was deluged by every wave as the bows pierced the white foaming crests before plunging down into the trough of the sea ahead. However, due to the extraordinary amount of spray hitting my face, and having uncharacteristically forgotten my visored helmet, I was frequently unable to see the oncoming waves and this was proving increasingly frustrating; in turn, this problem made it all the more difficult to judge the correct pace and angle to safely negotiate the seas.

Having pushed on well into the 'trouble zone', I was rapidly beginning to doubt the wisdom of my decision to head for home. The situation was getting pretty serious, but it was also clear that turning about in order to extract myself from these very confused and angry seas could be even more of a dangerous option. Knowing these waters well, I was aware that the worst of the overfalls were only about a mile across, so I kept going at a reduced pace until the seas began to moderate upon clearing the Little Russel channel.

Although the seas were now less steep, it was still rough and the wind seemed to be increasing; my mind wondered at the prospect of an uncomfortable five to six hour 'bash' if I sought to continue my passage across the English Channel. Prudence and the fact that I was now very wet (I was only in yachting gear and not my usual drysuit) caused me to think again about pressing on regardless; plus, knowing that the seas would be behind me if I returned to the safety of St Peter Port, it seemed prudent to return there. I carefully chose a gap between the waves to turn the craft and, having safely reversed my track, once again headed for the dreaded Little Russel overfalls.

Overfalls can be breeding grounds for black holes and rogue troughs.
© **RIB International Magazine**

Being buried to this degree can destroy windscreens and wheelhouse superstructures. © Safehaven Marine

With the wind astern and running in a big following sea, things quietened down for a short time, and I was pleasantly surprised with the way the trimaran handled the conditions. Surfing down the backs of the waves she didn't show the slightest sign of stuffing into the back of them. By the time I reached the overfalls I was really quite enjoying myself and was almost looking forward to seeing what the boat would do as she ran in the opposite direction through the maelstrom directly ahead. Her ability in these conditions was nothing short of breathtaking, and with every wave successfully negotiated in such stunning style my confidence grew.

Freak wave, rogue trough, 'black hole' in the sea, call it what you will; as offshore boaters most of us experience something like this at least once in our seafaring lifetime. Whatever the name, the fact is these seas invariably take a vessel by surprise due to the instantaneous nature of their arrival. It is difficult to know what else I might have done faced with the situation I was now rudely thrown into, but what happened next confirmed to me that the sea is always capable of producing the unexpected.

At around 15 knots the craft started climbing a particularly large wave, which seemed to sap the power from the motor, so that by the time it reached the crest the boat was barely moving. It was as if a huge magnetic force was trying to drag the boat backwards, despite the RPM of the motor remaining virtually unchanged. On top of the crest the RIB hovered momentarily, pivoting on a knife-edge, with its bows clawing at open space. Then, as the craft cleared the crest, the centre of balance shifted and her prow went into a headlong nosedive, straight into what appeared to be a massive black chasm.

As the craft started its dramatic descent, I quickly shut down the throttle, but to no avail, for she gathered remarkable pace and went into free fall in an almost vertical dive. Although probably only a few seconds, it seemed an eternity before we reached the bottom of the trough, by which time I had braced myself as best I could in anticipation of the big moment. As the bows buried themselves into the black depths, the boat filled immediately and I recall everything going dark as the wave behind then broke over the boat, completely burying us both beneath tons of water. I held my breath, awaiting a glimpse of daylight, but felt peculiarly calm, in the knowledge that the buoyancy of the boat would eventually overcome the weight of water and the craft would rise to the surface, with me hopefully still attached. Everything seemed to be happening in slow motion as I surfaced to see white foam all around me, but to my astonishment no boat! My automatic lifejacket had inflated, forcing me to the surface, and alongside me was the RIB's auxiliary flexible fuel tank, with my dry bag floating just in front of me, but the boat was absent: just white foamy water where, only an instant earlier, there had been an 8m RIB!

It was probably only a few seconds but it seemed like an age before I felt myself being lifted by something pushing against my stomach; a momentary panic hit me as I tried to work out what was happening, until I realised I was lying atop the stainless steel surround of the console windscreen. As the boat re-emerged, I found my legs astride the steering wheel and I quickly extracted myself from this less than favourable position to get behind the helm. Unsurprisingly, the boat was full of water, my flexible fuel tank now floating between the seats, my dry bag floating up in the bow and I was thinking, 'no, yes, yes'!

It was in the 1993 record-breaking run around Britain that I first practised the 'no, yes, yes' procedure for checking crew and boat after an incident, so I automatically reverted back to this simple, yet fundamental checklist. No one is injured or missing; Yes, the boat is still afloat and seaworthy; Yes, the engine is still running – the safety cut-off lead was still attached to my leg and obviously the distance I had moved during the incident was not greater than the fully stretched lead, but it must have been a close-run thing. Congratulations to Evinrude for a totally waterproof engine cowling, and to the riggers of the craft for a 100% waterproof setup; nothing broke or failed to work, despite the severity of the incident and the significant amount of salt water searching for any weaknesses.

I quickly had the RIB moving forwards again, and in the process the water began to flood out over the transom and through the two 4 inch transom scuppers. In little more than two minutes the entire deck was clear of water, thanks to the sensibly sized transom ports, and what little water did find its way beneath decks was soon gone thanks to an efficient in-hull bailing system that, likewise, continued to operate due to the electrics remaining intact.

After gingerly completing the last of the overfalls I was confronted by no more than a moderate sea, which allowed me to cruise the remaining short distance to St Peter Port at speed. I moored to a pontoon berth, gathered my belongings and headed up the gangway to the road above, but as I squelched my way onto the pavement with my dry bag over my shoulder, I was taken aback by coming face-to-face with my wife. Thinking I was well on my way across the Channel, she was equally surprised to see me. 'You look as if you have been swimming!' she exclaimed, and with bedraggled reluctance I had to agree...

LESSONS LEARNT

There were many lessons learnt from this experience.

Clothing: Firstly, the huge benefit of wearing a drysuit over a sailing suit when getting constantly covered in spray but, more importantly, to provide total waterproofing in an emergency, such as happened to me. Had I been hours from land and in cool conditions, I would have become very cold, very quickly, with possible dire consequences.

Helmet/goggles: The value of a lightweight visored crash helmet to protect one's eyes from flying spray and to keep the head warm. At the very least, a pair of goggles allows good vision, particularly when raining.

Kill cord safety attachments: The importance of engine safety kill switches with lanyards of practical length cannot be overemphasised. I have known a number of people who have been thrown into the sea while helming a fast craft alone and have managed to climb back aboard and continue to safety.

Bailing: Large-diameter scuppers are essential in ensuring that the craft is capable of shifting unwanted water from the decks swiftly. A craft with water on its decks can become sluggish to respond and the water may find its way into the electrics.

Engines/ancillaries: The soundness of modern outboards was more than proved in this incident, as was the integrity of the console design housing the vessel's battery and electrics. If the electrics fail through water ingression, then everything stops working: motor, radio, navigation equipment, electric bilge pumps, lights, etc.

Hull design and integrity: The degree of bow lift generated by different hull designs can have quite an effect on how a craft deals with a following sea, but from my 40 plus years of offshore powerboating I have found all craft are vulnerable to burying themselves if the conditions are severe enough, or the odd rogue wave puts in an appearance.

Passage-making decisions: I made my decision to proceed with my cross-Channel plan based upon my previous experiences of this sea area and the forecast on the day. Furthermore, the angry seas found in overfalls are common around our shores and, while uncomfortable, are not usually impassable if prudence is taken negotiating them.

Because I test RIBs for a living and there were no crew that I had to think about, I was probably driving this unusual craft faster than was necessary to evaluate how she handled the conditions. In hindsight, despite the boat handling the seas in a confident manner, my speed was probably too high and I should have let the rogue wave go ahead of me instead of cresting it. The wave that finally delivered the near *coup de grâce* was totally different to the others and caught me completely unawares. It therefore goes to show the importance of remaining alert and putting prudence ahead of bravado.

It is clearly impossible to predict the unexpected, so having a boat beneath you that is strongly made, well-found and properly equipped for its intended duties is fundamental for safety at sea. There is a fine line between exhilaration and catastrophe, and it takes a wise person to know the difference.

SINKING IN THE ATLANTIC (Alan Priddy)

We arrived in Stornoway at 0400hrs to be greeted by the police, Coastguard and officers from the fishermen's mission – feeling glad to be alive but very cold. Stripping out of our drysuits, they could not believe how much water spilled out from mine due to having put it straight over my soaking wet clothes after our transatlantic swim!

After a quick debrief with all concerned, we were whisked off to a local hotel where our wet clothes were taken from us on the promise that they would be returned by 1000hrs that morning. They knew we did not have anything to our names, and by taking our clothes and leaving us naked in our rooms we could not run away – not that we would! Tuesday morning was a manic time with the world's press camping on our doorstep. It never ceases to amaze me how the media simply devour a disaster, but all too often prove wholly lethargic about reporting a good-news story. Our 10m cabin RIB,

Spirit *underway off Land's End.* © RIB International Magazine

Spirit, had been one of the most successful powerboats of its generation, yet she gained hardly any press interest at all during the course of her many record-breaking exploits until she sank, putting in jeopardy the lives of all hands aboard and the rescue crews that raced to save them.

We had, by any standards, a lucky escape; just another ten minutes and circumstances would have prevented us from being picked up by helicopter at all. On top of that, we were very fortunate that the RFA *Fort George* warship was relatively close to our position, being just 100 miles away on exercise. Fortune continued to smile on us as there was a flight engineer crew in Stornaway able to service the rotors on the helicopter. If there hadn't been, the aircraft would have remained where it was due to having exceeded its serviceable flight hours, and would not have been able to respond to our MAYDAY call.

Thank goodness, too, that the pilot had just got his qualifications to alight on the deck of a ship, otherwise ditching in the sea might have been a distinct possibility, bearing in mind the craft had far exceeded its maximum operating distance to effect the rescue. In fact, the first words I heard in my headphones from the flight engineer upon being winched into the Sikorsky were 'you may have a worse situation on your hands than the one you've just left – this is the furthest offshore rescue the RAF have undertaken; we might have to ditch if we can't make the deck of the *Fort George* in time!' If we had not been making our passage in a RIB, I am convinced we would never have returned to the surface, and although badly damaged and waterlogged, she remained afloat long enough for us to be winched to safety. Our own 40 years of knowledge and experience also paid off when it mattered most. Following the loss and our subsequent rescue, I and the rest of the *Spirit* crew spent a good amount of time appreciating the value of life. We were all very well aware that we had pushed what life normally allows us in terms of escaping certain doom to the absolute limit. The media attributed the catastrophe to something I had said immediately after being rescued, which was that we had hit something. On reflection this was unlikely to have been the case.

Firstly, we had been running at a comfortable cruising speed and in perfectly reasonable conditions when the incident happened; we struck neither an underwater object nor a wave of any stature. We were actually running in a following sea which, as you will appreciate, rarely presents impact complications unless the conditions are severe or the boat is travelling at very high speeds. Indeed, the crew and I are now of the firm belief that the wave we were traversing literally collapsed underneath us –

An unusual phenomenon: a breaking sea collapses to expose a 'hole' on its rear face. © **RIB International Magazine**

causing us to fall into a very deep hole. The crushing of the vessel's cabin was therefore caused by the wave behind and the wave in front falling in on top of us. This resulted in *Spirit* plummeting down to an estimated depth of some 30 feet almost within a split moment. Of course, this theory is difficult to prove categorically, but nonetheless, upon gathering all the evidence available and gaining the individual experiences of each crewmember involved, I am confident the facts concur with 'black hole' phenomena. Quite simply, she just went down as if someone had grabbed her by the spray rails and whipped the sea away from beneath her hull. When she did resurface, her shorting electrics started a fire that added to the drama and shock of the moment. Reeling from the chaos, we had just enough time to don our survival suits and grab the satellite phone. If we hadn't located that phone, all means of calling for help would have been denied us – with possibly the worst of consequences. Thanks to such technology, however, contact with the outside world was successfully made and an eight-hour rescue operation ensued.

As this book reveals, scientists and learned men such as Ted Pitt and Michel Olagnon are endeavouring to prove the theory behind rogue waves, reverse waves and so-called 'black holes': phenomena they now feel could account for the swallowing of entire boats and their crews. In fact, out of the 114 ships lost in the North Atlantic every year, it's notable that a total of at least eight disappear without any trace and even without a distress call being made. Could black holes and the like be responsible for such a substantial loss of life? Furthermore, could they be far more common than we ever realised? As for *Spirit*, she was left drifting in the icy currents of the North Atlantic, heading north-east on her way to Canada via the North-West Passage. How long her sponsons kept her afloat is anyone's guess. One thing I know for sure: it was because *Spirit* was a RIB that we returned to the surface alive.

LESSONS LEARNT

Having vital lifesaving equipment stowed in a location that can be accessed in an instant is critical to survival. In an emergency every second counts, and making the right decision first time can make the difference between life and death. Technology plays an essential role in saving life these days, and items such as a satellite phone, an EPIRB, even modern survival suits, are all 'must haves' on any serious offshore adventurer's inventory. Such essentials saved our lives and, besides being able to lay our hands on them without delay, knowing how to operate them even amidst the chaos of the emergency was absolutely critical. Therefore, the need for advance familiarisation of equipment and the emergency procedures needed to be taken on the part of all the crew cannot be overstated.

Hugo Montgomery-Swan

DESIGN AND ERGONOMICS

POWERBOAT DESIGN AND CONSTRUCTION

BY PAUL GLATZEL AND BARRY DEAKIN

Leading marine journalist and powerboat instructor Paul Glatzel investigates the key factors involved in the business of building powered craft for use in adverse sea states. Additional material is from Barry Deakin of the Wolfson Unit for Marine Technology and Industrial Aerodynamics.

There is a saying about operating in more challenging conditions that goes something like 'The crew will fail before the boat.' Given the strength and capability of many boats this is surely true, and I have come across plenty of situations where the helm and crew struggle to cope in seas that their craft can survive with some ease. It is easy to be overly critical of a helm and their crew in such situations; however, a more objective view raises the interesting question of how powerboat design and construction contribute to both the longer-term survival and comfort of the crew and, of course, the craft.

Much has been written over the years about sailing craft in heavy weather, perhaps because sailing boats are more prone to being caught out through being unable to outrun adverse conditions. Here we'll focus on powerboats and the specific issues they face. Whilst sailboats exist fundamentally for leisure use, whether cruising or racing, powerboats are put to a far wider range of uses. RIBs are used for local pleasure trips but equally for long-distance cruising, offshore racing in rough seas and, of course, in the case of lifeboats, for rescue in potentially extreme conditions. While there are plenty of sports boats and motor cruisers that will never put to sea in anything other than relatively calm conditions, there are other motorboats, such as fishing vessels and pilot, police and harbour patrol craft that don't have the luxury of choice.

So what are the factors that make a craft highly effective in rougher conditions? The actual hull design is, of course, critical, and there are many hull shapes to choose from. But in addition to the overall shape of the hull, elements such as chines and strakes can be added to affect the handling and balance of the craft. The materials and method of hull construction play a key part too, with a balance needing to be struck between the weight, cost and speed, according to the use of the craft. In this chapter we'll aim to explain, in a straightforward way, how these various factors impact on handling and seakeeping.

HULL SHAPE DESIGN

Ten minutes spent in any boatyard will highlight the huge range of hull types available, each with its own advantages and disadvantages.

Deep vee hulls: Hugely popular and found on craft from 4m to above 40m. Deep vee hulls are, by definition, V shaped and are characterised by the 'deadrise' of the hull – those with significantly less deadrise would be referred to as having a 'shallow V'. The deadrise is the angle between the horizontal and the hull and reduces from the bow to the stern. The higher the deadrise at the bow, the 'sharper' the V, and so the better it will be at slicing through waves. The price, though, of higher

deadrises is less lift and consequently a need for greater power to both get onto the plane and remain there. Deep vee hulls will also have a reduced forefoot (see photo), again improving ability to slice through waves by having less lift at the bow. The disadvantage of this lack of lift will be noticed in following seas, where keeping the bow up is key, so designers may introduce a flare in the bow or design the position of the chines to create extra lift.

RIBs couple a deep vee hull to an inflatable collar to create a highly effective rough-water craft. The tubes act to absorb wave impacts; they provide buoyancy which can be very helpful at the bow, and the all-round fendering lends itself to use as rescue and safety craft. Available from 3m to 20m, the versatility of RIBs ensures they are hugely popular with both leisure and commercial users.

Stepped hulls: A variant of a deep vee hull, these have become increasingly popular over the last few years and are commonly found on race boats and some smaller family 'runarounds'. Stepped hulls are considered to offer a more efficient planing surface than 'simple' deep vee designs, with better stability and extra lift created through air pockets behind the steps. Stepped hulls appear to offer a marginal increase in speed for some craft, but potentially at the price of a more complicated hull build and thus greater cost and weight.

Displacement hulls: These displace water rather than ride on it and, although slow, with a good hull design they can be very seaworthy indeed.

Semi-displacement hulls: A popular design, balancing the benefits of a flatter hull to create lift with a fine bow to improve the ability to slice through waves. Typically heavier and more solid craft, semi-displacement vessels will need overly large engines to achieve much more than 22–26 knots.

Cathedral hulls: Often found on dory-type craft. They are not typically good rough-water boats as they are prone to 'slamming'. They have great load-carrying capability, though, and are good general-purpose boats.

Catamarans: These consist of two hulls and are very popular in the commercial world for dive and fishing charter operations. They offer a large deck space and a stable platform and are typically highly competent in rougher conditions. The stability and performance they offer have led to them being common in the race boat world.

Clearly each type of hull has particular virtues, and in choosing the hull type for a boat the designer factors in the various requirements of the end user.

HULL CONSTRUCTION

There is no point having a great hull design if the construction is not up to the job in hand. The construction of the hull can be considered to comprise two elements: the materials used and the way in which the hull is built to create the necessary strength for the forces the hull will take.

A variety of materials is available, each with their own pros and cons. In choosing the materials to build with, the boat designer must balance the need for strength against cost and weight. The usage of commercial craft may often lead to some damage that will need repair, so building in materials that require very specialist skills and facilities (given the craft may operate in an area where there are neither) may not make much sense. Most leisure craft, and a good number of commercial craft, are built using composites, most commonly glass reinforced plastic (GRP). GRP comprises fine filaments of glass in a material to which a resin is then added. The application of a resin is a common feature of all of the composites. Aside from GRP, both Kevlar and carbon fibre are also used, in high tension and high compression areas respectively, reflecting their key properties as materials. By using a combination of materials, 'less can be more' and weight can be kept down, the compromise perhaps being the overall cost and the complexity of the build.

Another material in common use is aluminium, although this can be quite a difficult and thus expensive material to work into complex hull shapes. Overall it is likely to be heavier than a composite but has the advantage that it can be repaired with comparative ease.

When you consider that in rough water the force exerted on the hull might be as much as 70–100psi, the need for a method of construction to withstand these forces is critical. The forces acting on a craft come from all directions and, in addition to 'simple' impact forces, are also trying to twist and bend the structure.

Those designers credited with creating some of the most capable craft in rough water argue that a craft with a very high degree of stiffness, able to withstand these bending and torsional forces, is the best suited to these conditions. To create a strong, stiff hull there is a need for a mixture of stringers: beams running fore/aft and frames positioned transversally like ribs. The number of stringers and frames will vary from boat to boat, and designers find an optimal balance for their craft that creates the required strength and stiffness in relation to weight and cost.

Stepped-hull boats can create their own challenges, as the difficulty of constructing a very stiff hull, given the existence of the steps, can offset the perceived benefits in respect of speed and efficiency.

RIBs, too, have their own particular problems. Whilst fundamentally the hull is just the same as any other deep-V hull, there is the additional challenge of the positioning and attachment of the tubes. Most RIBs have tubes constructed from a material called Hypalon, although a good number are made from PVC. The quality of both materials is now excellent.

Tubes are either bonded to the hull or are attached by means of a track-like system, where a part of the tube is slid into a runner. In the case of some military/commercial RIBs, a flap of the tube is screwed to the hull. As with other aspects of hull design there are pros and cons with each, with those designs with a removable tube being the easier ones

RIB tube attachments must be first class for use in demanding sea states . © **RIB International Magazine**

to repair away from specialist facilities. Whichever method is chosen to attach the tubes, the designer will have either decided to have the tubes sitting proud of the water at rest or touching it. Equally they will have designed the craft in such a way that at speed the tubes either just touch the water or sit clear. At rest, tubes touching the water create a very stable platform, which can be useful in work and safety boat environments. Under way, tubes touching the water can create drag but can equally soak up some of the wave impact hitting the craft. Those with tubes proud of the water under way don't create drag, but if the craft heels over as it hits a wave the tubes can create lift and absorb some of the impact.

*Dunk and stability tests are a legal requirement on virtually all vessels intended for commercial use. © **Pascoe International***

OTHER DESIGN FACTORS

There is still a variety of areas the designer needs to actively consider when developing their chosen hull.

CHINES AND STRAKES

Chines exist at the intersection of the almost vertical topsides and the angled hull beneath, and are designed to create lift and stability. As the craft increases speed so the chines at the bow create lift, helping it onto the plane. Once on the plane the chines further aft continue to create lift, with those forward doing so as the bow encounters waves. For designers the challenge is to create a chine wide enough to provide an appropriate amount of lift, but not so wide as to present a flat surface to slam against the waves. Chines add to stability by creating an upward force on either side of the hull as the craft comes down. Some craft have what is known as an inverted or reverse chine, where the edge of the chine curls downwards. This can create greater lift, but the price may be a harder ride.

Strakes are known as 'running strakes', 'lifting strakes' or 'spray rails'. Similar in many ways to chines (albeit positioned between the chine and the keel), strakes also create lift and stability. They usually run from the bow to about two-thirds of the way along the hull, and due to their shape have the effect of pushing water away from the hull, reducing friction and thus increasing efficiency. Not extending them fully to the stern has the benefit of reducing water turbulence in the area immediately ahead of the prop(s).

STABILITY, WEIGHT AND BUOYANCY

In designing a powerboat suited to rougher conditions there is undoubtedly a compromise to be achieved in respect of weight, buoyancy and stability. For some craft, speed is the essence of their existence, so whatever can be done to reduce weight is critical. This may take many forms, from the construction methods used to build the craft to the items allowed on board. While, on the one hand, a decrease in weight may allow higher speeds to be reached utilising a certain level of power, the reduction in weight may make the craft more of a handful in rougher conditions as it becomes 'flighty'. In contrast, a heavier boat may tend to hold the water better and offer a softer and more forgiving ride. For example, craft such as those used by pilots or for patrol may not need such outright speed but will need the ability to plough onwards almost irrespective of the weather.

The 'Bedford', an early pulling lifeboat, was employing cork sponsons to aid buoyancy in the late 1800s. © **RIB International Magazine**

The stability of a craft is a function of the relationship between its weight and its buoyancy. Understanding the basics of how it affects a craft is essential for a skipper, as it impacts on both his management of the craft and how he handles it.

The weight of the vessel exerts itself downwards through its centre of gravity (CG). For a vessel sitting at rest, then, the CG is a fixed point. However, the positioning of fuel, people and kit affect the CG and designers seek to find an optimal layout for their craft that positions the CG to give the best handling characteristics. The skipper that puts two heavy liferafts on the roof, or adds a radar arch where one has not sat before, may affect the CG and potentially the stability of the craft.

Designers can contribute to how the boat handles by designing the craft to have a low CG positioned 'correctly' fore and aft to ensure the weight of the vessel contributes positively to its capability in head and following seas. Getting this positioning right can significantly reduce the yawing that could otherwise be experienced.

Acting in the opposite direction to the weight of the vessel is its buoyancy, which acts vertically upwards from the centre of buoyancy (CoB). Sitting at rest the CoB remains static; however, as soon as the vessel begins to move through the water and waves, so too will the CoB move around the vessel. As a vessel heels over, the CoB moves (as a different part of the hull is now underwater) to create a moment that rights the vessel: the 'righting moment'. As the bow enters a wave the CoB moves forward, and so on. This happens continuously and, as different elements of the hull are under the water, the CoB is constantly moving.

It is here that different hull designs create different reactions. The bow of a craft with a very deep vee hull and a reduced forefoot contains little volume in contrast to the more rounded hull of another vessel with a fuller bow. As the bow of the deep vee craft enters the wave there is less of the volume of the craft actually in the water, and thus the CoB does not move quickly forward to lift the bow up the wave, helping it to slice through. In contrast, the fuller-bow vessel will experience its CoB moving rapidly forward as a greater percentage of its hull is in the wave, thus creating the effect of lifting the bow up the wave. Conversely, therefore, that same deep vee hull heading downwind suffers from the lack of buoyancy that its sharp bow gives it.

Designers can further contribute to handling characteristics through the design of lifting strakes, chines etc into the hull. The lift produced can help the craft right itself as it pitches and rolls by creating a righting moment in addition to the one generated via the movement of the CoB. Likewise a designer can introduce a slight flare in the bow of the deep vee craft to create lift to compensate for the lack of buoyancy in the bow.

Another consideration for designers is ensuring that a vessel's stability is not compromised by it taking water on board. As already mentioned, the CG stays stationary unless crew, fuel and stores are moved around a vessel. A wave taken over the bow that brings water on board can suddenly and dramatically alter the CG. In addition to the volume of water and extra weight this adds, the water sloshes around rapidly, moving the CG around the vessel. Just such a scenario occurred in 1987 when the ferry *Herald of Free Enterprise* capsized off Zeebrugge with the loss of a considerable number of lives. Water taken on by the vessel was able to move around, and as the CG was not balanced by the upward effect of the CoB this had a catastrophic effect on stability, and led to a capsize. In a powerboat, a key design consideration must be the ability of the craft to rapidly dissipate water taken on. This can be achieved in many ways, from large scuppers and big pumps to simply not allowing anywhere to retain such water by having a closed wheelhouse and flat decks.

Water in the bilges can cause the same effect, so alarms should be fitted, along with pumps large enough to deal with the predicted inflow in the event of the failure of seacocks in the engine bay.

DYNAMIC LIFT

As mentioned in the previous section, the weight of a vessel exerts itself through its CG, and the buoyancy created from its hull shape exerts itself in the opposite direction through the CoB. At rest, the craft is in equilibrium, as these forces are equal and opposite, otherwise it would either sink or fly away! The other key force that comes into play is that of dynamic lift. Take the example of a planing craft. As power is applied the hull is pushed through the water. The undersides of the hull are at an angle to the water surface and interact with the water flow to create an upward force on the hull. This leads to there being less buoyancy, as less of the hull is in the water; however, the combined effects of lift and buoyancy act against the weight of the vessel and keep it operating on top of the water. This lift is known as 'dynamic lift', as its effect and magnitude are changing second by second, acting through the centre of lift (CoL). Our planing craft is now running with just its rear section in contact with the water; this area is referred to as the 'wetted area'. The actual size of the wetted area will vary according to the shape of the hull and how the helm uses the mechanical instruments available to them to affect the craft. The trim of an outdrive leg or outboard, and/or the use of trim tabs or throttle, can alter the attitude of the craft, leading to a repositioning of the CoL and the CoB. Both dynamic lift and the buoyancy of the craft are changing constantly as the craft moves, and so too are the positions of the points through which they act. These changes are not noticed by the helm/crew, though; they occur automatically and constantly balance each other.

This fast rescue craft depends on maximum lift in its hull in order to compensate for its diminished sponson design.
© *Paul Hollander*

SPRAY CONTROL

Some boats are renowned for their wetness, which may be due to green water shipping over the bow or, more likely, to poor spray control. If the former is a problem it is likely to be a fundamental design deficiency, such as insufficient volume or flare in the bow sections. There is little that can be done to the boat to reduce it, the only solution being a change of speed or heading. Poor spray control may be improved in some cases, though.

Spray is generated by high pressure at the spray root, the point at which the water surface intersects the front of the hull of a fast boat. The trajectory of the spray depends on the deadrise of the hull, its curvature and the trim of the boat. With a high deadrise the spray will be directed well aft, and with a low deadrise it will be deflected to the side, or even forwards in extreme cases. Chines and spray rails detach the sheet of spray from the hull and, hopefully, constrain it to a low trajectory where it will not be blown onto the deck or superstructure, or impair visibility from the helm. Problems can arise if the spray rails are poorly located or of the wrong shape.

The spray sheet reduces in thickness as it spreads away from the spray root so, if the spray rails are located too low, or are too narrow, the spray sheet may be too thick for them to deflect effectively. Often the rails flare out to nothing at the bow of a boat and, if the boat is trimmed down by the bow, the spray sheet will be generated well forward, where the spray rails may be too narrow to deal with it.

In these circumstances spray may rise right up the topsides and be carried across the deck, but the situation may be alleviated with a small increase in trim, perhaps by movement of people aft, by reducing the angle of trim tabs, or with a small increase in speed.

To be effective, the undersides of the rails must be horizontal, or perhaps angled downwards by a few degrees so that the outer edges are lower, and the edges must be sharp. If these conditions are not met, the spray trajectory will be upwards and it is likely to be blown on board.

Another problem, more often seen on semi-displacement boats with rounded hull forms, is that the rails or chines may be located just above a region of the hull with significant convex curvature in the sections. In this situation the spray may start to separate from the hull before it reaches the rail, so that it impacts only the outer edge of the rail. The effective rail width will then be inadequate, and the spray is likely to be deflected upwards.

In most cases, when spray control is a problem despite the presence of rails, the simple solution is to increase the width of the rails. This will usually be much simpler than relocating them.

Barry Deakin, Wolfson Unit for Marine Technology and Industrial Aerodynamics

Typical 'rapid response' seating in this military craft. Note the good grab points and well-padded seats, but no suspension system.
© FB Design

SEATING

As already stated, if helms and crew are to be able to withstand the punishing effects of a rough sea it is essential that the vessel is fitted with appropriate seating. RIBs are typically specified with 'jockey seats', allowing the helm and crew to stand astride a seat they can also sit on. Jockey seats are highly effective as they use the flexibility and shock-absorbing properties of the knee, hip and ankle joints to cushion the ride, although this can only be sustained for moderate periods of time. Some commercial, military and more expensive RIBs have jockey seats with inbuilt suspension. Apart from RIBs, helm and crew seats with inbuilt suspension systems are common in those commercial craft regularly operating in rough water, such as pilot vessels and charter boats. In recent years, shock mitigation deck surfacing has also been developed to provide cushioning underfoot. This can be a very effective addition for high-speed craft and has been employed by Special Forces units, for example, to help protect their personnel from extreme fatigue and injury caused by the often considerable shock-loadings imposed upon their bodies by the hull's interaction with the water's surface.

The multiple chines in this vessel's hull will provide a sure-footed ride, but in some instances can also increase the hull's wetted area and induce a less sea-kindly ride. © Ribeye/John Apps

EXTERIOR LAYOUT

Topside, boat layout varies according to what type of craft the vessel is and what use it is being put to. For example, pilot boats tend to require an enclosed wheelhouse and an outside deck that can be easily navigated whilst wearing a safety harness. The flat deck has the added advantage that green water taken over the bows is dissipated immediately.

Basics such as locker lids that are easily secured and stay put in rougher seas seem a fundamental requirement but, when present, are often evidence of a boat designed by an individual with real experience of using the craft and of being clouted by that same locker lid in years gone by!

A forward rake to the windscreen will afford better water drop-off. © Redbay RIBS

RNLI boats are good examples of considerable thought having gone into the real use of a craft. The kit that is needed is easily accessible, easy to release with cold wet-gloved hands, but above all else is the best for the job. For example, the items that contribute to safety are perfectly placed, such as the drogue at the bow of the Atlantic Inshore Lifeboat. This can be instantly released in the event of engine failure, as opposed to requiring a crewmember to scrabble around in a locker, unpacking it and attaching the rope. Simple things are often what make a craft great.

ERGONOMICS

Though we deal with this subject in some detail elsewhere in the book, suffice to say that a craft designed to operate in the toughest conditions commercially will, of course, need to satisfy some pretty tough build requirements from the relevant certifying authority. This is only part of the picture, though, and as research in the world of the motor vehicle has shown, the ergonomics of the interior design and layout contribute materially to the comfort and thus stamina of drivers and passengers. In our world, a well-laid-out helm position is critical, with instruments positioned to be easily visible without obscuring vision in any way – large chart plotters can be particular culprits here. As already touched on, a decent shock-absorbing helm seat/position is key, as is the position of the throttles relative to the seat and steering wheel. Designers must not forget the other crew either, with good positioning for them being essential, so they can contribute positively,

A well laid out helm station in a typical modern motor yacht, but note the distance between wheel and throttles!
© Redbay RIBS

either by means of easy access to the navigation equipment (instruments should not just be usable from one position) or through simple but critical tasks such as keeping a lookout. On vessels likely to be at sea in rougher conditions for any period of time, designers must also consider how the basic comforts, such as food, drink and toilet facilities, can be provided safely and consistently.

To drive a boat hard in adverse seas requires all elements of the craft's helm point, cockpit layout and design to be finely tuned. © Euro Offshore

CASE STUDY

Pilot vessels, by their nature, tend to need to satisfy a range of criteria. Firstly they must be excellent sea boats, able to withstand gale force conditions when travelling out to meet inbound ships or to recover pilots from those departing their domain. Often, though, they will also act as a patrol craft and need to be able to carry a lot of people and kit and must be happy pottering around patrolling an area. As with any design, getting a craft to excel in all areas is a challenge. Frank Kowalski has been building such craft at Safehaven Marine for many years and readily admits that, over the years, designs have evolved to tidy up real or perceived areas for development on previous craft. For his craft he considers a bow with a fine deep vee essential, giving the ability to slice through waves while reducing the vertical movement of the bow by keeping the buoyancy in this area down. The design of the hull is married to an extremely strong, stiff hull built from readily available materials, ensuring that when repairs are needed they can be made in many shipyards.

CONCLUSION

In summary, in this chapter we've looked at how designers can influence the handling of their craft through, initially, the very fundamental choice of hull shape. Once the hull shape has been decided upon, many other factors come into play to create hulls that are revered for their seakeeping qualities, as opposed to those that never make it past the prototype stage. There is a lot for designers to consider, and inevitably it is a slightly inexact science in some areas, but the importance of getting it right is obvious, especially when it comes to designing craft for use in heavy weather.

ERGONOMICS IN HIGH-SPEED CRAFT

BY DR TREVOR DOBBINS AND PAUL LEMMER

Dr Trevor Dobbins, of STResearch, looks at the challenges facing the human frame in relation to high-speed travel aboard planing craft. Design and build issues are also considered, from the perspective of both the builder and the user. An additional contribution is made by offshore powerboater and marine consultant Paul Lemmer.

High-speed craft, or HSC as we shall refer to them, are undoubtedly one of the most enjoyable forms of offshore vessel in existence – especially in good weather amidst blue skies, balmy heat and alluring flat water. In such conditions there are few challenges to either helmsman or crew if good sense is the rule of the day. But change this perfect scenario into one where the wind is driving up ominous iron-grey seas, the sky is darkening by the minute and heavy squalls begin beating their icy rain drops like shards of glass on the faces of the crew, and this environment can begin to feel threatening and dangerous. Besides the obvious psychological effects, it stands to reason that in such conditions the demands on the human body also start to increase dramatically.

In terms of challenging offshore conditions, what should be of greatest concern to powerboaters is navigating in difficult sea states at night, poor visibility through deteriorating weather conditions, a worsening sea state, the effects of being cold and wet, or perhaps being generally weakened by seasickness. We shall consider these elements in some detail within this chapter, but it is important to first make clear that although HSC have been in existence for many years, and the demands on the crew of a seagoing vessel are generally well recognised, at the same time few designers or boat manufacturers have really shown any genuine desire to improve or even understand the ergonomics of their craft and how these relate to the challenges we have just described.

DESIGN

In the marine industry, the value of aesthetics is often placed above the need for good seagoing design, with the latter playing 'second fiddle' to the former in order to maximise sales under the glitzy lights of a boat show stand. However, it is also worth noting that the automotive industry spends vast amounts of money on resources to ensure the science of ergonomics is optimised wherever possible – with not only aesthetics and styling in mind but also functionality and safety.

In the marine environment, it can be argued that the greatest issue with HSC is the motion that the crew and passengers have to endure in adverse sea states, but so often this basic fact appears to be ignored in the design of many craft – including commercial vessels. This has many important consequences and includes the following issues:

- Fatigue
- Injuries, both acute and chronic
- Difficulties in operating the craft effectively and safely
- Exposure to the elements

The battering that HSC occupants suffer during transits in poor sea conditions is one of the worst and potentially most hazardous 'rides' that can be experienced on any form of transport. It is held that the often severe motion of HSC should be described as 'repeated shock' rather than 'vibration' – although when the detrimental effects of vibration occur, especially within the confines of a wheelhouse, the influence of the vibration is relatively minimal when compared to the severity of impacts and the overall shock loadings that are frequently encountered on a high-speed planing craft.

For example, when an HSC launches itself off a wave, it generally re-enters the water with an unpleasant impact – often on the flat of its chine, with the resulting level of impact being up to 25G, and potentially even greater. A common comparison involving humans coping with high G loads relates to racing drivers and fighter pilots. Racing-car drivers can repeatedly experience cornering and braking forces of up to 4G during a race. Fighter pilots, undertaking aerial combat manoeuvres, can be exposed to a variety of acceleration loads, potentially of up to 10G, for a few minutes at a time. These G-force exposures are different to HSC as they have a slower onset rate and last for much longer. Probably the closest analogy is a fighter pilot who ejects from his cockpit in an emergency, exposing his body to something in the order of 16–20G in the process. The difference between a pilot ejection and an HSC impact is that the ejection lasts for around twice as long as the equivalent boat impact. Although of shorter duration, the HSC exposes its occupants to repeated impacts during a transit rather than the single ejection impact. This, in turn, may easily amount to hundreds, if not thousands, of impacts on a single transit or extended passage.

Repeated shocks seriously degrade the performance and health of the occupants. Anecdotal reports from boat crews describe them feeling physically 'shattered' following passages in adverse sea states, and recent research has demonstrated that post-transit running performance in fit military personnel can be reduced by over 25%. In fact, there are many examples of individuals suffering acute injuries as a direct result of the effects of 'shock impact' aboard HSC, and these even include seriously fractured vertebrae.

In addition to acute injuries, there are many reports of chronic injuries caused by long-term exposure to repeated shocks, including damage to backs, knees, hips, necks

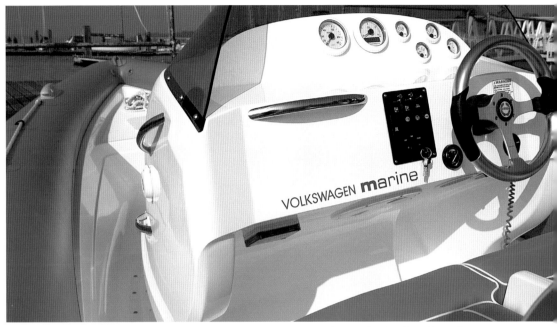

Well laid out helm console with everything nicely to hand: good wheel to throttle position and a clear view of the dials. Note the grab handle for the navigator.
© RIB International Magazine

The stresses on the human frame can be significant at speed in adverse seas. Designing the correct seating and helm positions for the crew is essential if personnel are to avoid injury or undue fatigue. As this picture indicates, severe lateral movement has to be considered in terms of the seating/bolster design to negate the harsh effects of the craft landing on the flat of its chine © Mindworks.

and shoulders. Both acute and chronic injuries can leave the sufferer disabled, continually dependent on painkillers, or in financial difficulty resulting from having to seek early retirement from their chosen profession. Legislation in Europe now requires a reduction in the exposure of humans to harsh motion in all professional environments. Unfortunately, though, especially in the marine world, designers, manufacturers and operators have not yet engaged with this legislation, and so crews and passengers continue to suffer. Nevertheless, solutions do exist to help reduce exposure to repeated shock and whole-body vibration, so it makes sense for these to be designed into HSC right from the build's inception. Such items include shock mitigation decks, suspension seating, mats, padded bulkheads and sufficient grab points.

In addition to increasing the risk of acute and chronic injuries to HSC occupants, it stands to reason that rough sea conditions make it more difficult to operate the craft. But in its pure form, 'operation' comprises two issues, namely 'command' and 'control'. Firstly, the 'command' element includes the ability of the crew to understand their environment and position – this is known as 'situational awareness'. The crew have to 'read' or judge the sea conditions so that they know what steering, throttle and trim inputs to provide. They must also be able to read the instrument displays within the craft, ie the chart plotter, the radar, engine gauges and so forth, so as to make sense of the information these provide. Increasing speed has a big bearing on situational awareness: the faster the craft moves, the more difficult it is to have a full understanding of the environment. Research using eye tracking (monitoring what a person at the wheel is looking at) suggests that at 20 knots the coxswain is able to take in and comprehend his surroundings to a reasonable and generally safe degree. At 50 knots, however, just over double this speed, the coxswain has to focus on the oncoming waves, navigation marks and other craft to an excessive degree – in fact, almost to the total exclusion of being able to check his own craft's instruments. More speed, therefore, equals a greatly reduced concentration field, with the focus of the eye and brain narrowing significantly in an effort to ensure sufficient attention is given to the immediate distance and the influx of information the high-speed experience is generating within this 'zone'.

Reflexes and decision-making response times are likewise naturally sped up as the brain processes the rush of information bombarding it from every quarter. Here again priority rules, so that which is considered secondary in terms of importance will either be rejected or 'set aside' in preference to that which is more pressing, ie the next wave or approaching rock!

As mentioned above, the motion generated by either high speeds and/or adverse sea states also makes it much harder to read the craft's instruments. Unfortunately, instrument suppliers also appear to design their systems to look attractive under the spotlights of an exhibition stand or for use in user-friendly conditions (eg moored in the marina). As the surface of the sea roughens and the motion of the boat becomes more exaggerated, it becomes harder to read instrument displays, especially if the numbers, icons and letters on them are too small and discreet in the first place. The difficulties associated with this mean it takes much longer, much more concentration and more effort to decipher the information so vital to the helming of the boat. This, in turn, will ultimately compromise the boat's safety.

In addition, all of these issues are exaggerated, of course, when operating at night or in poor visibility. In any conditions, when forward vision is reduced it makes it harder, if not impossible, for personnel to anticipate the motion of the craft. If they can't see a particularly severe sea, for example, how will they brace themselves sufficiently, flex their legs in time, duck, or take some other measure intended to limit damage to their bodies? Where you might have military personnel, for instance, all sitting in line on jockey seats, not being able to get a clear view ahead without adopting an uncomfortable posture, this lack of forward vision to the sea ahead will almost certainly result in physical injury or, at the very least, heightened fatigue. Good visibility aids 'postural stability', with the latter also being dependent on suitable and adequate seating, handholds and bracing points, such as footplates and foot straps, which really do need to be optimised throughout the craft. Many of them can be integrated into such components as the backrests of seats or grab rails affixed to ceiling bulkheads, but all must be positioned in such a way so as to not require stretching, and to ensure that strains or injuries are not caused by their use. Their positioning is therefore critical to their effectiveness. Tubular grab rails can even have hot water pumped through them via the engine's cooling systems, preventing cold, cramping hands on an open boat. But here again, initiatives such as this need to be considered at the very first stages of a vessel's design and build.

Seat belts or harnesses, though generally only to be worn within the confines of cabins, may also be a necessary addition in vessels such as lifeboats or race boats – allowing the user to reduce the degree of effort he exerts by letting both the seat and the harness do the work for him. They also reduce the risk of increasing the magnitude of the shocks due to secondary impacts.

Of course, the helmsman has the best and most secure position of all. Firstly, he can read the sea better than anyone and anticipate or alter its effects more readily due to his contact with the controls. Secondly, the wheel can be one of the best and most substantial grab points available. Thirdly, he is in the best position by far when it comes to taking evasive action. And fourthly, invariably being located on the starboard side, he is also positioned on the most favourable side of the boat in relation to prop torque and the resulting consequences of a boat landing more heavily on the flat of its port chine. Being aware of these facts, he should therefore drive accordingly, employing a sympathetic helm technique and acting in the knowledge that if he's finding the going hard, his fellow crewmembers will likely be finding it even tougher – particularly if the coxswain is located at the rear of the craft!

In my view, designers should take more account of postural stability issues, even for the coxswain. If the wheel and throttle are badly placed, for instance, causing either undue stretching or even finger traps between the two, this will make controlling the craft in adverse sea states very difficult – even compromising the safety of the boat. In addition, when designers integrate shock mitigation systems (especially suspension seating) into the boat, they need to consider carefully how the crew will operate the craft, and its various systems, as the seat moves relative to the fixed controls and displays.

In addition to the design of the boat and its components, it is essential that the crew are trained to operate the boat in testing sea conditions. Research has shown that the coxswain's input to operating his craft is principally centred around steering and throttle use, and of these, throttle control has been shown to be the most significant factor in the generation of a comfortable ride. Unfortunately, there are very few training courses that teach novice coxswains and crewmembers how to employ the proper use of the throttle in adverse sea states, and in turn maintain the safety of their craft and its occupants.

ENVIRONMENT

Around the world, ideal conditions at sea are rare, and the combination of wind chill and water can be a deadly mix. Though a cold/dry environment is relatively easy to cope with, wind chill from travelling at high speed hugely increases heat loss. Then, when the spray starts to fly, the risk of cold-related problems enters another dimension altogether. So what can be done to negate this type of problem? Where the craft is used in conditions other than warm climes, consideration may well need to be given to providing some form of cabin, or at least screening, to protect the occupants from direct wind and water, the design of such protection features, of course, being specific to the use of the craft in question.

SCREENS

In the case of windscreens, though this feature may be common on many types of powerboat, in reality few provide any real protection, but rather are added by the builder to assist the boat's aesthetics and provide the customer with something he expects to see included on the standard specification list. Screens can be very effective, but much depends upon their height and their shape. One of the best screens I've seen was on a British-built RIB, where the screen was just below eye level but featured a forward curvature to its leading edge. This deflected the airflow, actually lifting it over the people standing behind it. This meant that the screen stopped the gale rushing into the crew's eyes, even though their faces were largely above the screen, hence ensuring good visibility. This design was so effective that it was even still possible to wear a baseball cap at 50 knots, and for the coxswain to communicate to the navigator without shouting! Impressive, I think you'll agree, and it shows what is possible with a little care and the application of good design.

One last point on the matter of screens: a screen's leading edge can be as lethal as a knife. People have had large sections of their face removed in the most horrific accidents when a boat has stuffed into a wave, bringing it to a sudden stop – with the result that its occupants have either been thrown forward of the console or, worse still, into the leading edge of an unprotected windscreen. This is why increasing numbers of boatbuilders are now introducing stainless steel grab rails to the tops of screens, firstly as a means to provide another handhold, and secondly in an effort to provide protection against the potential impact of plexiglass, or its plyglass equivalent, on flesh. But hitting a stainless steel grab rail with your face at 40 knots will still have an unpleasant outcome, so designers need to develop user-friendly solutions.

CABINS AND CLOTHING

Fatigue is reduced massively when a crew is able to gain protection within a cabin, cuddy or wheelhouse. Removing the element of wind from the equation makes a huge difference to the crew's comfort. Anecdotal comparisons of crews making 100-mile offshore passages in identical weather and sea states in both open and cabin HSC indicated a reduced level of fatigue in the individuals who had the benefit of travelling within even an open-backed wheelhouse or cuddy.

Where the craft is of an open design it is essential to provide the crew and passengers with the appropriate degree of clothing for both warmth and safety. A big problem with increasing the number of clothing layers is that it reduces the individual's mobility, making it more difficult to move around the craft and undertake command and control tasks. Foul-weather clothing often restricts head movement and vision, which in turn compromises the safety of the craft. A solution to this is the use of heated underclothing, which reduces the need for a large number of clothing layers. The advantage of this solution for HSC is that there is an on-board power source to supply the clothing's heating requirement, but the boatbuilder and operator must ensure that the electrical systems have the appropriate level of safety.

Going offshore in open boats, or even when aboard wheelhouse/cabin craft in extreme sea states (ie in a lifeboating scenario where the crew will be moving to and fro from the cabin to the perils of the exposed deck), requires the use of proper drysuits in conjunction with the mandatory wearing of a lifejacket. Foul-weather clothing of the traditional variety, despite all its high-tech claims, will not prevent water getting in unless it features neck and wrist seals made from materials such as latex or neoprene. In addition, this form of typical 'sailor's clothing' will not keep the wearer dry and protected if he falls overboard. Breathable materials such as Gore-Tex have made wearing drysuits much more bearable in recent years, and this form of clothing remains the only option if the wearer is to be guaranteed protection from the dangers of water ingress and the hypothermia this can induce. Even so-called 'immersion suits', as used by many within the offshore oil and gas industry, offer limited protection compared to that given by a drysuit; but getting the base layers right

Even a lightweight drysuit such as this will afford great protection in the offshore environment. © Crewsaver

is paramount when wearing the latter. Leading clothing suppliers should be able to advise on the correct wickable underclothing/base layers needed to make drysuit apparel effective.

Besides the dangers related to cold, keeping the body at a comfortable temperature to ensure it doesn't overheat can be challenging too. Unlike a sailing craft where the crew are active for a high proportion of the time, aboard an HSC relative inactivity can be the order of the day. Crew will invariably dress to keep warm, but when called upon to resolve a mechanical problem or some other task that requires physical energy, the crewman in question can quickly overheat in his drysuit or heavy waterproofs. This 'overheating' problem in turn will greatly speed up the onset of seasickness, particularly when the boat is loitering, rolling and pitching to and fro. Also, sweat will condense inside a drysuit, and once the crewman has returned to his 'passenger' state of reduced activity, the moisture within the clothing will increase the cooling process and he will soon begin to become cold and uncomfortable. Once again, the correct type of base layers, capable of wicking the moisture away from the skin, is key in helping to negate the problems associated with the body overheating.

Protecting the extremities of the body is also essential. Gloves, for example, will only prove effective at keeping your hands warm and functioning if they remain dry inside. Therefore, gloves must be waterproof and possess a latex wrist seal. The types of glove used by professional North Sea divers fulfil these criteria but can reduce dexterity, making it difficult to operate controls unless they are designed for use with thick gloves. Alternatively, wetsuit gloves should be considered, along with travelling with numerous pairs of gloves so that wet gloves can be regularly exchanged for dry. Cold, stiff hands can pose a major threat to safety.

Likewise, getting the headgear correct on an open boat is essential. There are times when a woolly hat may suffice, but once this gets wet it becomes more of a hinderance than an aid in retaining body heat. Waterproof hats with extending side flaps for ears and neck can be good, but generally it is a lightweight helmet that will give the maximum protection. It's flip-up/bubble visor will allow forward vision even amidst rain and flying spray, while the helmet itself gives protection both from impact and the effects of heat loss. Specialist marine safety helmets are used by the emergency services and other professional users, and are built to a recognised standard. Race boats generally require full-face helmets, along with other mandatory personal items such as UIM-approved lifejackets with lifting points, and even a flameproof suit in some instances. Helmet weight increases the stress placed on the neck within the high-G HSC environment; helmet users should understand how the weight of the helmet will increase the risk of neck injury when exposed to high-G impacts. Less weight, combined with strength, is the ideal combination. The detail design of the helmet is also important. Peaks may help to shade the eyes from the sun, but if they are firmly fixed in place they can act as a brake if the user falls overboard at speed, causing the head to be snapped back on entry into the water. Professional operators will undertake a risk assessment to understand the safety risks and therefore identify the aspects and level of protection required. All HSC users should likewise undertake the same process.

SHOCK MITIGATION

One of the most important concepts for HSC designers and operators to grasp is the requirement for shock mitigation to reduce the risk of injury, degraded health and serious fatigue. The best solution is to deal with the problem at source – in this situation this would be the vessel's hull and how it re-enters the water. This is where discussions related to hull type – monohull or multihull, deep vee or medium vee, displacement or semi-displacement – as well as vessel size and geometry will all come into play.

The next step in the chain is the deck itself. The advent of suspended-deck technology means that a significant amount of the impact's magnitude may be removed before it even reaches the human frame. This technological solution will become of greater significance to the HSC sector as the legal requirement of operators to protect the craft's occupants becomes more recognised. This has the potential to change the focus of the development of HSC hulls and even the vessels' structure. The craft should be designed around the requirements of its deck, for example the deck's actual dimensions – the shock mitigation requirement for the load it has to carry along with the boat's displacement criteria. These factors will then shape the design of the structure along with how and where any specialist deck surfacing is to be laid.

The use of suspension seats on craft with fixed decks is an easy partial solution to reducing repeated shock exposure. For a boat with a fixed deck, suspension seats should be one of the core design elements around which the rest of the craft is designed. Suspension seats generally come in two forms: those where the individual's total weight is taken by the seat, and those of a straddle design where the individual has their feet on the deck and can use their legs as part of the suspension system. Each type has pros and cons, with the choice being made dependent on the use of the craft. In the case of fixed jockey seats, the width and the height of these should be adjusted to the user. Also, the depth of padding to the seat needs to be sufficient to provide protection from impact, and its backrest should be of the right height and design to provide support for the user, whether they are sitting or standing.

Once the shock mitigation system has been chosen (ie deck and/or seats), the command and control system should be designed to fit the various crewmembers. Designers and manufacturers fail too frequently in this area: too many HSC craft are fitted with consoles that are simple-to-manufacture boxes into which the instruments and controls are bolted, glued or screwed. With the appropriate expertise it's possible to develop a console that works efficiently with the crew, thus increasing their performance, safety and comfort. In some instances, this means that the controls can even be attached to the suspension seat, while other solutions work with the more traditional setup of the steering and throttle controls being mounted to the console itself. It's something of a paradox, though, that all too often the more expensive the boat, the poorer the ergonomic design of the helm, crew and passenger positions. Aesthetics take over the design, and the effectiveness of the command and control functions dramatically degrade in the process. This problem particularly applies to some of the luxury motor cruisers being built for the leisure market.

An excellent example of good design and ergonomics. Each crewmember's needs have been considered individually – note the attention to detail in terms of each specific position. © **RIB International Magazine**

CRASH

An issue that is almost completely ignored in HSC design is crash safety. Cars and other forms of transport have for many years been designed to protect the occupants in the event of a crash. Unfortunately, the majority of HSC designers and manufacturers have dismissed this safety issue and therefore leave the occupants of their craft at an increased risk of injury.

Reading reports on HSC crashes evokes memories of car accidents before the introduction of seat belts and the use of energy-absorbing materials. Occupants in these incidents have been reported as dying from injuries sustained by hitting the craft's console, steering wheel or sharp-edged structures – with fatal injuries including multiple broken bones, severed arteries, broken necks and internal chest damage. All such injuries are typical of those sustained in automobiles many years ago. Cars have for a long time been designed to minimise injuries during a crash. Although HSC are fundamentally different to cars crashes, there are also many similarities – and these beg the question: Why is more thought not given to the need for safety features to be designed into HSC? The answer may lie in a lack of understanding and the investment needed for developing design solutions.

In addition to reducing the risk of injury during a crash, a boat's design features should also help to reduce the 'bumps and scrapes' that HSC occupants often receive when experiencing a rough ride. These safety features should also address the needs of the post-crash condition of the boat to ensure that the safety of the boat and its occupants doesn't further 'degrade': it's no use surviving the crash with minor injuries only to die from drowning as the craft sinks!

CONCLUSION

Where does all this leave the HSC designer, manufacturer and operator? Looking at this subject from a positive stance, much can be achieved by the introduction of a few simple concepts which, if followed, will do much to enhance HSC: these include designing the craft 'around the person', and initially focusing on the requirement for shock mitigation to reduce the risk of injury, degraded health and fatigue.

The high level of injury risk requires that operators comply with their duty of care to their employees, particularly in the European Union, where legislation dictates this. Systems should be put in place to track both operator exposure to repeated shock and whole-body vibration, and their health status.

HSC operators should undertake a recognised training programme to ensure that they are qualified to operate an HSC in poor sea conditions. This recognises the link between the coxswain's skill in driving with his human cargo in mind, and a desire on his part to limit the problems associated with repetitive strain on the human frames of his valuable crew.

AN OPERATOR'S VIEW

Paul Lemmer now discusses the importance of ergonomics from the viewpoint of the operator and the relevance of design 'in the field'.

Having been to sea in powerboats since 1964 I have seen countless new designs coming to the market, each one purporting to be better than the last and invariably offering more seaworthiness and comfort than its competitor or predecessor. While there is no denying that most modern designs have significantly improved in terms of performance and seaworthiness, there remains much potential for the development and application of ergonomics within powered craft.

Combining the modern deep vee hull concept with the latest high-tech materials has meant that even some of the smaller cruisers can now safely travel at sea in quite inclement weather, providing the crew know what they are doing and that the vessel is equipped with the right safety and navigational equipment. However, while we should applaud the performance, finish and layout of many of these craft, sadly the same cannot be said for the helm positions on many of these boats. It never ceases to amaze me how designers and manufacturers can get helm ergonomics so horribly wrong; it is as if they have spent their entire budget and 'thinking time' on the appearance and finish of the craft – then, as a last minute exercise, thought about how to pilot the beast! So what have ergonomics got to do with boats? Basically everything!

The Collins Dictionary defines ergonomics as 'the study of the relationship between workers and their environment, especially the equipment they use'. However, what it also says under 'ergonomic', as opposed to 'ergonomics' is: 'designed to minimise physical effort and discomfort, and hence maximise efficiency'. This latter definition is particularly pertinent to waterborne craft.

Today's car manufacturers spend millions getting the driving position right, so why does the marine industry so often overlook the importance of functionality and good ergonomics? Take a look at some of the best-known luxury motor cruisers and you will see how poor the helm position ergonomics are. On one particular well-known make, incorrect placing of the throttle and gear levers required the helmsman to get up from his driving position and stretch right forward over the wheel at arm's length in order to reach the controls! It appeared that having put a plethora of instruments, gauges and switches on the dashboard, the designers had forgotten about the engine controls and just put them on the next adjacent space they could find. Not only is this inconvenient, but it could be deemed dangerous if one had to take sudden evasive action in an emergency, let alone control the speed of the craft in congested waters or heavy seas.

The positioning of the helmsman in relation to the steering wheel and the controls is crucial for proper control of the craft. Too far from the wheel and one's arms are unacceptably stretched, leading quickly to tired muscles when the going gets tough; too close and one cannot move the wheel without 'feeding' it, and if wearing a lifejacket this can catch the wheel, leading to serious manoeuvring problems. Ideally, one's arms should be comfortably bent at the elbow to provide leverage, yet extended sufficiently to allow swift movement for quick correction of the wheel. The throttle and gear controls should fall naturally to hand and not be placed too high or forward, forcing the helmsman to lean uncomfortably; neither should they be located so that they are too low or, even worse, slightly behind the helmsman's arm. Ideally, assuming one's hands are positioned at 'ten to two' on the wheel, the controls should be within a few inches, with just enough clearance for gloved hands on the wheel.

Though much has been said already in this chapter on the matter of windscreens, I will just add that many motor cruisers suffer from poor cabin windscreen design. Rearward raked screens, though they may look sleek, can often be poor at ridding water from their external surface. Some boats of this type have insufficient wipers to cope with heavy weather. You may have noted that many pilot boats and lifeboats feature

Good ergonomics at work, enabling this lifeboat crew to operate their craft to its optimum in heavy seas. © **RIB International Magazine**

forward-raked screens. This is because a forward-raked screen is far more effective at naturally shedding the water that strikes it. It may not look so sexy but it is often the preferred choice in craft designed for adverse sea states. Within the cabin, glare from instrumentation lights, as well as the cabin lights themselves, can reflect on the screen's surface, impairing vital forward vision. Detail of this type has to be given appropriate consideration by the vessel's designer.

The positioning of such key items as the ship's compass, the chart table and the navigation screens is often so hopelessly poor that from a functional point of view, especially in heavy weather, their use can become almost impossible without the skipper of the vessel compromising his helming to a dangerous degree. How many craft have you seen, for instance, where the compass is set to the centre of a large helm console, so that the coxwain has to virtually leave his seat in order to get a proper reading? Try doing this constantly in a heavy sea where an accurate bearing is essential to a safe passage. I have, and it can become frustrating in the extreme!

Seating is often another area that can come in for criticism in heavy weather, especially in smaller craft. As previously mentioned, it is not only important to have the positioning correct for the helmsman; it is equally important for the crew. Having handholds that fall naturally to hand helps passengers feel more confident and relaxed, which in turn reduces stress, fatigue and injuries caused by overbracing. Similarly, the height and type of padding used in the seat base, the positioning of the backrest, and the manner in which these items all combine are crucial for the comfort, confidence and security of the crew.

Prior to undertaking a 4m Round Scotland RIB Challenge from Inverness around the top of Scotland and back to Inverness via Cape Wrath and the Pentland Firth, it became obvious from the first sea trial that a modified seat top would be required for the RIB's sit-astride two-man jockey console. The standard seat provided was far too low and wide in its design to provide a safe posture. Once again, those who had designed this part of the boat's anatomy were evidently not experienced users themselves. The new seat that Hugo Montgomery-Swan and I designed not only added the required height and additional cushioning but was also tapered in form and incorporated a raised pillion section to its aft end. The difference this made was outstanding, both in terms of comfort and in relation to how much better the boat could be driven from this modified driving position. With the addition of some anti-vibration deck matting, a high-performance stainless steel propeller and the transferring of our auxiliary fuel decks to the forepeak, the boat could now be driven to its optimum. These few 'mods' transformed the driving experience beyond all expectations. And with the raised pillion section to the new seat top, the second man could see over the head of the cox without knocking his teeth out on his companion's skull every time a wave was leapt!

Poor positioning of controls and mediocre seating may be accepted by some when cruising up a river or meandering down the coast on a calm day, but when confronted with a change in the weather and a rapidly deteriorating sea state, the difference between a well-designed craft and a poorly laid-out or equipped boat can make a significant difference to the well being and safety of the crew.

Assuming that everyone is equipped with an up-to-date, modern, approved lifejacket of the correct floatation rating, clothing is another area that should be more carefully studied, especially for the more adventurous in open powerboats or RIBs. The Coastguard and RNLI are well versed in accounts of craft that, although seaworthy, have required assistance due to the crew being ill-equipped and making wrong decisions because of their exposure to the elements.

As skipper of a craft, especially an open boat, keeping one's body at a comfortable temperature is essential if rational and safe decisions are to be made. A cold body means a slow mind, with slow response times and even a confused mental state. Hypothermia can sometimes set in without the sufferer being conscious of its creeping effects. Too hot and dehydration can develop, and in extreme conditions sunstroke, both of which can lead to the brain, once again slowing down, and in some instances even shutting down altogether! Keeping the body at the right temperature is, therefore, not only essential to the process of operating the boat's vital systems adequately but also plays an important part in the coxswain being in a fit state to take care of his crew.

From years of experience, through trial and error, I have narrowed down what really works for me when helming open craft offshore, and for the head an adjustable balaclava under a lightweight marine safety helmet fitted with a clear visor has proved ideal. The type of balaclava I use has a long neck section that tucks well in and has an adjustable elasticised face aperture that allows it to be pulled down from over the head to rest comfortably around the neck. This simple piece of clothing can be used on its own or in conjunction with a helmet, and offers superior wind protection and comfort in colder climates.

Invariably, rough seas equal overcast and dull weather conditions and moderate-to-poor visibility, so think twice about tinted visors and even tinted windscreens. I made this mistake when racing recently around the shores of the British Isles – I will never forget the feeling of not being able to read the instruments and waves properly due to the impaired vision created by my tinted visor. In adverse sea states you need everything working in your favour, and things such as response times can represent the difference between negotiating a wave safely or getting it badly wrong, potentially resulting in damage to both the boat and its crew.

A craft in difficult sea conditions, suffering from poor ergonomics, will tire its crew much more quickly than a well-set-up craft, and this will undoubtedly lead to mistakes on the part of the coxwain through fatigue. Getting something right can be as easy as getting something wrong, and ultimately it comes down to the correct selection of equipment and the correct set-up of a craft as to whether your seagoing experience is a safe, manageable affair or one that spirals into a battle for survival.

Think through your vessel's construction and fit-out with the greatest care. Try to get the end result right before even taking delivery of the craft. Then, when the boat is in your possession, take the time to sea-trial her in a variety of sea conditions while remaining in a controlled environment to the fullest extent possible, ie your home patch, with good contacts notified ashore and even another support craft to hand on standby. Try not to be too forgiving of the vessel's shortcomings. Remain objective. Make notes on where the boat could be improved and set about working through your worksheet. Remember, it is so often the small things, the ancillary items, that, upon failing, are the cause of a major incident. So do not underestimate the need to give the fullest attention to detail. Think through the small things and the big things will take care of themselves. Do not be satisfied with just providing a solution: think how you are going to actually execute that solution. If it means a few sleepless nights, that is far better than grappling with an unknown scenario you hadn't anticipated or thought through properly in the real environment, where lives are involved. It's all well and good carrying an auxiliary outboard, for example, but have you considered how you might rig it on your boat's transom in a difficult sea state?

CONCLUSION

How well your craft is laid out, what equipment it carries, what backup systems it possesses and how efficient you are at operating them – all these elements play a major part in surviving adverse sea conditions where chaos rules. Your responsibility, either as the one who signs off the final specification or the person who takes charge of the vessel in the real environment, is a weighty one. As such, your contribution to the vessel's welfare when the going gets tough could well make the difference between life and death.

SECTION 04
HULL TYPES IN ADVERSE SEA STATES

FLYBRIDGE CRUISERS AND SUMMER GALES

BY PETER DAVIS AND PAUL MERRITT

Peter Davis and Paul Merritt, both very experienced Yachtmaster professional skippers, relate separate accounts involving flybridge cruisers being caught offshore in dangerous sea states. Peter Davis opens this chapter with an essential commentary on the realities of coping with heavy weather aboard leisure craft of this type.

There is a well-known saying among sailors that succinctly gets to the heart of heavy weather at sea. It goes: 'It's better to be in here wishing we were out there than to be out there wishing we were in here.' Only a masochist could say they enjoy really severe weather, and being caught out in heavy seas can, particularly the first time, be a very frightening experience. Many modern powerboats can cope reasonably well up to a certain level of weather. However, the transition from being a 'coping' vessel to a vessel in outright danger can be very rapid indeed. The idea, often quoted, that the boat can take a lot more than the crew can, holds true with some designs, but it is by no means a universal truth. I have been in planing boats that have performed better in full gales than some semi-displacement hulls have in force 5 winds. Size, underwater profile, available power and a vessel's trim will all be influential in both comfort and overall safety. I would add that the skill of the helm is of equal importance. The examples I give in this chapter demonstrate not only the influence of the design on handling but also the all-important human input when helming in heavy weather.

Trying to pigeonhole what constitutes heavy weather is an issue in itself; nothing could be truer than the statement that one man's force 5 is another man's gale. It is how we as individuals perceive the weather and how it directly affects us that is important, rather than an arbitrary sea state measure or Beaufort scale number. As a very broad guide, the Beaufort scale can only give us an indication of conditions in the open seas. Trying to translate wind strengths to conditions inshore and in sheltered waters will be, to say the least, hit-and-miss. I have been more uncomfortable in a south-easterly force 4 in Lyme Bay heading east than in a north-westerly gale off Plymouth. With that in mind I will desist from labelling heavy weather as starting at any specific Beaufort number. I will, however, try to give wind strengths and sea states as best my memory serves me. Actual wave heights are notoriously difficult to assess at sea, and the truth is that wave heights are frequently wildly exaggerated. I will try to relate the heights of waves to the actual height of the top of the wheelhouse in the boat described, as I believe this will give a much better picture of the size of waves encountered.

Of the two hull types described here, I will try to compare not just the safety but also the relative comfort of each type. The examples shown all involved building sea conditions.

The issue of safest hull type often comes up. Champions of fast planing hulls will point to their ability to outrun bad weather and, by using their power, get up on top of any sea and magically skim across the waves. I have to say at this point that I have found very few occasions at sea where I have either been able to totally outrun bad weather, or where the wavelengths have actually allowed me to bridge successive wave crests and skim over the top. All too often progress has been a series of sickening falls into troughs, producing nerve-jangling and back-breaking slamming, a constant playing of throttles required, alternately backing off and then accelerating to maintain safe progress. Yes, there will be occasions where the wavelength will closely match the waterline length of the boat, particularly so in the case of some larger-sized planing boats. Progress might then be made at high speed to windward. Frequently, however, this will not be the case. Where progress can't easily be made, helmsmanship will start to have significant influence, and I will try to examine the helming strategies adopted in the examples that are shown below. Advocates of the full-displacement hull will talk about steady progress and point to the design of big ships and commercial fishing vessels, which are almost universally of full-displacement design. 'But we've got the best of both worlds' will be the cry of owners of semi-displacement hull types, pointing to pilot boat and lifeboat designs. The truth, of course, is that all three types can be good or bad sea boats. There is no universal rule to say which design will be the best in practice.

However, in conditions where progress can only be made at displacement speeds, with equally good designs and equivalent sizes, the full-displacement design will usually be the safest. Generally, the planing and semi-displacement hulls will not handle as well as their full displacement cousins. When it comes to heaving-to under power, ie heading more or less into the seas at tick-over revs maintaining steerage way, lying to a sea anchor or simply drifting, more often than not it will be the full-displacement design that is ultimately likely to be the safest.

The point should again be emphasised, however, that despite the above there will be some planing hulls that, even at displacement speeds, will be more comfortable than some semi-displacement designs, and equally some semi-displacement designs that will be better than some classes of displacement hulls. There really is no hard and fast generalization that can be made regarding this, and it is simply a matter of experience telling you which is and which isn't a good or a bad hull although, of course, all boat sales literature makes sweeping claims about the seaworthiness of their craft. It would be extremely unusual to see a manufacturer claiming his particular product was only good in sheltered waters.

How then, in practice, do these designs perform for real? In Displacement and Semi-Displacement Hulls (chapter 10) I relate two accounts involving displacement and semi-displacement hulls. In this chapter we look at two separate accounts involving planing hulls. The following account of a late-season cruise in the English Channel illustrates how quickly the weather can change, the oft-mistaken and dangerous belief in being able to outrun weather and, crucially, the vital importance of fuel system integrity.

ST PETER PORT TO TORQUAY (Peter Davis)

The weather had been bad all week, with a succession of lows sweeping the country. Sitting in the office and picking up every available forecast, it rapidly began to look as if the late summer cruise would be off. The Channel Islands in early September, as the last of the summer sun blazed, had always been a favourite destination. Listening to the rain coming down outside it seemed that summer was rapidly vanishing along with the cruise. Suddenly, a lull in between the lows was forecast for the coming night. A hurried call home and the trip was brought forward. With work straightened away and bags hurriedly packed, we got to Torquay just in time to catch the fuel dock and fill the twin tanks of our 38ft fast planing motor yacht.

The plan was to wait until after midnight to give the seas time to settle. A night passage to St Peter Port at around 17 knots should give us an early arrival. Decca would provide us with a series of fixes and we would use Start Point and the mid-Channel and Les Hanois lights as reference points. It was a trip we had done many times, and in reasonable conditions it posed no problems. In the event all went to plan, we had a lovely night crossing in bright moonlight, with seas that flattened out all the way. We arrived at St Peter Port in time to catch the sill, tied up in the marina and enjoyed a good breakfast in the Harbour Café.

That evening the weather set in again and we spent the whole week wet and miserable staring at a harbour wall. In total there were six of us on board. Along with my wife were my teenage son and daughter, each with a friend. The weather during the week was truly awful: a succession of gales with heavy rain as warm fronts swept across, followed by all too short brighter periods as the associated cold fronts rushed across, only to be replaced by the next depression. All thoughts of a run to Alderney or down to St Helier in Jersey for a few days went completely by the board. As the week ran out we started to get anxious as to whether or not we would be able to get back at the weekend. The thought of leaving the boat in Guernsey was not appealing. Aside from the cost, other commitments would mean we would have to wait at least a month before we could get back. Additionally, we could just as likely catch another bad spell then and be delayed again.

Trudging back time and time again to the marina from the harbour office with the latest forecast, I really did start to regret setting off on the trip in the first place. The forecast for the next few days was plainly grim: poor visibility, heavy rain and force 6 to 7 winds, north-westerly backing westerly. This was no weather for a 38ft planing powerboat in mid Channel.

Then suddenly, as happened on our outward trip, the weather unexpectedly changed; the depression tracked more to the north and, as the wind dropped, the sun shone. The evening forecast showed a steady improvement and the following day's weather was

Very challenging conditions for this flybridge cruiser. The aft deck of such a craft can be a vulnerable area, as can the doors to the main cabin off the deck – strong cabin doors are a must in heavy weather. © Safehaven Marine

giving force 3 to 4 northerlies backing westerly and increasing 5 later. Not ideal, but handled sensibly definitely possible. With hindsight we should have taken more notice of the backing of the wind given in the forecast, a sure precursor of yet another warm front approaching. The barometer on board appeared steady, however, and a plan was quickly conceived to start as early as possible in the morning.

Leaving the security of our berth in the by now relatively gentle winds, we motored over to the fuel berth and topped up the tanks. A call to the harbour office and we were able to berth for the night outside on the waiting pontoons. Full of nervous anticipation we had a hurried meal on board and settled down to an early night. Promisingly, the wind continued to die down, and as we lay in bed we could see the stars for the first time in a week through our forward hatch.

Early the next day we awoke to be greeted by a thick, clammy atmosphere and visibility down to about 70 metres. What wind there was still blew northerly and as best as I could tell the barometer was steady. All thoughts of an early departure, however, were put aside as I didn't fancy the tricky pilotage around the island's south coast in such thick fog, and we took the decision to go ashore in the dinghy for breakfast and to pick up the latest forecast.

The harbour staff were as bemused as we were by the conditions. The forecast was now giving local fog patches slowly clearing, and the wind force 4 backing later to force 5. This would not normally be a problem for a sensibly handled 38ft fast planing boat. Downwind the boat would perform well, upwind in a full force 5 we would need to throttle back but, with the seas taken correctly and with attention to the helm, I knew the boat would cope reasonably well, although it would be uncomfortable at times. However, I was also aware that as a force 5 built it could all too quickly become the yachtsman's gale, but optimism, as so often happens, won through and the decision was made to go once the visibility improved. The boat, like most powerboats, handles head seas best if they are taken obliquely to the bow at an angle of around 20° to 25°. This effectively lengthens the wavelength and gives a far better ride, often eliminating the worst of any slamming. Looking at the chart, to achieve those angles would mean us taking a number of tacks. Firstly we would slip round the southern end of the island around 4 to 5 miles offshore, and then head north-north-westerly towards the end of the mid-Channel shipping lanes to the mid-Channel light. With the wind in the north, the seas should be just off our starboard bow at around the correct angle to give us the best ride. By the time we were there I anticipated the wind would have backed westerly, as we swung more north-westerly towards the English coast. The seas should by then be forming just off our port bows, giving us the most comfortable ride. The fog was by now visibly lifting, and without further ado we all got our lifejackets on and, with me conning from the flybridge and my son acting as lookout, we left St Peter Port.

As we made our way down the Little Russel the conditions did not seem too bad. We could see well over a mile now and the sea had an oily sheen. We encountered a long, easy swell and I estimated the height at around 8 feet, but the length was such that we were able to power ahead at a good speed.

We had a good run along the south coast, enjoying the ride. Both engines sounded healthy and we all started to relax a little. Setting ourselves 5 miles off Les Hanois by a

Decca fix we turned north-west, with the swell now coming at almost the exact angle to enable us to make good progress. There were no signs of any white horses as such, just the odd patch of white to be seen here and there. A quick conference and the vote was taken to go on. We settled into our normal routine; one of us on the helm with a lookout while the rest of the crew rested. As skipper I was also responsible for the navigation and was able to plot our position from the Decca, which seemed to be behaving itself. Our course was to take us towards the mid-Channel light and the traffic separation scheme, and I estimated that it would take around two hours or so, depending on our speed.

We throttled back to around 15 knots for both comfort and economy. The odd cross seas we encountered were setting up a slightly uncomfortable roll for us, and this speed, which kept us just on the plane, was comfortable. I still estimated the wind strength to be no more than the top end of a force 3, maybe a 4. After about an hour, with about 15 miles to run to our waypoint, we noticed a distinct change in the seas: they were getting shorter and the number of white caps had increased significantly. As I came down from the flybridge to do a fix I saw my wife in the aft cockpit; her expression told me all was not well. 'They've just given an imminent gale warning,' she said. 'Westerly 7 to gale 8 for Portland and Plymouth.' Imminent is within six hours. We went inside and looked at the chart; we had around 60 miles to run, approximately 4 hours at 15 knots. It was a good 35 miles back to St Peter Port. We had every sailor's worst dilemma – to go on or turn back. Many times I had turned back and the weather had failed to live up to its promise. We really wanted to get home so we voted to go on. Our reasoning was that we had four hours to beat the worst of the weather. The flaw in our thinking, of course, was in assuming that 'within six hours' was going to be nearer six hours than, say, three. It was difficult to tell the wind direction accurately, but I was sure it was backing a bit, going anticlockwise, more to west-north-west. The barometer was also showing a sudden fall: it was down to 997 from around 1000 the last time we looked. That much of a fall in the last three hours or so was confirmation of the forecast weather. I still felt that, providing all went well, we could maintain 15 to 16 knots and be able to outrun the worst. Even if we had to cope with a force 6 for the last 10 miles, we should still be able to keep the seas at a fair angle to our bow. With hindsight it is obvious that at this stage we should have turned back, run comfortably with the seas behind us and tucked ourselves back into St Peter Port. However, optimism always seems to take over in these cases and we plugged on.

The next hour saw us reach our waypoint and we turned onto our new heading. The swell was now quite confused and, far from sitting on our port bow, was virtually dead on the nose; the wind had backed, but nowhere near as much as I thought it would. The seas now were much more intimidating, with typical force 5 or 6 open sea waves, a good 2.5 to 3 metres. We started to slam into them and had no alternative but to drop down a few knots; this brought us into semi-displacement speeds, and even with full trim tabs applied to lower our bow we were still riding bow high. The relatively full fuel tanks added to our bow-high attitude. Even at this reduced speed our motion was becoming very sharp. I could see from my wife's and daughter's expressions that they were beginning to feel uncomfortable. Looking to port I could see the outline of jet-black clouds to the west and I really started to doubt my judgement in sailing. I checked the chart: 35 miles give or take to Torbay, around three and a half hours to the safety of the marina. The skies continued to darken and the first few drops of rain fell, mingling with the spray which by now was flying constantly over the flybridge. Even within the last five or ten minutes the sea had seemed to become much rougher: we were in a true mid-Channel force 6, the small-boat gale! We plugged on, throttling back on the bigger seas and creeping back to 12 knots or so when we could. Occasionally, an extra big wave reared up in front, and even when we immediately throttled back, the motion still became very violent. Each time I throttled back the loss in speed caused us to wallow in the troughs and once or twice the waves came in such quick succession that we seemed to be physically knocked back .

There was no way we could drive from the flybridge, as by this time water was continually coming over the top. Inside it was a mess: the floor was strewn with bits of kit and it was difficult to hold on. Looking at the seas ahead, I judged that the biggest of them was not far short of the actual height of our flybridge, which was a good 15 feet above the waterline. Suddenly, without warning, the port engine stuttered. The revs dropped back and the additional power on the starboard engine slewed us to port. I dropped back on the starboard engine to compensate and was able to use the helm to bring us back on course. I advanced both throttles and both engines picked up to their normal levels. My wife and I glanced at each other. I could sense through her calm exterior she was uneasy. My son and daughter and their friends had gone to their cabins, 'to wait it out'. We resumed our routine, me steering and my wife sitting in the nav position, monitoring the instruments. We did not have an autopilot and steering manually was becoming very tiring. Whenever I could I tried to keep the seas at that magic angle to the bow of 25° or so, but each time I did we ended up pointing into Lyme Bay, away from our destination. I kept hoping for the wind to back more and hopefully take the seas with it. Still, despite the scare with the engine we made progress, albeit probably at an average speed of no more than 8 knots. Our destination, instead of getting closer, was as far away as ever. With both engines seemingly running well I began to doubt if the port engine had actually faltered so badly; perhaps a bit of dirt or a momentary glitch with the injector pump? Even as I thought this, we came down off a particularly big wave and the port engine faltered again. I pulled back on the starboard throttle to compensate and glanced at the log. It showed us doing barely 5 knots, with the port engine clearly labouring.

I slowly advanced both throttles and the revs built gradually and speed picked up again. All seemed OK for around five minutes when, this time, the starboard engine stuttered and dropped a good 1,000 revs. Again, pulling back and letting the revs slowly rise seemed to help restore power. I noticed, though, that each time we suffered this the final rate shown for each engine on the same throttle settings was always slightly down by about 100 revs. It became clear that we were slowly losing power. We still had nearly 30 miles to run due to our reduced speed and the various course deviations I had made. I wondered if an autopilot would have held a better course than me in those seas, but my experience of them in other powerboats was such that I doubted it. On top of that, the sea was clearly worsening. Helming below was very difficult as, with the constant spray being thrown up, the wipers were struggling to cope. The symptoms we were suffering clearly pointed to a fuel issue as both engines were affected. With around 25 miles to run at 10 knots, I thought we might just get in, as at this reduced speed the engines seemed to be settling down. The idea of trying to look at the system at sea was not appealing, as being down in the hot engine bay trying to avoid getting burnt and swapping filters was guaranteed to bring on seasickness, and with the violent motion we were experiencing, an injury was a real possibility.

At that moment the world went dark. Through the windscreen I saw a truly massive wall of black in front of us. I throttled back and yelled to my wife and down to the kids to hang on as we hit. The bow started to rise as masses of water poured over us. How the windscreen held I don't know, but later I realized how lucky we had been. If the windscreen had gone in those seas I am sure we would have foundered. There was a cry

Forward vision can be hugely impaired by flying spray in foul weather. If windscreen wipers fail in such conditions it can present a very big problem. Reading the seas to work the throttles is essential. © Safehaven Marine

from below as my daughter was catapulted from her bunk. We seemed to be rising for ever, then we burst through the top, and as the wave passed under we toppled down. High waves, more often than not, equal deep troughs, and we seemed to fall for ever. I estimate that we fell at least 20 feet, so the wave itself was probably approaching twice the height of our flybridge. As we hit the bottom the entire boat seemed to shudder, not quickly, but for what seemed a prolonged time. My son, daughter and friends all came up to the saloon and I could tell that they were now very scared indeed. I pushed both throttles forward in the hope that the bow would lift to the next wave and not bury her nose in. Nothing happened: the revs refused to rise on both engines, we were down to just 6 knots and in the worst position we could be in: a south-westerly gale among horrible seas with some very large waves – like the ones we had just negotiated. We all now gathered in the saloon. It was clear that we had several choices here: we could run at this reduced speed and limp our way in, which could be very hit-and-miss, particularly if we encountered any more really big waves; we could declare an emergency (a PAN PAN, not a MAYDAY, as I didn't feel that we were in grave and imminent danger), or we could try to fix the fuel problem and make an advisory call to the Coastguard, informing them of our situation. I had spare filters on board, and it seemed that to attempt a fix after advising the Coastguard at Brixham was the correct decision. We did not want to declare an outright emergency but it was clearly prudent to advise them of our actions. I have often thought about this decision since then. Some might think that we should have sought outside assistance. The weather was very bad and could get worse, we were some 15 miles offshore and help could probably have been with us within an hour. On the other hand, we were fairly sure we knew what the problem was and had the means, with care, to potentially fix it. We had survived a massive wave, were watertight and still making 8 knots, no one was injured, we had a liferaft prepared for quick deployment and were all wearing lifejackets. My son and wife agreed we would try and see if we could change at least one filter; the port one, as that had seemed the worst.

We shut down the port engine, and with the starboard engine set just above 1,000 revs my son's friend took the wheel and tried to hold us steady. This speed was too fast for us to heave-to into the seas and we dropped back 100 revs or so. This allowed us to slowly head into the seas at approximately 4 knots. At this speed it was initially surprisingly comfortable compared to what we had experienced before, but working below would still be very difficult. We eventually managed to change the port filter, with my son doing the hard bit while I held onto him and did my best to keep him away from the starboard engine. The filter was very badly clogged with black detritus. I've seen this before and it is, in fact, a diesel bug – if that's the right term for it – which can easily block fuel pumps, injectors and filters. Bleeding the engine, which should have been a simple job, was a nightmare, and my son was lucky not to get burnt as he leant head down, spanner in hand, pumping the lift pump. The port engine fired up after a fair bit of cranking, and it was soon clear that the filter change had worked. The engine would rev to its maximum and we could now make a good 8 knots on the one engine. I thought of changing the other filter but it was just something I couldn't bear to do. We would have had to crawl around the side of the engine to reach the filter and the risk of being burnt was just too great. We throttled both engines up and watched our speed rise to

10 then 12 knots. We informed the Coastguard and, as we pointed the bows home, we saw the first sight of land through the murk. There was no more drama to report; the seas gradually eased as we approached the land, both engines ran without a falter and our spirits lifted.

We eventually arrived at our destination, wet and tired, and to our surprise lots of our friends on the marina turned out to catch our lines and welcome us back.

Left: *Making good progress in heavy beam seas, but keeping a good lookout for breakers or 'rogues' remains essential.* © *Safehaven Marine*
Right: *A 31ft motor cruiser shows its ability to punch through heavy seas close inshore.* © *Offshore Powerboats*

CONCLUSION AND LESSONS LEARNT

The fuel system needed a complete clean out to get rid of the bugs, which had probably accumulated over time. Now I always filter my diesel as I refill. The boat took a gale, but only by running at displacement speeds for much of the voyage. At that speed, gently motoring ahead as we changed the port filter, it was reasonably comfortable, but at 8 knots the slamming was severe and planing speeds were impossible. Early on, despite the high-running bow angle, we were able to make progress at semi-displacement speeds once we had the seas running around 25° to the bow. The boat took a number of large waves, probably 10 to 12 feet high, with corresponding troughs. It took a singularly large wave of around 20 feet, and a subsequent investigation showed that part of the forward bulkhead had cracked and shifted. Without the fuel problem we could have probably outrun the very worst conditions, but we had no choice at the speeds we were forced to drop down to. With our fuel problem we simply did not have the power to outrun this particular gale. This, by the way, was not particularly severe, as gales go and in truth I doubt we had many sustained gusts much above gale force strength. The seas were certainly confused, and the week's poor weather prior to our departure from Guernsey probably contributed towards that, and the odd really large wave was very daunting. The fact that the occasional wave could form which was at least twice the height of the normal waves was worrying. What was very apparent was the difficulty in working on the engines at sea. As an aside, a friend and I really struggled to change all the filters again, particularly the starboard one, when back in harbour. Changing the port filter at sea was difficult but not impossible for two people. Knowing that it really had to be done if we were to get back under our own steam certainly spurred us on. From that day, care of fuel has always been my number one maintenance item.

On reflection, I guess we would have preferred to be in St Peter Port wishing that we had gone, rather than being out there really wishing we hadn't. It is all too easy to adopt an optimistic view about weather and view local conditions as indicative of what it will be like 'out there'. The truth is that small boats, faced with windward courses, must appreciate what force 5 winds and seas can be like in open water. Our desire to get back probably clouded our judgement and, when we should have made the decision to return to St Peter Port, optimism held sway. In any kind of heavy weather, power is the key; lose it and problems can multiply very quickly. When interpreting forecasts it is important to appreciate two things: firstly, they are predictions, not cast in stone, and secondly, they often refer to ranges. If weather is forecast as imminent it actually means within six hours. In our case we encountered severe conditions within three hours. Wind strengths can also vary, in that the extra wind strength between the top and bottom of a force 5, ie 17 to 21 knots, can be significant in terms of the sea state. Sailors are well aware of this difference as they frequently refer to reefing sails 'before the top end of a force 4' or 'at the bottom end of a force 5'. Any forecast of a backing wind is a sure sign of the approach of a depression, and we should have considered not going when we read this. The fall in the barometer was another indicator of the blow coming in. The idea of outrunning bad weather is fine and, had our courses taken us downwind, we might have succeeded: our motion would have been less, sediment in our fuel might not have been so agitated, and we might not have suffered any issues. 'Mights' and 'mays', however, don't really have any place in prudent seamanship. We could have had these problems regardless of our course. Poor engines equal poor performance, and poor fuel means limited performance – and that is the last thing to have to cope with in a gale!

FROM PUERTO RICO TO AGADIR (Paul Merritt)

We arrived at Gran Canaria on 14 July and took a taxi to Blue Ocean, a Fairline Squadron 55 lying at Puerto Rico. I had delivered her down to Lanzarote the previous October and it was a once in a lifetime passage: the seas were so flat that we slowed to 6 knots in the Biscay to have a barbecue on the flybridge.

This time I was with a friend, Ian, who was making his first delivery trip. The owner, who had been chartering the boat, wanted her delivered from Puerto Rico, on the south side of the island, back to the UK. The plan was to leave at 0630 the next morning to head to Las Palmas to take on fuel and fill the four 150 litre drums which we would carry on deck for the 338 nm passage to Agadir, Morocco.

The forecast was very poor and we eventually left Puerto Rico at 0945. There wasn't a breath of wind on the south side of the island but we had to return to base less than two hours later, after taking quite a beating into a head sea as we rounded the south-east corner of the island. The rest of the day was spent exploring the town. The boat's charter skipper hired a car and made two trips to Las Palmas to collect the drums and deliver them to us, ready for an early start the next morning. Unfortunately, by the time the drums had been delivered the fuel berth had shut.

We tried two more times to leave Puerto Rico but the seas were too big. We finally managed to get away on 19 July. It was extremely rough but we covered the 54 miles to Las Palmas in around three hours. The biggest problem in this area is the north-easterly wind that funnels down between the islands, increasing in strength as it goes.

We did have one stroke of luck in Las Palmas. We were sat in the Match bar and met a young Dutch lad named Mick. Mick was crewing on a catamaran heading across the Atlantic and through the Panama Canal. It was clear that there was a conflict of interest aboard the boat and sure enough, the next day, a note with a CV attached was wedged in the aft-deck door, asking if he could scrounge a lift to Gibraltar. He promised that he would scrub our boat daily with his toothbrush if it meant a free passage! We decided to let him come along as far as Gibraltar.

On Thursday we got the forecast we wanted, or rather one that at least allowed us

A flybridge cruiser's 'top hamper' will create substantial windage – even more so with a fast planing hull. This semi-displacement flybridge is about to take a heavy landing! © Safehaven Marine

to leave – north-east force 4. We knew it wouldn't be smooth but it was the best we could hope for at this time of year. We left at 0500 that morning and had a reasonable trip across to Rubicon on the south of Lanzarote, where we took on 2,000 litres of fuel for the crossing to Agadir in Morocco.

We cleared Rubicon at 1115 and had a leisurely trip along the south coast of the island, giving us time to cook and eat something before heading north up the east coast, where we were sure to meet the northerly breeze that had been forecast. The sea here was like glass, but slowly grew as we neared Cabo de la Palon, and it wasn't long before we were heading into a short, sharp sea with the winds blowing a good force 5 to 6. At this time we were slamming quite heavily and were down to 12 knots.

Off Puerto del Castillo it was decided that we should put into Sociedad, a port on the island of Graciosa on the north-west tip of Lanzarote. I knew we were in a sea breeze and thought that the sea would probably be better some miles out, but the boat was taking a terrible bashing, not to mention us too. I therefore decided the best time to leave would be about three or four the next morning for the long trip across to Agadir. But as we progressed up the east coast of Lanzarote the wind eased and I made a final decision to turn to starboard and go for Agadir. It was to be the longest 230 miles of my sailing life.

Just to check, I spoke to my wife Wendy, back home in the UK, who relayed two conflicting, but acceptable, forecasts. The Spanish report was giving north-east force 4, and the French south-west force 4. Whoever was right (I hoped it was the French), the weather was certainly nothing to worry about.

The sun was shining and the sea was getting better as we cruised towards Agadir at 19 knots. Then, at about 160 miles out, we noticed a change in sea conditions. The swell was increasing, with more white horses appearing, and it wasn't long before we eased to 16 knots.

The problem with long ocean passages on planing hulls is that you either go at over 16 knots or less than 10. Anywhere in between and the hull is just squatting down, using valuable fuel. At 8 knots I knew the range of a Squadron could be increased by 100 to 150 miles, but it would also give the weather more time to change from favourable to extremely unpleasant.

As dusk fell the swell had increased to a good 10 to 15 feet with white horses, and we were down to 8 knots. But there was no question of turning back. It would mean refuelling again, and besides, the weather forecast hadn't been so bad.

At 2200 and 130 miles out, the storm struck. It had built up almost without us knowing. We were now in a considerable swell and the boat was bucking and slamming wildly. From the saloon, we were looking out of the port windows and all we could see was angry sea, a massive swell with white horses bearing down, looking awesome in the reflection of our red steaming light and then breaking on the fore and portside deck.

I had been in worse seas, but not so far from land. I knew it was going to be a long night so I decided to snatch an hour of sleep on the seats in the saloon. I had not been asleep for long when I awoke, full in the knowledge that we were in a good force 9. By this time cupboards had opened, spilling the contents, doors were opening and slamming shut, and the whole boat was in a terrible mess. Mick had been on watch for over two hours. He was a sailing man through and through and it was his first time on a motorboat. It was only later that I learnt he had survived a major yachting disaster two years previously in which his skipper had drowned. If I had known this before I would have been completely spooked!

The boat was climbing some pretty steep waves and the speed was down to 6 knots as I took over the helm and wedged myself into the seat, staring out into a dark and stormy night. The windscreen wipers were on maximum but it was nowhere near enough to clear the spray. With visibility so poor, breaking waves were not visible until they were almost dropping on the foredeck. From a skippering point of view there was little to do but slow down to take them on the port bow, which meant working the throttles continually.

There was no other way out of the situation. We had to maintain a general course towards Agadir. There is no other port on that coast to head for, and if there had been, I was certainly not going to come round to starboard and take the full force on the beam.

At about one in the morning, three gruelling hours since the storm struck, a huge wave broke over the flybridge, wiping out our plotter antenna and also the autopilot.

A confused and dangerous sea in rising conditions well offshore.
© Murray Macleod

Great – a raging storm and now we had lost our easiest means of navigation. Fortunately, I had transferred fuel from the drums into our tanks before nightfall, so we had plenty to reach Agadir and were now over halfway across, so turning back was beyond our range. To say the least I was pretty concerned. Then it got much worse.

Suddenly the whole boat was airborne, seconds later coming down as though someone had lifted her about 4 feet and let go. The engines raced as the props came clear and, as she hit the waves, doors were forced open and came off hinges. At the same time the fuel filter alarms came on, warning of water in the fuel. Everything in the boat, including the seating and furniture in the saloon, came adrift.

Almost immediately a huge wave hit us on our port side and forced us like a matchbox down the side into the trough. The boat was almost on her side and through the window I could see the starboard deck was underwater. At this point I thought my time had come. I said to the lads, 'I think it's about time we at least carried our lifejackets with us.' Ian replied that he did not want to prolong the agony: 'If she goes down I want it to be quick.'

For the first time in 35 years of boat delivery I can honestly say I was scared. I thought about making that call home, the one that says hello but means quite the opposite. This was turning into a bad dream, but I had to stay focused. My mind raced. What were the options? I thought of running with it, which would have been safer, but that meant pushing further out to sea and running out of fuel, wherever we ended up. We pushed on.

It was an endless night, steering by hand and taking a terrible beating. The flybridge was awash, water was coming through the saloon's deckhead light fittings and the aft deck was sometimes under a foot of water, if not more. On several occasions my stomach and I did not think the boat was going to recover from the severe rolling and pitching as she slid down the waves.

We arrived in Agadir at 0630 in the morning, 8 hours after the storm hit and 13 since we left Las Palmas. After mooring up we surveyed the damage. On the flybridge the helm seat had been washed away and the fridge door had been knocked open but had somehow remained attached. Below, four doors had ripped off their hinges, both shower doors had walked off and every locker had spilled its contents. The boat looked a tip and we looked a mess. We were exhausted.

The radio started to crackle with news of other disasters, and we soon realized that we had been through the tail end of a hurricane across the Caribbean. Reports of stricken tankers and lost yachts abounded. We were lucky. A Squadron was not designed to be out in those conditions, and 55ft felt very small indeed. I do not think anything smaller would have survived. These were the worst sea conditions I had ever encountered. And to think they were apparently only a force 4 – so much for weather forecasts!

After the thrill of the storm, and the endless hassles with Moroccan port officials and fuel suppliers that followed, it was with great relief that we entered the Straits of Gibraltar with 'only' 1,100 miles between us and Hamble. We had made it back to Europe, and whatever was thrown at us could not compare to what we had just been through.

CONCLUSION AND LESSONS LEARNT

1 Always have a detailed passage plan, and source possible bolt-holes in advance of setting off. Carry paper charts in addition to your GPS.

2 Never leave port without plenty of fuel. About one third more than the passage strictly requires is really the minimum quantity that needs to be carried in order to provide a safe margin.

3 Secure everything on board before setting off, especially any heavy items that could damage the fabric of the vessel if they happen to break free. Beware of internal doors and furnishings breaking free. These and the contents therein will cause serious distraction and even injury if they are not secured.

4 In head seas, you'll want to avoid 'stuffing' the bow into waves; apply throttle as the crest approaches and ease off as it passes. 'Reading the waves' is essential and therefore forward visibility is critical.

5 In very rough weather and big breaking waves, avoid a beam sea at all costs.

6 Don't trust weather forecasts implicitly. The 1979 Fastnet Race was proof of this. Though forecasting technology has since improved, it's still not infallible. Trust your instincts and err on the side of caution. Cruising or passage making on a tight schedule can prove a killer. Best to wait and stay alive than take a chance on an offshore passage and suffer the loss of your boat, or worse still, the lives of your crew.

7 Understand the design and operational limitations of your boat.

DISPLACEMENT AND SEMI-DISPLACEMENT HULLS

BY PETER DAVIS

Displacement and semi-displacement hulls have a tradition of being favoured as designs highly suited to heavy weather. Peter Davis, a man with many years of professional boating under his belt, relates his key experiences of such craft proving their strengths in testing scenarios.

INCIDENT OFF CAP D'ANTIBES, FRANCE

This narrative refers to a genuine semi-displacement design based upon the renowned Nelson hull, considered by many to be one of the very best ever built. A semi-displacement hull will generally give a soft and comfortable ride in heavy weather if kept to a sensible speed: for vessels in the 10- to 15-metre range I have found this to be around 13 to 16 knots. Reasonably good and relatively comfortable progress can be made to windward, providing seas can be encountered at an oblique angle (similar to planing boats at around 20° to 30° to the bow) as opposed to head-on. Trim tabs, if fitted, can be used to lower the bow, which will further enhance the comfort of the ride.

During the early part of the 2000s I was involved in running a training vessel out of Antibes in the south of France. The Nelson-based boat was 35 feet long, powered by twin 180hp turbo diesels, with a maximum speed, lightly loaded, of around 22 knots and sensible cruising speeds of around 14 to 15 knots. We were mainly involved in doing Yachtmaster preparation courses for the superyacht fraternity, and also providing the vessel for them to sit their exams. Of the two incidents described here, I was present for the first but have relied on the recollections of one of my colleagues who witnessed the second. I have included the second incident as the conditions were very similar: both occurred in the late autumn, the weather had been fine and warm and the Yachtmaster preparation courses had gone well. We had four candidates on each course, which ran from Sunday to Thursday on consecutive weeks, with exams starting on Friday afternoons for two candidates, working into the night and finishing sometime on Saturday. The remaining two would be following the same pattern but starting on Saturday after lunch. On Thursday morning the good weather we had enjoyed all week changed. The wind swung around to the south-west and built to a good force 5. With the wind in that direction the Cap itself can give a good degree of protection in its lee. Looking to seaward at the end of the Cap, however, one could sense the sea building steadily.

In the late afternoon we decided to go to sea and do some final MOB practice and a few navigation exercises. There was a 2-metre swell running which the boat was able to take in its stride as we motored out. The daylight was slowly fading and turning to twilight as we worked our way west towards the Cap. The further we went, the easier the seas became, as we came under the influence of the land creating a lee for us.

We ran some man-overboard drills and navigation exercises without any problems.

This semi-displacement hull is performing with a very level running attitude. The vessel's good balance and fine entry enables superb handling in these breaking head seas. © Safehaven Marine

Being fairly close to the Cap we could sense there was a lot more south in the wind now and we could make out a line of white at the end of the Cap. It was clear that to proceed southwards would be inadvisable, but where we were in the lee the seas remained reasonably good and sufficiently palatable for us to continue. We worked our way slowly east, further away from the Cap and the lee it formed, doing some position-fixing exercises.

The more we moved towards the east the more the seas built. The swells were now a good 3 metres and the seas themselves were much shorter. Even at 3 metres the Nelson hull was superb, and at 14 knots, which we had dropped down to, the ride was bumpy but had none of the slamming associated with typical cruising planing boats. The reflective wave patterns of the seas swinging around the Cap produced a set that allowed us to have them hitting us just off our starboard bow. Our course being east with a touch of north at the time, this was the ideal angle for us for the best progress and comfort.

The boat had an easy motion for most of the time and we could see the lights of Antibes off to the north. Given the performance of the boat we decided to do one more exercise and we turned the boat around back towards the Cap on a north-westerly heading. It was clear that in the hour or so we had been out, the wind had strengthened considerably, and by now there were some heavy gusts coming through. The seas were quite a lot shorter and we dropped down to 12 knots as our rise and fall was starting to turn just a bit too violent at times. The consensus was that we didn't really have a lot more to gain by being out there and – sensibly, given the deteriorating conditions – we decided to abort any more exercises and return to Antibes before it got really dark.

As we made ready to turn around, I stood in the aft cockpit and was fascinated by the way the seas rose up alongside the boat, looking as if they would dump themselves into the cockpit, only for the boat to lift to them and the seas power on their way under us. The light was fading but we still had reasonable visibility. As I glanced towards the Cap, which must have been about 3 miles away, I could make out a lot of spray towards its end where the seas were breaking against it. I suddenly sensed something strange: the Cap seemed to have grown much darker. Then, with horror, I realised I was not seeing the Cap but a massive wall of black water bearing down on us. This wave was huge, at least twice the size of any that we had seen before. I could make out its top which was flecked with white.

To take this wave at speed and at the angle it would most likely hit us would be extremely dangerous, and I called to the helm to come into it and reduce speed dramatically. There was simply no time to take over, and to the credit of the young student at the helm he had already turned us towards the wave and throttled back. This wave towered above our wheelhouse, which was around 10 feet above the waterline, and I estimate that it was a good 20 feet from trough to crest. We started to rise. Even at 5 knots the motion was very abrupt and we seemed to be pointing skywards as solid water swept our decks. We continued up until gravity took over and, with a truly sickening fall, we plunged down to the bottom of the trough. The rogue wave we had encountered sped on into the night and the seas resumed their normal 3-metre size.

A valuable sequence showing the attributes of a modern displacement craft at every stage of its successful negotiation of this large on-coming sea. The manner of the vessel's performance is impeccable. © *Safehaven Marine*

With enough drama for the evening we made straight back to port as quickly as we could, inspecting for damage on the way. The boat had taken this rogue wave very well indeed: there was no obvious damage that we could see, and a later inspection showed nothing broken bar a couple of mugs that had smashed as we came down off the wave. In my view the student helm had performed excellently, and I am pleased to say that he went on to pass his Yachtmaster exam the next day. The Nelson hull lived up to its reputation for safe and dependable seakeeping. As far as the wave itself was concerned, on reflection I am happy with the estimate of its size. Why such a wave should form within an established pattern of seas is a bit of a mystery. I tried to find any other reference to a rogue wave occurring that night but I could find none. The swells, as they swung around the Cap, were being reflected off it back out to sea both southward and eastward, and there is no doubt that some of these seas would have combined with some of the new wave patterns approaching. In most cases one would expect some of these combinations to cancel each other out, but I suspect that two sets may have got into some synchronised pattern which effectively doubled the wave height. I also wonder whether a swell had been formed out to sea, possibly from a large ship, which had combined with the reflected sea to produce our rogue wave.

Interestingly, the same weather pattern was present a few weeks later when a colleague of mine instructing on another course experienced exactly the same conditions as we had: in seas of around 2 to 3 metres with a force 5 rising wind and in an almost identical location as we had been, they encountered a similar huge wave, at least twice the height of the regular ones. This time the wave part-broke over the boat, and its force was such that the Nelson was so submerged that it fired the hydrostatic release to the liferaft, which launched itself, along with its very solid wooden mounting brackets which the sea had ripped out! Recovering this liferaft took at least an hour.

As you can imagine, some valuable lessons were learnt regarding picking up casualties in bad weather. This occurrence was so similar to the one I encountered that both my colleague and I searched to see if there was a documented history of rogue waves off this particular part of France. While we could see reference to the Cap producing the type of reflective wave patterns described, nowhere was there mention of this area producing rogue waves of the size we both came upon. Experts such as Michel Olagnon and Tedd Pitt, for example, have undertaken much research into the subject of rogue waves, and without doubt such seas can be of truly enormous size. As to their actual cause, however, there is still much debate. The fact that we encountered waves of this height so close to land, and not in overly severe winds, would point to this phenomenon not simply being a deep-ocean occurrence but one that can happen anywhere. Nevertheless, the bottom line is that the semi-displacement hull proved its worth in this situation and took care of all aboard in reassuring style.

CONCLUSION

It is a somewhat frightening realisation that abnormal, freak or rogue waves, whatever we call them, can and do pitch up without warning. The waves we encountered were very close to land and were in the vicinity of a major headland. I have a strong belief that the reflected swell, combined with the general set of the sea, caused the waves we encountered. The fact that we only experienced these waves twice does not mean that there are not more occurrences. Care should always be taken when navigating close to headlands, even more so in tidal conditions. Driving relatively comfortably in, for example, 8ft seas, and gaining a consistency in angle of encounter to waves, simply cannot guarantee that much bigger waves will be able to be taken on the same heading. I was once taught that the best method is to try to concentrate on the wave pattern and size, one or two sets after the most imminent wave. That would give you time to reduce speed, which you will undoubtedly need to do, and adjust your angle, which initially needs to be around 20° off the bow, allowing you to luff up to the crest. Unless you are unlucky enough to have a wave rear up literally dead ahead, astern or abeam, you will have at least some time to react.

Keeping the power on when meeting a sea of this magnitude is essential if the craft is to not only climb the steep gradient but also avoid being knocked off its face and rolled. © Safehaven Marine

NO SAFE HARBOUR

My second example of powerboats in heavy weather concerns the delivery of a fairly traditional displacement 32ft trawler yacht design from the River Thames to the West Country in August 1992. This particular account centres on the difficulty of entering harbour in rough weather and the problems that can be encountered, even when supposedly tucked up safe inside, when really heavy weather strikes.

Every bit 'the little ship', the trawler sat in her berth at Canvey Island on the Thames. The tide was making, and although the forecast was poor with gales forecast for later, we had calculated that we had time to run down the Thames Estuary around North Foreland to Ramsgate before the bad weather hit.

With the sun shining and a force 4 blowing from the south, we made good progress downriver towards the estuary, Margate and North Foreland. The water was building into a good chop and we could sense the wind definitely rising. By the time North Foreland itself was in sight and we had turned towards it, the sea was beginning to get reasonably big. The little displacement boat rose up and down the swell very purposefully, pushing aside some quite big lumps of water. However, her roll was typical of a displacement hull, slow into it and then more sharp on the way back; not that uncomfortable at this stage but still requiring vigilance and a sympathetic hand on the helm.

Like many boats she was most at ease with the seas off the forward quarter, which had the effect of lengthening the swell and generally making the ride more comfortable. With North Foreland dropping behind us the sea roughened up considerably; the wind by now was almost due south and was starting to heap the seas into quite considerable-sized waves. Fortunately, the fetch was relatively short as, with the weight of wind we were now experiencing, had the fetch been greater the seas would have been building to a very rough and uncomfortable level. It was clear that the forecast gale was coming in a lot sooner than we anticipated. Ahead lay Ramsgate and shelter, or so we thought.

The seas by now were directly on our bow and the motion far too uncomfortable. We waited for a relative lull in the seas and thankfully turned inland towards the west of Ramsgate. The little trawler obliged and answered the helm, and with the entire 120hp of her single diesel engine working flat out, she came around to our new heading. With the sea now off her port bow the motion of the boat became slightly more comfortable, though it did take on a corkscrew motion from time to time as it slid off to starboard down the back of the larger waves. This required considerable concentration by the helm to hold her steady. The autopilot, which we tried in order to give some relief to the helm, proved not only inefficient in the size of seas encountered but dangerous as well, as the time taken for it to react meant that the boat could easily have broached. Steered manually, we could react much faster to the first signs of any tendency to broach to leeward.

Several of the crew were by now feeling sick, and none too soon we were able to open up Ramsgate Harbour entrance. As the next lull came we swung the wheel hard to starboard and started to come round. The seas were now on our port quarter; the corkscrew motion was still there, but for some reason the boat seemed to prefer the seas on that quarter. As we approached Ramsgate the seas themselves also became markedly shorter and, as the depth decreased, we began taking quite large amounts of green water into the rear cockpit. However, the oversized scuppers on the boat coped very well in shifting any water. The entrance to Ramsgate itself was very rough, with seas a good 8 feet high. We adjusted our heading so as to open up the whole of the entrance, and with the seas raging behind us the trawler tracked straight and true. With walls of water piling up on her stern, we surfed in, with the log nudging 12 knots. Once tied up on the outside pontoons we settled down with a good cup of tea to go over what had been quite a testing little trip.

We were not the only boat seeking shelter: the pontoons were almost full with an assortment of both power and sailing craft. Every vessel was beginning to ride up and down on the swell which was coming in from the harbour entrance. As the day progressed it was clear that this was going to be more than just an ordinary gale. The wind was gusting very strongly now, at least to a severe gale force 9, and at times it felt as if we were nudging storm force 10. Inside the shelter of the harbour we could see the entrance, which by now was just a complete wall of white broken water. The swell inside the harbour was very severe indeed and our boat was riding up and down quite violently, putting a tremendous strain on both our warps and cleats. The particular make of boat we were on, however, was renowned for the strength of its fittings, and I felt if any cleats were going to fail it would be the ones on the pontoon. We put out extra fenders and additional ropes, and as the afternoon drifted on it was clear that we were going to be in for a very uncomfortable period indeed until we had enough water to get into the inner marina. The west and east marinas, with their wavebreak pontoons, had not been installed, and in those days there was a simple horseshoe shape of holding pontoons just outside the inner marina.

Some of the boats that were moored broadside to the incoming swell were being driven up and onto the pontoons themselves, and it was clear that everybody would need to help everybody else in order to make our stay safe until we could all enter the inner marina, about 4 hours away. By this time the harbour authorities had examined the state of the pontoons themselves, which were snaking up and down in the swell, creaking and generally making a very frightening noise. All the time the wind was rising, and with it the swell inside became more and more untenable. We could see that some of the yachts were in a very precarious position. One yacht in particular, about 50 metres ahead of us lying on the cross-section of the pontoon, was suddenly lifted completely out of the water and deposited with a sickening crunch onto the pontoon itself. The crew on board were clearly very distressed, and it was obvious that the yacht in its present position would sustain heavy damage, so we all helped to move it around onto our pontoon so its stern was facing the swell. Eventually, after a very anxious and uncomfortable few hours, we were able one by one to get ourselves inside the inner harbour as the clearance over the sill increased.

One by one the vessels were directed by the harbour staff and made their way inside until we were amongst the last left. By this time the pontoons themselves were beginning to break up. In some sections they were snaking up and down a good 5 to 6 feet, which meant that standing on them was now physically impossible. Fortunately, we had prepared for this situation and had re-rigged our warps so we could slip our lines from on board. While the engine was ticking over we slipped all warps bar our bow lines and

An offshore displacement fishing vessel operating in Alaskan waters. A high degree of buoyancy in her bow affords excellent recovery out of a trough to punch through the next sea. © Ben Reynolds

engaged ahead, the starboard helm allowing our stern to move out as our bow turned in towards the pontoon. With the wheel amidships we engaged astern and increased revs to back away, but even at almost full revs we hardly moved against the weight of the wind and swell. It seemed impossible for our boat to travel astern; however, after what seemed an eternity, she gradually began to make way. I reversed towards the white maelstrom that was the harbour entrance, thinking that I did not want to get the boat anywhere near the broken white water, but at this stage I had no choice. I just had to reverse towards it. Putting port helm on and moving through neutral to full ahead she responded and, breathing a sigh of relief, we started to move towards the entrance of the inner marina. By now the swell inside the harbour was very uncomfortable and I estimated its height to be at least 5 feet. As we came into the marina entrance we surfed over the sill. I swung the helm hard to port and at the same time gave a silent prayer that the boat would answer it and come around to port and safety, away from the boats berthed dead ahead which seemed to be just feet away. True to her pedigree she swung around, and the only drama was when we caught one of our aft dodgers in the steel davits of one of the moored cruisers to our starboard and ripped it.

Tucked up inside the inner marina we were able to observe the weather in safety. Through the night the wind gradually eased off from severe gale through to gale, and then down further to just a good breeze. On inspection we had suffered surprisingly little damage, though the same could not be said of some of the yachts. We decided that we would have to leave the boat there for a week and come back and resume our delivery later. The story of that delivery is an interesting tale in its own right, as it took us five weeks in total with many stops and maintenance problems... So how, then, does a fairly traditional displacement hull behave at sea compared to both planing and semi-displacement hulls? The trawler-type boat we were on was an early wooden-hulled version and she possessed most of the design characteristics of the true full-displacement hull form. Her performance, given her size of 32ft, was surprisingly good: her motion out of the roll was somewhat sharper than one would have liked but, given the seas, probably as good if not better than other designs. Certainly, when corkscrewing, with the combination of pitch, roll and yaw, the ride was uncomfortable, but in truth we never felt in danger. This motion, though, did cause seasickness among certain members of the crew – a condition that cannot be minimised in terms of its debilitating effects. It was clear that sensibly driven, and with the seas taken on the right quarter, the little trawler was well able to cope with the conditions. The autopilot simply didn't have the same type of almost intuitive reaction as a human hand on the helm, and it's interesting to note that, 15 years on, some autopilots are still struggling with these types of conditions, particularly so when seas are on the quarter. I recently undertook a delivery in a 44ft semi-displacement motor cruiser in force 5 conditions, where using the autopilot became more tiring than steering manually due to the excessive corrections it made, despite being set to what we felt were the correct levels of sensitivity.

Havens that are considered to be safe are not always so, and in severe weather it is very easy for vessels to suffer damage and become difficult to both berth and then extract themselves when required to do so.

I tried to get some detailed weather records for the gale we encountered, but aside from a mention of gales in the Irish Sea and along the Channel at that time, nothing particularly interesting was reported. However, this trip took place not long after the final stages of Hurricane Andrew in the United States, and I suspect that our gale was a spin-off from that. The synoptic chart for 30 August shows a low centred in the Irish Sea, producing somewhat tightly packed isobars and giving us the southerly winds we experienced. The seemingly abnormally strong winds we encountered appeared local to just that part of the coast and were not typical of the general gale as it passed through the Channel. Our speeds, a maximum of 7.5 knots, were dictated by our hull design, and in the early stages, as the weather built, a semi-displacement or planing hull might have got us into Ramsgate faster. I suspect, though, that once inside they would have been even more uncomfortable.

A modern semi-displacement hull achieving an impressive 20 knots in rough water. Note the level running attitude of the hull. © Safehaven Marine

CONCLUSION AND LESSONS LEARNT

It's easy to believe that a harbour equates to a safe haven. Frequently this is not the case and much damage can be caused within them due to the proximity of other vessels or because the mooring or berthing facilities may be poor or too old to cope with such fierce weather. It is wise to carry more large fenders and warps than you think necessary, as you will undoubtedly need them. The strength of our fittings was a great comfort, but not all modern vessels have sufficient size or security in terms of their cleat fixings. I would always want to check the methods of fastening cleats to boats to ensure that suitable backing plates and substantial bolts were used. The other part of the equation is the strength of the cleat you secure to the dock. If you are in any doubt whatsoever in heavy weather or, for that matter, even benign conditions, don't use that particular cleat. A big swell from a passing vessel could easily produce sufficient surge to rip a cleat out. Cleats are heavy, and pinging through the air could have a massive or even fatal impact on an unsuspecting head or body, Sometimes, however tempting it may be to make harbour, the old adage of going out to sea to find sea room can be the safest option.

With this in mind, displacement hulls and their semi-displacement counterparts are invariably more able and better suited to 'riding out' a storm than their fast planing cousins. Hence, the practice of 'dodging' as practised by the coxswains of the heavily built, displacement hulled, Scottish fishing trawlers, who are known for their survival technique of applying just enough power to maintain a 'head to sea' position in the teeth of a gale. Displacement hulls can be vulnerable when running before a very big sea as they lack the necessary agility and speed to avoid the dangers astern. Efforts to negate the effect of waves travelling faster than the vessel's movement through the water have thus involved the 'double ender' or 'canoe stern' design. Such designs, long used by the herring fisherman of Scandinavia, have been considered by many as some of the most seaworthy displacement hulls ever developed. But with low-revving diesel engines and long range fuel reserves, these forms of powered vessel are known for their exceptional abilities in the most extreme sea conditions.

Hugo Montgomery-Swan

No safe haven here, even in this trusted natural harbour. Note the deserted mooring buoys in the central foreground. © Murray Macleod

WORKING IN A STORM
Commercial Fishing Vessels and Heavy Weather
Ben Reynolds is a USCG licensed captain and Alaska commercial fisherman

As summer ends and the sun's energy on the high northern latitudes weakens, two prime global breeding grounds for winter tempests strengthen, ready to produce their massive low-pressure storms. One of these is the Icelandic Low in the North Atlantic off the coast of Greenland. The other stretches from the icy Bering Sea into the vast Gulf of Alaska. This is the Aleutian Low. From September to April this low draws moisture from the Bering Sea while warm tropical air collides with frigid Arctic air masses, producing winds in excess of 150 miles per hour and waves reaching 20 metres. These same waters produce incredible amounts of life and sustain the most productive fisheries on Earth. For those whose livelihood depends on venturing out into the ocean here, handling your vessel correctly during heavy weather is of paramount importance.

Fishing vessels from 30 to over 130 ft go out year round to harvest crab, cod, pollock, halibut, salmon and herring during their respective seasons. Methods of catch include bottom trawls, pots, ground lines, seines, gill nets and trolling. While this wide array of vessels includes many different boat designs, there is one important aspect that differentiates them from most other full displacement hull vessels: a fishing vessel's stability changes throughout its voyage. This is primarily through the operation of its gear and the catch it will haul aboard. Thus, to manoeuvre and handle the vessel one must understand how each aspect of the sea state, as well as the fishing methods being used, will affect the stability of your vessel. This is especially important during times when there are many external capsizing forces working against the positive stability of the vessel. Stability is a fundamental aspect of proper boat handling as it determines which course of action you will take under any given circumstance. There are several key factors that can contribute to an originally stable fishing vessel becoming unstable over the course of a voyage while under way, during fishing operations and in heavy weather.

1 Added weight from fishing gear, boarded water, icing and the catch itself. These will raise the centre of gravity of the vessel and lower the available freeboard. The rails will submerge at lower heel angles.
2 Lifting weight off the deck or from over the side transfers that weight's effective centre of gravity to the tip of the boom or winch, immediately raising the vessel's centre of gravity. If the weight is from over the side this will also add a heeling force. Always minimise the time lifting heavy fishing gear from over the side, such as retrieving purse seines, and do so in sheltered areas.
3 Heavy fishing gear such as stacked pots can shift during heavy weather, leading to a loss of overall stability.

4 Free surface from slack tanks, fish holds, cross-connected tanks, water trapped on deck or progressive down flooding. Free surface is the term used to describe the motion of liquid to the low side of a vessel when it heels over. This causes the vessel's centre of gravity to move further outboard, leading to a reduction in the vessel's righting arm curve.

5 Towing fishing gear. This would include bottom trawls and purse seines. Several factors combine to inhibit the manoeuvring and stability of the vessel. The tow adds weight, reducing stern freeboard, and raises the centre of gravity to the towing point aboard the vessel. The towing point should be as low as possible and directly off the stern, especially in bad weather. Avoiding beam or quartering seas while towing will reduce the shifting from side to side of the towing load. Always maintain a means for quickly releasing any towed or lifted gear in case of snagging on the bottom or of the fish diving, to prevent capsize.

6 Icing is a major concern to fishing vessels during winter, especially those with large superstructures, shelter decks or gear such as pots. These large surface areas allow sea spray to form into ice, rapidly reducing overall stability. Running downwind with the seas reduces the ice formation from spray but also increases the risk of broaching and capsize. Proper throttle control and riding on the back side of the preceding wave will help prevent the vessel from doing so.

In severe heavy seas, when the safety of the vessel and crew is at stake, the prudent course of action would be to head into the seas and maintain a bare steerageway until the weather lessens or protection can be sought. Carrying a sea anchor will allow you to maintain this heading in case of propulsion failure.

Commercial fishing in Alaska or any other high latitude combines not only good seamanship but also a knowledge of the working mechanics of your gear and the effect it has on your vessel, the stability of your fishing vessel in all situations you will encounter, and an awareness at all times of the fast-changing weather systems these areas of the world produce. Fishing is not just a matter of travelling from point A to point B, but a way of life where you work day after day in a harsh environment. When you are exposed to heavy weather you must strive to manage the risk by taking every necessary precaution and by staying vigilant to the handling of your vessel in its current state. By doing so you will safeguard your vessel, your crew and yourself.

COASTAL OPERATION

OPERATING WITHIN THE SURF LINE

BY PETER ADAMO
With additions from Paul Hollander, Hugo Montgomery-Swan and Edward Wake-Walker

Peter Adamo has a lifelong association with the sea and in recent years has gained huge specialist experience in the field of high-surf rescue through his work with the NSRI – South Africa's leading maritime rescue organisation. This chapter not only explores the techniques employed by some of the world's most experienced high-surf boat handlers, but also includes invaluable experiences gained by professionals operating within the surf line.

In this chapter I will draw upon my experiences gathered over many years as an inshore rescue boat coxswain operating along South Africa's surf-swept coastline. The information that follows is not exclusively mine, however, for I also draw upon the experiences and collective knowledge of many of my peers, a number of whom I regard as experts in the techniques of working powered craft close inshore, often amidst high surf. This chapter will also touch on ergonomics and safety where appropriate, as well as different hull types and how these relate to operating within the surf line.

THE IMPORTANCE OF HULL DESIGN IN HIGH-SURF

I have a love of wooden boats, partly because the first boat I ever owned, or part-owned, was an 8ft marine-ply rowing pram. Four of us, all 12 years old, bought the boat for just under one pound sterling! But as humble as it was, we learnt much of our seamanship in her, handling the boat in all types of conditions. There was no formal sea rescue then, so if we got into difficulty we had to get ourselves out of it. As I grew older I bought a fibreglass boat and then, a little later, built my own wooden ski boat. In latter years I have built boats for a living, and my love of all things wood has remained with me to this day.

Being a boatbuilder by trade, I'm very aware of the importance of hull design and the benefits, as well as the disadvantages, of the various forms available, whether they be planing, deep vee, medium vee, semi-displacement, displacement or cathedral. Each, of course, can come into its own under certain conditions and depending upon the specific role being undertaken. But when it comes to the matter of employing a boat for use in high surf, the hydrodynamics of these hull variants must be understood, not only to distinguish the right hull for the job, but also to get the best out of that design in the real environment.

I may be guilty of generalising here, but it could be said that in many cases northern-hemisphere craft tend to be built with narrower beams than their southern-hemisphere counterparts. This is because of the shortness of the northern seas. When I did my national service in the Air-Sea Rescue Services of the South African Air Force we had two German-built 96ft boats, which were similar in design to the old wartime E-type boats. In the long swells off our South African coast, these narrow-beamed vessels would corkscrew horribly, rolling off the top of a swell to one side, and rolling back as they hit the next swell. The momentum would force them to carry on rolling on the opposite tack, and then back again, a very tiring and unpleasant experience. You had to be wide awake, with feet braced, and ready to anticipate the roll to counteract its effect on the helm. Short spells on the wheel were the order of the day. Nonetheless, it goes to show how important it is, in operational terms, to ensure that the right hull, indeed the right boat, is employed for the task in hand. This is no less true in the business of high-surf operation, where the peculiarities of steep seas, white water, shallow depths and rapid response times collectively make for an environment of extremes.

RESCUE IN HOUT BAY

It was 1630 when we launched the large offshore rescue boat, *Spirit of Rotary*, from Hout Bay. She was an 11m diagonally planked wooden boat with two 375hp Caterpillar after-cooled turbo diesels, which gave her a speed of 34 knots on trials. She was also 28 years old and a grand sea boat, designed by the late Bill Edwards, a man who had tremendous experience of the seas around the Cape of Good Hope. There are still plenty of his boats around, and all the owners and crews love them. A boat needs to be designed for the seas it will endure, and in South Africa we have the long South Atlantic rollers, normally from the south-west, and when our big winter storms hit they can be up to 20 metres high. Our boats are beamy planing hulls; the centre of gravity is very low, with the engines giving the craft stability, and there is very little top weight, which reduces the amount of rolling.

The first of our autumn fronts had just passed through, and the wind had swung from north-west straight into a south-easterly and was gusting between 25 and 30 knots. The sea was confused, with a 5 to 6 metre south-westerly swell and the chop of the south-easterly sitting on top of this. The area we were headed for was the notorious 'Dungeons' (34 03 36S 18 17 48E chart SAN 150), famed for its huge surf. The Dungeons are traditionally home to one of the world's top big-wave surfing championships. Its location is just behind the popular tourist attraction of Seal Island, which is famed for its white shark gatherings. Just behind the Dungeons a 24ft GRP hard chine yacht, *Renette*, with three aboard, had set off a distress flare. The yacht had been bought by the three amateur sailors a few days earlier; they had no knowledge of sailing and very little of boating in general, but they were motoring the yacht around to Hout Bay where they had hoped to learn how to handle her. The problem was that the motor was not powerful enough to push them against the wind and they were being driven back. Finally, the boat had been pooped once too often and the engine cut out. Without power, *Renette* was blown into a mass of low-lying reefs and boulders. Two fishing boats now stood off, unable to enter the area.

I went in between two breaking waves and turned into the oncoming swell. I began veering down on to the yacht, with my crew ready with a messenger line attached to our towline in order to pass to it. An incoming wave helped what our starboard turning props were already doing, pushing the boat to port. I immediately put the gears into neutral and then ahead. With that, I felt the controls go slack; in fact, it felt as if they had snapped. Now I had lost all control of both engines!

The breaking wave threw us over on to our beam ends, and the crew were almost thrown overboard. As I ran from the upper control station down to the cabin I heard the terrible screams of the three yachtsmen as their yacht was pitchpoled and rolled right over, flinging them into the sea where the water temperature was 9° centigrade.

I established control of one engine but was in no position to help the yacht, as I first had to get complete control of the boat. The yacht had been pushed closer to the shore and I could not approach it from the same direction anyway. The yacht was swamped; the air trapped inside was keeping it just afloat. The crew had scrambled aboard again and were sitting on the coach roof.

I went out the same way I'd come in, and after some manipulating I regained control of both engines. We proceeded to the west and then north to get around the area. We again approached from the shore side and manoeuvred between the semi-submerged rocks to get close to the yacht. The closest reef was about 3 metres from us, and the incoming and outgoing swells were pushing us in all directions. We got close enough to pull the female crewmember onto our boat but had to beat a retreat as huge swells rolling in made it impossible to get close again. The sun was going down and we were determined to go in once more to pull the remaining casualties off. I briefed the crew and, as we waited for a break between sets of waves, our small 5.5m RIB, with its shallow draught, arrived on the scene and was able to take the other two crew off and transfer them to us. We were all soon back at base.

There are several lessons here. The gear-control cables consist of an outer and inner cable; the outer cable is clamped in position and the inner one is pushed forward or back against the clamped outer cable to change the gear position. The clamp was made of plastic and was unable to take the load; unknown to us, the manufacturers had made a modification, as by then a brass one was standard. Fortunately, we had an extremely well-designed boat which could handle the rolling without being seriously compromised. But the failure of a little piece of plastic could have caused the death or serious injury of up to eight people in a lesser craft possessing a reduced degree of lateral stability.

During my time with the National Sea Rescue Institute of South Africa, one of my functions was to teach others how to handle boats. The one thing I stressed was that sea time was useless unless you did something positive while out on the water: you can drive a boat around all day on a flat sea and learn absolutely nothing. Rather, we spent time manoeuvring in and out of marinas, coming alongside other boats, dropping buoys in the water and coming alongside a supposed casualty, as well as experiencing a range of different sea conditions. This way people learnt just what their boat was

The South African lifesaving RIB crews are highly skilled high surf operators.
Throttle control and quick reflexes are the order of the day. © Simon
Everett/Optical Art

truly capable of. It was just this type of basic knowledge and experience that enabled us to work in potentially very dangerous situations with some degree of confidence.

KNOW YOUR BOAT

Knowledge of the boat and all its components is also vital for quickly and accurately assessing a problem when it first arises. I do annual safety surveys on yachts but sadly am no longer surprised when I ask an owner or skipper where a certain bit of equipment is and he looks at me blankly and says: 'Do I have such a thing?' I tell people to go through their boats from stem to stern, to find out where everything is, why it is there and how it works. More importantly, when it goes wrong they must know how to fix it or get around the problem in an emergency. I then give them a sketch of a hull and ask them to draw every piece of equipment from memory. Try it yourself; it's good discipline!

The value of this type of thinking was impressed upon me some years ago – back in the early 1970s, in fact – when the NSRI was still in its infancy. In those days we had fitted a new hydraulic steering system to the 6m rescue boat at Bakoven, located about 12 miles south of Cape Town. It was a beach-launching rescue base. We were called out one day to a reported drowning off Llandudno beach, some 5 miles further south. There was a 2 to 3 metre breaking surf off the beach and I was making my way in and out of the waves, heading out to sea every time a wave started peaking. Suddenly, the steering jammed and I could only go to starboard. It had given us innumerable problems previously and the agents were trying to find the solution. To free the lock, there was a screw on the back of the steering box that had to be undone, then with the wheel centralised the screw had to be tightened again. To make this process easier, a tee-shaped piece had been brazed on to the screw so it could be done by hand. With the deftness of speed inspired by fear, I was under the deck, undoing the screw, while a crewmember centralised the wheel. Then I tightened it up again – all within about 30 seconds! The steering was working again, but I was caught in the surf line and unable to turn into the wave quickly enough.

Llandudno beach is about a mile long, and the surf starts breaking out to sea on the northern side, just where, in fact, we happened to be. Looking out to the far side of the beach I could see this was probably the only place we could attempt a decent breakout. Running with the wave, I accelerated along, towards and across the beach. Then I turned to seaward in order to meet the wave on the far side, going through it just as it broke over us. It was a nasty moment, but by understanding the problem and being able to fix it without delay we got out of trouble. (We replaced the steering immediately after that incident.)

As skipper, you will probably helm your own boat for the most part. But whether it's you or a crewmember, you want to be able to see all your engine instruments, as well as your navigation screens. In addition, there is the critical need to observe all that is happening around you. The steering position, particularly in the case of surf rescue craft, is also critical, since human response times need to be so fast. Everything, therefore, needs to be working in the favour of the helm. Thus, before buying or building a boat or fitting instruments, try drawing or making a dummy steering position so as to ensure all your instruments will be within easy reach. One of the biggest problems I have had with all instruments is the

What might be termed a 'death sea'. An extreme and violent body of water capable of crushing a boat and killing its crew. © Murray Macleod

reflection or glare that makes them virtually impossible to see at times. The sales lads will tell you the latest instruments all have high resolutions and that poor screen clarity is a thing of the past, but frequently, with all but the largest hi-definition screens, this is not the case. So try also to minimise the effect of glare by holding the units at different angles and in different light conditions before fixing them in place.

CREW SAFETY

It goes without saying that a crew working within the surf line needs to be well versed in the techniques of riding a craft at speed and being able to read the sea in order to minimise the effects of extreme motion.

All need to know their roles and have a secure position aboard the vessel. This may be a suspension seat within a wheelhouse or a particular position on a RIB sponson. Whatever or wherever a crewman's position may be, it needs to be known to them and be suited to the individual concerned. Handholds, footstraps and the like all need to be strategically placed. Even in a cabin environment, just a rope running fore and aft along the roof bulkhead is a simple but practical way to provide additional safety for crew moving about. This negates having grab rails where your head can hit them or where they protrude and can smash into your hip. If the sea is big enough, as it invariably is when on a rescue mission, bruises and knocks are a frequent reward for one's efforts. All the crew appreciate the operator minimising this.

Jackstays running fore and aft down the outside of the craft are necessary if you have personnel working in severe conditions on deck. Likewise, wearing a good harness with crutch straps, clipped on to the jackstay, is important. Beware, though, when working within the surf line, that if the vessel were to capsize, any securing devices of this type could well be the cause of injury or even drowning. In some extreme incidents, being thrown clear of a craft can be a safer option than being held to it. When aboard a craft with an enclosed wheelhouse, the instructions to my crew are to never leave the safety of the cabin in rough conditions, be it night or day, without clipping on to a jackstay. It goes without saying that lifejackets with safety lights and reflective strips are a must. They are particularly crucial if an MOB incident occurs at night.

HIGH-SURF HELMING TECHNIQUES

When launching into surf, RIBs up to 7.3 metres in length can usually be launched manually or semi-manually off a beach, depending on the expertise of the personnel involved and the equipment available. Boats of an overall length greater than this simply become too heavy and cumbersome to manage. (The RNLI's Mersey Class and their FCB2 prototype are examples of large craft that are, in fact, carriage-launched into surf utilising a semi-submersible tractor system. Beach-launched vessels of such great size and mass can, of course, only be launched by complex mechanical means into the surf line. Typically, then, RIBs of 5.5 metres tend to be the limit for manual launch.)

Launching into and through breaking waves can be one of the most dangerous and demanding aspects of boatmanship. It requires experience, knowledge of the prevailing conditions and nerves of steel. Once committed it is impossible to turn back and the only way out is onward. To illustrate: 'The Wilderness' is a stunningly beautiful area along the Garden Route of the Southern Cape in South Africa (lat and long 33 59.712'S 022 34.834'E). The beach there has continuous surf running all day, 365 days a year. Nonetheless, it is the only place to launch a boat in the vicinity. Of course, the height and severity of the surf depends on the weather at the time, and the National Sea Rescue Institute has a station that rescues many holidaymakers every year. It is also used as a training base for other surf-launching stations around the country. The NSRI Training Officer, Hennie Niehaus, sent me a copy of their operational training manual, which I feel has some pertinent points worth repeating here:

1   With high-surf helming techniques, hard and fast rules are few; hence the training manual offers guidelines as opposed to rules.
2   No one person knows everything. Learn from each other. There will always be something new to learn.
3   Practise riding in the surf under safe conditions. Use the guidance of more experienced people to help you gain experience.
4   Always think in terms of 'safety first'.
5   Treat all waves as you would big waves. Watch out for the third wave: behind two smaller waves there is invariably a large sea advancing toward one and growing in intensity and size with every metre gained.
6   The second wave is likely to be the one that flips you. Why? Because you might be able to jump a large wave, but it won't help if you stall the engines, lie abreast or cavitate in front of the second wave.

7 Watch out for beach breaks, ie waves that break right on the beach. These waves have a devastating effect on the launching of a boat. They can swamp and flood boats, kill engines and flip even large vessels with ease.

8 Hold the nose of the boat directly into the surf. If this isn't done, one small wave could push it to one side, allowing the second wave to flip it.

9 When holding a boat in surf, never approach the boat directly from behind. If a wave pushes the boat back, the propellers will inflict massive injury. If the wave hits the side of the boat, and you are standing on the shore/lee side, do not stand with your body against the sponson/tube. Hold it at arm's length – in doing so you will minimise the chance of being pinned down.

10 As the wave approaches, push the boat towards it to provide some momentum.

11 Do not let the boat drift backwards.

12 As the wave hits, the front crew should jump on to the boat. This adds more weight to the front of the boat, keeping the bow pinned, and it also serves to lift the engines.

13 As the wave hits, pull your body onto the sponson and then drop back down as the wave passes. Do not try to hang on to the side of the boat when a big wave strikes: the boat will be ripped out of your hand.

When launching into surf, every member of the crew or team needs to be perfectly clear in their minds as to their individual function. It's good practice and common sense to choose the smallest wave, with the helmsman already in the boat with the engines running. The crew should next push the boat into the water as deep as possible before boarding themselves. Accelerating as close to the line of the first breaking wave comes next, giving the boat just enough speed to penetrate the wave and break clear to the other side. Too much speed will result in the boat flying off the crest and landing heavily in the trough beyond, to the detriment of both craft and crew. Keep a wary eye out for the waves behind this first wave, for these are unknown quantities. The helmsman should aim to hit a wave before it breaks. If the engines get caught in a breaking wave the propellers will likely cavitate due to the profusion of aerated water. If this does occur and the engine RPM races, pulling back throttles to allow the prop to slow while the air dissipates will then allow one to slowly, but determinedly, throttle up once more, with the propeller biting again in the process. This corrective action needs to be done instinctively and with speed, but too much haste will simply cause the prop to continue spinning devoid of any grip.

The sponsons on a RIB push out a huge cushion of air ahead of them. With fine entry bows and the natural buoyancy of the sponsons atop of this, a RIB can have excellent seagoing properties both in head-to-sea conditions and following sea states. Invariably, though, especially at slower speeds, the weight of the boat's engines may cause it to squat in the water and travel with a bow-up attitude. This makes the importance of correctly balancing the boat by means of proper weight distribution all the more critical. In operating in and around the surf line, this factor becomes all the more vital to get right and could well mean that in some circumstances the skipper might send one or two crew up on the foredeck to help keep the bow down. If this is done, and it would generally be the case only on smaller, open craft, of say 5 metres in size, then adequate handholds etc must be available to provide the necessary security.

Several years ago NSRI Hout Bay was asked to take fuel out to a boat that was on its way into the bay. They were having problems with blocked fuel lines. I used our 5.5m RIB, *Queenie Payne*. It was a wild Easter weekend: a front had come through and the winds were veering and backing from south-west to south-east continuously, gusting up to about 50 knots. We went out of the harbour, but within a relatively short distance it was impossible to venture any further out to sea. We had the spare 25 litres of fuel in the bow, and as the wind gusted I moved the crew up into the bow and then aft again as the gusts died. Even with weight of this degree working in our favour, as we came up over the steep crests and the wind got beneath the hull I could feel the boat lifting, her bow almost floating in the air, before she descended into the trough beyond. We got back safely into the confines of the harbour, but it was surprising how much forward weight this small RIB needed in this particular head-to-sea scenario.

Like the majority of launches that involve negotiating surf, the key elements required to ensure a safe exit and entry are: (a) a competent skipper (this includes an inherent confidence in one's abilities and equipment), (b) a detailed knowledge of local conditions, and (c) patience.

A single-engined RIB punches its way out over a bar and its breaking seas. Preventing the boat from flying can be difficult as large amounts of power are required – power not speed is what is needed here. © RIB International Magazine

CAPSIZE IN THE SURF by Paul Hollander

As part of my work as a professional boatman with the Netherlands Coastguard, an organisation whose operational zone is confined to the relatively shallow, cold and often storm-tossed waters of the North Sea, I was engaged in a training exercise aboard an outboard-powered 5.4m offshore RIB.

On this particular day my crew and I were operating among a line of small breakers, nothing of any apparent consequence, caused by a south-east-going swell which was heaping up in the shallows just a short distance from the shore. The location was very familiar to us, the weather was fair and we were practising our steering techniques amidst the breaking seas as each one took his turn at the wheel, duly switching places on the three-person jockey seat in the process.

All went well at first, with the RIB displaying its typical agility in these conditions; that was until the keel of the boat hit a sandbank in the midst of the surf. At that very moment, too, a comparatively small wave struck the vessel broadside and instantaneously flipped the RIB clean over. During the capsize my two crewmates had swung out of the RIB, but I was thrown backwards off the jockey seat, and in the process had forced my right foot hard into the deck foot strap, right above the ankle of my drysuit boot.

The violence and suddenness of the accident and the predicament of being trapped underneath the upturned hull with my foot held fast was frightening. My lifejacket, of course, had fired up and was also holding me firmly up against the boat's upturned deck in the narrow gap between the seat console and the sponsons. Fortunately, this was the one section where an air pocket lay. Amidst the confusion of my bedarkened world I then grappled with the jacket's fittings in order to dump its unwanted air, since I had no need for such buoyancy.

Being familiar with capsize drills and surf training, as well as being a strong swimmer, at least I was used to being comparatively orientated under an upturned craft. But it was not only my foot being trapped that complicated this scenario: the situation was made worse still by all the fuel that was spewing out of the tank vent. In fact, it appeared that each time the RIB was rocked in the surf, the action aided a siphoning effect that resulted in petrol being pumped out of the fuel tank from underneath the jockey seat. The stench was nauseating. (We had recently moved the fuel vent to this rearward position after getting fed up with the stench of fumes issuing from the breather's previous position – namely, up on the helm console.)

The fuel flowing around me made it impossible to breathe, and I couldn't swim away since my foot, despite my struggling, remained stuck in the strap. When my crewmates were able to touch the bottom in 2 metres of water they managed, with huge effort, to lift the tubes of the RIB clear just a couple of times between the rhythm of breaking seas so I could breathe. Every time they managed to lift the tube clear of the water I could see about me and take a gasp of salty air while trying like mad to jerk free my foot.

It took a huge amount of effort to finally break free, and this was only done by wriggling my foot back out of the boot and into the leg of my bulky work suit. Then, using my knife, which fortunately I kept on my right side, I proceeded to cut the boot off. This was no easy job as you can imagine– beneath the boat, in the dark freezing water and being trapped in the position I was, using the knife in earnest was awkward in the extreme. But then again, I was under no illusion that I was, in fact, fighting for my life.

Upon swimming free and into fresh air, though the whole experience had lasted minutes it had felt like an hour! Having lost our handheld VHF in the capsize, with the use of a CD-ROM as a makeshift heliograph we managed to attract the attention of our colleagues, who by now were already looking for us. After sighting us and the dark outline of our upturned boat amidst the dumping surf and sandbanks, a KNRM RIB was dispatched to go to our aid. Upon reaching the scene, after much manoeuvring and muscle power a gang of us then managed to successfully right the craft and its severely drowned engine.

Would an activated self-righting system have saved the day and provided the mechanical help required to extract me from my predicament? I believe that if a self-righting bag had been deployed, the sudden action it would have induced through the boat righting itself could have caused my leg to be either broken or dislocated. Others have suggested a spare air bottle might also have provided enough inhalations to enable me to either work more freely, or alternatively provide a life-sustaining supply until help arrived. Many debates were held following this incident but the following observations are likely very valid.

■ Having a knife on your person can save your life.
■ In some instances, depending on conditions and boat type, a manual lifejacket could be preferable over that of an auto-inflation type.
■ A handheld VHF should be both waterproof and securely attached to your person.
■ A self-righting arch mast has its uses but in this instance could have been the cause of serious injury. These systems are of value both in shallow waters and in the open ocean – the latter amidst high seas which are breaking. But RIBs are inherently stable and generally only become vulnerable when power and/or forward motion is lost – as this particular incident shows.
■ A simple quick-release system that would allow a person to free a trapped foot from the confines of a deck foot strap could prove a real lifesaver. Mechanisms have been developed for stirrup irons on horse saddles, and there is no reason why similar thinking could not be employed for use aboard FRC and other open craft such as RIBs. A Velcro strap has many benefits in terms of its quick-release qualities. In any event, it is vital that foot straps should never be allowed to stretch and become too large through general use and wear.
■ Deck lights that activate automatically upon a boat rolling 90% or more would provide useful illumination. For professional operators, becoming familiar with the use of emergency equipment in the dark is always good practice.

■ Fuel breathers/vents could also be fitted with a non-return valve that prevents loss of fuel if the boat was to invert, or upon any occasion where fuel is likely to be ejected through the 'bitter end' of its breather pipe.

■ A drysuit protected me from the effects of hypothermia and thus allowed my body to keep working to free itself. Without this garment, all seven of the above points highlighted would be rendered obsolete.

■ Do not be fooled by an apparently harmless wave height. This accident occurred in conditions that were anything but extreme.

THE EFFECT OF SWELLS AND TIDES

The Kowie River at Port Alfred in the Eastern Cape (lat and long 33 35.696'S 026 53.457'E) requires craft to negotiate unpredictable swells and breaking surf. Like most estuaries, there are sandbanks that are dynamic, both in size and location. They tend to be bigger in winter because of the larger swells that prevail. Tides make a difference to the decision of where and how to launch. Generally it is easier to come back through the surf than launch through it. An incoming-tide launch, too, is easier to master, as the tidal waters enable the helmsman to station with the throttles engaged while facing the sea. Patience is essential, as is the ability to read the sea. Once a break or flat is spotted, a skipper must commit himself to the launch: at this stage indecision is your worst enemy. The ideal launch would be to proceed straight out of the mouth and at right angles to the incoming swell. The skipper must remain vigilant, as there are often more sandbanks outside the break.

An outgoing-tide launch is considerably more challenging under moderate-to-large swell conditions, as the tidal flow meets the incoming swell. This can create standing waves, which peak straight up and then break. They are not constant in size and frequency, and your craft can be battered and swamped without warning. Unlike the incoming-tide launch it is not possible to hold station unless one engages the throttles in reverse. This is not advisable unless the helmsman possesses considerable skill and experience, as the strong outgoing tide can turn the boat sideways in an instant.

Depending on the area, one could, of course, keep the power on and maintain headway by undertaking circles while waiting for the break. It helps if you have a fast vessel with plenty of power in reserve and there is a considerable period between sets. But another tactic to employ or add to this latter method is to quickly turn the vessel out of its turning circle to confront the advancing sea at the point one sees the likelihood of a break forming. If you mistime your exit badly, you must face the incoming swells and power through regardless, using just enough power not only to break through but also to prevent the bow from being knocked one way or the other. At the point the bow breaks through the crest, back off the power to prevent the boat from flying. The boat is certain to take a large amount of water over the bows, so big scuppers or an open-transom design is vital in quickly ridding the decks of any shipped water. If there is a large distance between the swells it's possible to run parallel to these and find a 'flat' to go out on. In the most extreme situations, if you run out of space you can turn to the beach and surf the boat back in on the back of the seas.

Riding a beam sea is still dangerous, but the secret to remaining secure is to keep the power on and to be positive in terms of one's helming techniques. High-powered planing craft excel in this sea type and so are much more able to operate under such conditions than their semi-planing counterparts. Being both nimble and of exceptional lateral stability in terms of their overall design, RIBs tend to make for very able craft within the surf line zone. In any high-surf situation, though, you're going to have to turn to face the sea at some point, and it is this last account, therefore, that is of special relevance.

A 9m RIB awaits its chance to power through the breaking seas off its bow. The nimble nature of a high powered RIB comes into its own amidst such water.
© *Murray Macleod/Seatrek*

FACING THE SEA

Some years ago the NSRI was asked by the South African Navy to assist in a number of sea-trial tests they were conducting on every type of RIB available. We were pushing these craft to breaking point to determine the abuse they were capable of taking in the hands of the military for their operational activities 'in the field'. The test took place in Hout Bay, in the Dungeons area, as described earlier. When the conditions are right, waves up to 60ft high break onto a reef about three-quarters of a mile offshore. The

A US Coast Guard 47ft motor lifeboat operating in the deadly surf of Morro Bay.
Note that though the vessel is capsized, its self-righting capabilities enable
its operational recovery.

waves were about 5 metres high that day, with some larger seas heaping up in addition to the predominant wave pattern. We were aboard the Navy's 6m boat, built as a heavy-duty work RIB. I had the helm, and with me were Bob Matthews, at that time Station Commander of Gordon's Bay Rescue Station, and one of his crewmen. Bob suggested we find a 'mother of a wave' to take off on in order to test the vessel's strength of construction. I set off a few times into the waves, each time 'bottling out' just before flying off the top of the crest. Bob was scathing in his remarks to me, so I handed him the helm. Twice he also pulled back at the critical moment, but then, after I had goaded him on, he took off on what was a truly monster wave.

I was sitting on the port side. With one hand I grabbed hold of the console with all my might, pulling myself down on to the sponson. I waited and waited as the boat came down, down and down; I knew we were in for a very hard landing. The boat crashed down hard as expected but I just managed to hang on. Bob, though, was screaming and pointing to his left leg. His ankle was at right angles to his leg. The massive slam had caused his ankle to actually push back into the leg between the tibia and fibula. We were now in the trough with another wave about to break on us. I grabbed the wheel and his crewman took the throttle on the other side, and we worked the boat over the wave before getting out of the surf zone. Bob was taken back to shore by the Navy and ended up in hospital for a week, then on crutches for two months.

It was found that the Navy had strengthened the deck by retro-fitting a sheet of stainless steel to it because of previous damage inflicted on the boat due it being employed to carry heavy loads. The net result was that there was no give in the deck, and a very different approach to landing was required due to this modification. Modern shock mitigation decking has, of course, proved itself to be of huge benefit on craft of this type in recent years, doing much to prevent injuries of this kind and the costs that go with them.

WORKING ON A LEE SHORE
by Hugo Montgomery-Swan

The danger of working on a lee shore with little in the way of sea room was brought home to me on a recent photo shoot I was involved with as part of my work with *RIB International Magazine*. Three RIBs were being put through their paces on this day for the benefit of the cameraman, who was positioned at the foot of the cliffs on the seaward extremity of West Loch Roag, Isle of Lewis. I was at the helm of a commercially spec'd 6.5m RIB going by the name of *Deep One*, a craft that I was relatively unfamiliar with and that was owned by Murray Macleod of Seatrek. My fellow 'pilots' were helming craft of similar type and length amidst the rough seas that were providing a suitable spectacle for the cameras that day. After 20 minutes or so of this 'fly past' routine, Murray Macleod and his brother, Kenny, aboard *Seatrek*, the biggest of the three RIBs, decided to have a short break and take a jaunt out to the adjoining bay. The conditions there were clearly quite lively, but then again perfectly within the limitations of both the personnel and the boats involved.

Passing through a narrow passage between the rocks, where the elements had caused the tip of the headland to break away and become a small isle separated from the main promontory, Murray, followed by Paul Lemmer at the helm of the second RIB, and then myself, alone behind the wheel of *Deep One*, drove out into the rough on the other side. Filing off the 'film set' last, and staying directly in the path of the wash of the leading boats, I emerged from the headland passage to be greeted by a very confused sea, which was due to both the incoming swell and the fact that the waves were rebounding off the cliff face and throwing up unpredictable pyramid-shaped seas.

Though exciting, a keen eye was needed to negotiate through this area of sea, for I was mindful of the strength of the waves and perhaps even the occasional 'rogue' that might catch the RIB broadside. I could also see Murray and Paul determining, perhaps, that this wasn't the safest zone to be sightseeing in, and hence coming round on a starboard arc in an effort to head back via the way we had all just come.

As I began to bring the helm over to follow suit and face my bows directly into the seas in the process, I glanced astern – only to see that the throwing line, made fast to the life ring tied to the arch mast, had come undone and was beginning to trail in the water just above the boat's propeller. Now I had a dilemma: should I take a chance and hope the rope wouldn't become entangled round the prop this side of the passage here on the lee shore? Or should I heave-to, leave the helm and go to the rear of the craft in order to secure the line, with all the potential dangers that might bring about – including the compromising of the craft with the wheel left unmanned? Neither seemed like a good option.

I quickly decided on the latter, left the motor in gear in order to keep the vessel's head to sea, and duly unclipped my kill cord so as to make my way astern. However, as I lifted my leg over the deck plinth just in front of the seat pod, I failed to notice that the kill cord cable had actually snagged under my bent knee, and as I swung my leg around, the cord was pulled taut to the point where it suddenly 'pinged' off over the side!

The engine stopped dead. I had to think quickly: radio the others or anchor first? I was only 50 metres from the foot of the cliffs and therefore speed was of the essence. I could not afford to make an error of judgement in terms of my priorities. I grabbed the radio mic and made one brief but assertive call for assistance. Without waiting for a reply, I then raced up forward to the anchor locker. Lifting the lid to the locker aside, to my relief the warp and chain were all ready for immediate deployment.

The boat was rising and falling severely in the near-curling seas which, with every yard they pushed *Deep One* closer to the cliffs, became more menacing, more unstable in their form. The wild motion on deck made it difficult to maintain a foothold, so I knelt as tight up into the forepeak as I could in order to get leverage over the heavy Danforth anchor. Out it came, and I heaved it over the side before it disappeared into the dark, green waters, with a rush of warp and chain chasing after it. By now the boat had swung broadside to the seas.

Bearing in mind my closeness to the shore, and the fact it was low tide, I was alarmed to see that every 'inch' of the 50m warp and additional chain was taken in a horizontal dive that clearly indicated the seabed was almost out of reach. In fact, by my estimate the anchor only had just enough line to bite home. Bite home it did, though, with the result that the RIB's bow was now pinned down to such an extent that the boat's sponsons up in the bow deformed under the strain every time she desperately tried to rise to the steep 15ft walls of water. Having put a halt to our continuing sideways march toward the rocks, and with the RIB now at the correct angle to the seas, it was with some relief that I saw the other two RIBs returning.

Murray at first directed me to the helm locker, where he said the spare kill cord was kept. I looked feverishly but couldn't see it. Under the circumstances it was decided to set up a tow; this we did, although freeing the anchor proved impossible. It had obviously struck a ledge, and under the strain of these

Disaster averted – the boat in question with Hugo Montgomery-Swan at the helm, being towed out of the 'danger zone'. © Murray Macleod

conditions, and the fact there was no power to help provide some slack, we had to make the decision to cut it free.

Seatrek pulled away, but downwind, toward the cliff face and the heavy seas that were crashing against it. With very little sea room, the towline went taut and then, without any warning, it seemed, a big sea rose up behind Deep One and began to carry her with uncompromising force directly toward Seatrek's transom. As I began the 'death slide', from my vantage point just below the top of the high crest I yelled to Murray, down in the trough below, to 'move it!' The two boats only just avoided striking each other and, with quick reactions and a firm hand on the throttle, Murray pulled away just in the nick of time.

Minutes later we were away from the lee shore and out beyond, into waters affording much greater sea room. With a blushing expression, I apologised for nearly writing off Deep One and for losing Murray's anchor to Davy Jones' locker, but there were some important lessons to be learnt here.

LESSONS LEARNT

No matter how brief the spell aboard a 'foreign' craft, it is good practice to familiarise oneself with a boat's key items, especially its safety systems. If, upon going to the anchor locker to deploy its contents, I had found it empty or the anchor warp in such a muddle it could not be deployed instantaneously, then the £50,000 vessel would have undoubtedly been wrecked on the foot of the cliffs. Likewise, unless I could have secured the boat by means of the anchor, the boat would have quite likely been capsized by the seas that were growing ever more fierce with every metre we closed on the rocks. Thankfully, due to his professionalism, Murray's thorough prepping of his boat ensured no delay was incurred as I sought to remedy my predicament.

Furthermore, the speed of rescue depended upon the radio working but might have also, under slightly different circumstances, called upon the use of flares. How vital, therefore, that such essential items not only work, but their whereabouts are clearly known by all aboard. In the particular scenario described here, speed was of the essence. There simply was no time to waste.

Equally important, and of key relevance to this account also, was the fact that I did not know where the spare kill cord was stowed. Even when Murray shouted its location to me, in the rise and fall of the seas I could not find it within the helm locker. This shows the wisdom of (a) having a spare kill cord, (b) knowing its whereabouts, and (c) being able to lay one's hands upon it without delay.

Hugo Montgomery-Swan

THE PENLEE TRAGEDY
19 December 1981 Gold Medal to Coxswain Trevelyan Richards

Taken from 'Gold Medal Rescues', by Edward Wake-Walker, with additions by Hugo Montgomery-Swan

The tragedy that befell the Penlee lifeboat six days before Christmas 1981, when all eight of her crew were lost together with the eight people they were attempting to save, had a profound and lasting effect on the RNLI and the British public at large. The shock and grief it caused in a small Cornish community is remembered to this day even by people who otherwise have had little involvement in the lifeboat service and who live nowhere near the sea.

The story is told here, not only because a gold medal was won in the rescue attempt, but also to show just how real are the risks lifeboatmen sometimes have to take and how dire the consequences when courage is not repaid by good fortune. Also, there are valuable lessons to learn from this tragedy, not least the design limitations inherent to the form of displacement lifeboat in use at the time of this disaster. The 47ft Watson Class vessel's relatively limited power compared to that of a modern lifeboat meant that her ability to manoeuvre in heavy seas along with her overall speed and agility/throttle response time was certainly not well suited to working amidst such high seas where sea room had diminished to a pitiful few metres.

It could be said that no vessel could have survived the conditions the Penlee lifeboat, *Solomon Browne*, faced that night. But though the Penlee lifeboat is central to this whole account, it would be unwise to overlook the vital lessons to be drawn from the fatal experience suffered by the crew of the *Union Star*. The cause of her breakdown appeared to be contamination of her diesel tanks with seawater via the breathers and fillers on her weather side.

The coaster's Captain, Henry Moreton, and Engineer George Sedgwick, worked feverishly to rectify the situation but were unable. With only emergency power and in the violence of the rising storm, they also misjudged their true position and rate of drift. A salvage tug tow was offered but the decision to accept 'Lloyd's Open' delayed acceptance and vital time was lost. Indeed the developing catastrophe was graded a PAN PAN and then a MAYDAY only in the final stages of the coaster's advancement towards the shoaling waters of the Mount's Bay coast.

When the vessel's anchors failed and the attempts of the helicopter crew to airlift the casualties off her heaving deck proved in vain, the lives of the eight aboard the *Union* Star depended solely on the efforts of the *Solomon Browne*. Vital time had been lost and, one by one, each option slipped through or was torn out of their hands. As this tragedy proves, even three miles out off a lee shore in bad weather constitutes very little sea room and affords very little time if things unexpectedly go wrong.

With no one surviving to tell the tale, details of precisely what happened on the night of 19 December are understandably scarce, but with the help of recorded messages to the coastguard and the eyewitness accounts of a Royal Naval helicopter pilot and a salvage tug skipper, a story of immense courage does emerge. It is told succinctly but movingly in the pages of the *Lifeboat* journal of the day:

'Penlee lifeboat, the 47ft Watson class *Solomon Browne*, with her coxswain, Trevelyan Richards, and all on board, was lost on the night of Saturday December 19 during a service to the 1,400 ton coaster *Union Star*, registered in Dublin.

Solomon Browne had launched in a violent storm to go to the aid of *Union Star* which had reported engine failure when eight miles east of Wolf Rock Lighthouse and which was drifting rapidly on to the cliffs four miles south-west of Penlee lifeboat station; there were eight people on board, including one woman and two teenage girls. The weather was atrocious. The wind, blowing from south by east, increased to hurricane force 12, gusting to 90 knots; there was a heavy ground swell and the mountainous seas were reported to be 60ft high; in driving rain, visibility was very poor. So bad were the conditions that in spite of many attempts a Royal Navy Sea King helicopter, piloted by Lt-Cdr Russell L. Smith, USN, was unable to lift off any of the coaster's crew.

Coxswain Richards repeatedly took his lifeboat alongside the coaster in these appalling conditions to try to rescue the eight people on board. Latterly on at least two occasions the lifeboat was lifted by a huge wave onto the deck of the *Union Star*, then sliding stern first back into the sea. Subsequently, Coxswain Richards drove her alongside once more and four people on the deck jumped into the lifeboat. The *Solomon Browne* was observed to have slammed hard against the coaster's side but was seen moving away, apparently still under control.

'The last radio message from the lifeboat confirmed that four people had been rescued and before returning to their base the helicopter crew saw *Solomon Browne*, then only about 50 yards off the steep and rocky shore, turn, possibly to make another approach. There was no further radio contact with the lifeboat, but her lights were seen to disappear some ten minutes later, at about the same time that *Union Star* was overwhelmed and laid on her side to the west of Tater-du Lighthouse.

'Despite many hours search through the night and the following day by the St Mary's, Isle of Scilly, and the Lizard-Cadgwith lifeboats, by helicopters, by HM Coastguard coast rescue teams and by fishing vessels, no survivors were recovered from either *Solomon Browne* or *Union Star*.'

To this day no one knows for sure how the lifeboat met her end. By the wreckage which was found afterwards it was clear that somehow she had been smashed to smithereens by some enormous impact. Whether it was the sea hurling her onto the jagged rocks where the *Union Star* had run aground or the effects of her being crushed by the capsizing coaster is impossible to deduce. Whatever the cause, there is no doubt that the lifeboat coxswain had pursued his increasingly impossible mission to the end and that on this occasion the sea had proved itself to be the ultimate master.

There is no question that Coxswain Richards employed every ounce of skill and boat handling ability possible amidst those impossible seas. It is evident too that he and his crew were expert in navigating the coast local to them, for as we have already made clear, the rescue had to be attempted at night, in driving rain and in seas that were of such a height as to continually obscure landmarks and the general coastline. Though the outcome was a total loss, nevertheless, it does not detract from the fact that skill on the part of all the crew, both in terms of handling their boat and operating its vital functions and components, plus a total ability to navigate amidst extreme conditions, is wholly necessary if any chance of survival is to be had.

The courage required by Trevelyan Richards to carry out the successful part of the rescue attempt when four people were taken off was enough to earn him the RNLI gold medal posthumously. His crew consisting of Second Coxswain/Mechanic James Madron, Assistant Mechanic Nigel Brockman, Emergency Mechanic John Blewett and Crew Members Charles Greenhaugh, Kevin Smith, Barrie Torrie and Gary Wallis were all posthumously awarded the bronze medal for gallantry.

Following the public enquiry into the disaster, the chairman commented in his summing up:

'The loss of the RNLB *Solomon Browne* and her crew was caused...in consequence of the persistent and heroic endeavours by the coxswain and his crew to save the lives of all from the *Union Star*. Such heroism enhances the highest traditions of the Royal National Lifeboat Institution in whose service they gave their lives.'

CONCLUSION

The most important conclusion we can draw from this chapter is that there is no substitute for real sea time experience if one is to become adept at working close inshore amidst high surf. Unfortunately, of course, we all start out with no knowledge or experience. The only way to gain it is to go out with an experienced skipper and crew and learn from them. So be a good listener and be observant to your surroundings. By that I mean work out what you would do in certain circumstances and then watch what the skipper does; ask him why he is doing it, and what would happen if he did it another way. Speak to the locals about the conditions and how to best handle them. Never feel inadequate about asking advice. You will still learn every time you go out, and the sea is rarely the same twice.

Also, take your boat out with the aim of getting a true feel of what it can do. Understand it, the good and the bad, the reaction time to opening throttles, going into, across, and with the swells. Do it at low and high speeds. Don't only think in terms of extreme sea state experience either; be determined to get the basics right first. Practise going alongside another boat, coming in and going out of a mooring. Practise with one engine only, and so forth. Learn to be observant and train yourself to think about the result of your actions before putting them into effect. Think safety as opposed to bullish determination in the face of danger. There is usually an alternative option, ie another launching place further away that's safer – even another way to negotiate a wave.

Peter Adamo

COASTAL EXTREMES

BY SHAUN WHITE AND HUGO MONTGOMERY-SWAN

As a commercial RIB builder and white-water RIB specialist, the late Shaun White was one of the key men involved in the earliest developments of the RIB through his association with Rear Admiral Hoare and Atlantic College in South Wales. Here he provides his unique insight into the helming of FRC (fast rescue craft) in extreme coastal conditions.

The ocean is an arena of unbridled force and momentum, an extreme testing ground for both man and RIB that can taunt, seduce and terrify us all. A huge part of its attraction lies in its unpredictability, yet the ocean's history is littered with the stories of those who have been ill-prepared for rising to the challenges of an underwater world haunted by the victims of poor planning and dysfunctional equipment. The ocean's tide-generated movements of water systematically and unfailingly respond to their lunar master, and if our only encounter was with wind-generated sea states travelling over a flat seabed, its victims would be far fewer in number. However, the seabed is anything but flat: it is littered with a vast array of monolithic structures of all shapes and sizes, from isolated rocks to whole strata of projecting plates, from veritable mountains to deep canyons. The one thing these obstacles have in common is that they all violate and intrude into our tidal currents, producing a microcosm of unique sea states in their immediate vicinity – a mirror surface image and caricature of the monsters that lurk below. To make matters worse, converging coastlines, headlands, islands and sounds add a new and random element to the equation. This presents our mariner with an ever changing theatre of opportunity, danger and doubt.

Let us assume that our mariner owns a RIB. A RIB is arguably the most proven small rough-water vessel invented, and if sound and well designed it is an object of excellence. Furthermore, in the right hands it's quite capable of surviving some very demanding seas. But anyone, no matter how ill-prepared, can purchase and go to sea in a RIB capable of 30–50 knots, straight into a force 9 gale, never to be seen again. While the right to choose must remain one of our cherished freedoms, the power of the ocean demands respect and prudence, and I hope this chapter may deny the force 9 another victim.

OVERFALLS

Here I am going to group together all tidally created waves of significant height generated by the geometry of the seabed. Amidst the apparent chaos and uncertainty of our subject, one aspect that is entirely dependable is the beautiful predictability of the tides so, in theory, a passage involving overfalls can be planned precisely by referring to your tide tables. Tide tables should close the file on predictability, and yet overfalls seem to have a mind of their own, and there is one crucial parameter we should treat with the utmost respect – wind speed and direction. As a rule, overfalls can be regarded as reasonably benign in light winds for the average RIB. In moderate cross and following winds, certain muscles start to twitch, but it's not until a wind-over-tide situation develops that the roller coaster really begins! Beware the perverse nature of overfalls even in the absence of a wind-over-tide situation. You can be easily seduced into a false sense of security. In Ramsey Sound, I have often witnessed our hitherto friendly 4 knot northbound incoming tidal stream, projecting overfalls of some half a metre, transformed in a wind-over-tide force 2 situation into standing waves of at least 8 metres by a wind speed of force 8. Now, one immediate danger is obvious: you have gone to sea, in our scenario, blissfully unaware that you have crossed to seaward of an overfall that is on a time fuse to explode when the tide turns. You have crossed the Rubicon, and you look back as that benign sea becomes a cauldron. You are trapped. What do you do? Travel along and outside the overfall until it peters out and you can cross? Await the end of the tide which may be hours away, with darkness falling or storm threatening? Maybe...but what about crossing it? Is your RIB seaworthy and, more importantly, do you dare?

This is now a motorway of juggernaut waves involving millions of tons of water, of smooth-sided mountains with awesome curling crests as the tidal stream strives to keep its lunar master happy. This is the spawning ground of black holes and whirlpools, and there are currents that are inclined to the vertical by some subterranean ski slope which explode on the surface into virtually unnavigable chaos. I have seen an inflated lifejacket taken 50 metres to the seabed by a whirlpool, only to surface half a mile away full of stones dredged from the seabed!

As you stare in awe, drained of all courage, you begin to notice something that is quite unlike one's usual perception of waves: oceanic wind-driven waves travel thousands of miles and require a very different technique to navigate safely, and you could be forgiven for thinking that these waves don't appear to be moving forward, so remember that what you are witnessing is the mirror image of the immediate seabed, but with the current running over it. This monster lurks on station in a clearly defined position. With a bit of luck, the regimented status of overfalls can be used to great advantage by the canny cox or skipper. Think of it as a mountain range laced with roads, but unlike the land equivalent, this tarmac is moving at a great rate, taking you rapidly up the side of the next mountain and tipping you over the cliff where you just don't want to be. While the waves may keep their station, the currents most certainly do not. You can experience 10 knot currents tracking over standing waves, and will need intense concentration if you are to compensate for side drift.

Onwards... You have decided to go for it! It is always better to start your run into

A RIB operating amidst the infamous 'Bitches' tidal race off Ramsey Island, South Wales. Big reserve power, a high degree of buoyancy and a shallow draft are all key factors in this craft's favour. Shaun White and Bear Grylls are pictured here amongst the crew. © Mindworks Marketing

overfalls from some way off. This serves several functions: it bonds the crew to the RIB as it begins to take up the motions of the overfall; the craft has time to assume the right speed and attitude; and you can pick your 'road' from a distance. Try to enter the overfall head-on to compensate for side drift. If you go in at right angles you will encounter a violent sideways movement by the bow as you hit the current. The demarcation line between a 5-knot tide and calm can be literally within a boat's length. This can severely compromise your safety, with crew possibly being flung into the water. But what if you do side-slip into this no-go zone? With a well-found RIB and compatible sea state there should be little problem provided you go directly into the wave. Go sideways and up and over at your peril, for the curling crest will cause you to fall very badly into the trough and could even capsize your craft.

With such fast-flowing currents taking you into the waves, whirlpools, black holes and general mayhem, chances of survival in the water are slim. SAR units have great difficulty in estimating your position and rescuing casualties in these conditions, and trying to enact a rescue with your RIB often ends in disaster and should only be attempted in moderate conditions. The problem is the fast-moving surroundings. There is a real chance, too, of the vessel crashing down on the casualty, often with fatal results; or there is the well-intentioned Good Samaritan crewmember making it 'times two' in the water. In this rescue situation, surrounded by huge waves that obscure the horizon, some form of quick navigation reference is essential – the benefit of riding the crest of a wave, when for an instant you are master of all you survey, is denied you within an overfall. A compass course is far superior to the slow take-up of plotters and radars.

So, you have managed to traverse the overfalls, keeping off the mountains, following the relative safety of roads and leads, and are out the other side and homeward bound. What about going the other way, along the overfall, either with or against the tide? Are you really ready for one of the most extreme hedonistic free falls man can experience? Be warned, you are in the grasp of a sea that never forgives. This is the battlefield from which 'ribsceptics' invariably emerge as total converts. This is where the manifestation of all the hearsay and hyperbole as to the virtue of a commercially/professionally orientated RIB finally sinks in: the high buoyant shearing bow to drag you out of that trough and stop you broaching and stuffing; the reinforced mechanically fastened tubes that do not rip off like a zip and transform that so very seaworthy boat into little more than a surfboard; the transomless stern that must evacuate several tons of water in the seconds between waves...or you capsize; the ergonomics of crew protection with superstrong handles at every turn; waterproof engines and electronics; so the list goes on... If you want peace, prepare for war!

You are pointing in the right direction, in this case into the wind, and the tide is with you. The roller coaster is about to begin. Keep the boat straight into the wave, which will hit you very quickly; the waves in overfalls are usually very closely spaced and the sheltered face very steep. Keep your nerve and bring total concentration into play. This is when timing and all the skills you have ever learnt in FRC handling will be most needed.

The RIB very often becomes airborne in this scenario, and it is very difficult to effect a gentle landing, thus avoiding the risk of damage and injury to boat and crew. It is essential, therefore, to have an even, lateral weight distribution, for if there is an imbalance the heavier side will tilt the RIB and you will land on the chine rather than the keel, with an even higher risk of damage. In the absence of superior hydraulic seating, the only way for the human frame to withstand these crushing forces is to adapt the semi-standing position, with knees slightly bent to absorb the vertical velocities. Many back injuries happen at this point, returning to haunt the casualty in later life.

A new problem is right in your face: the next wave in the series, and with little time to recover from your previous landing, the cycle repeats itself with breathtaking speed. Fall over the side here and it will be impossible to recover you until you are ejected out at the end of the overfalls – maybe many miles ahead. There is, however, one highly risky form of recovery, and that is to come in from the side of the overfalls with precise timing and speed to meet the casualty as he descends into the trough with its much calmer seas. Haul them rapidly over the side, aided by the RIB being down on the tube due to the rescuer's weight on that side, and then rapidly orientate the RIB through 90 degrees into the current to prevent going over the wave with all the perils that would bring. This should only be done in extreme circumstances, when conventional rescue services are unavailable and you are competent to carry it out. Practising with a float is very useful.

The level planing attitude of this hydrofoil-assisted catamaran makes light work of punching through these steep overfalls at the western end of the Solent.
© **RIB International Magazine**

Now try turning the boat around so as to experience going with the wind. This must be executed within the trough of the wave and with impeccable timing, otherwise you will be in our nightmare broadside situation again. Be ready to power up very quickly, as the current will have the stern of the RIB under the breaking crest of the windward wave in record time. This is where plenty of power is essential, otherwise you will not be able to climb over the back of the wave. In this downwind situation, you will experience the sensation of flying one second, surfing the next, tasting zero gravity, only to finally ride the beast with a rare harmony and sympathy that is indescribable. Of course, much depends on your natural 'gut feeling' and sense of survival, but one thing is essential: to keep the craft in a straight line with the direction of the waves – for all the reasons mentioned earlier. Deviating from this route invites broaching.

It is proposed by some that if in doubt, the action to take is to open the throttles and power on – rather than back off, which is likely to result in the craft dropping off the plane and losing the benefits of its greatest asset: its propulsive power. Nevertheless, when all is said and done, sometimes there can be little else left to one but to trust in your craft's integrity. Amidst inshore seas that are both chaotic and impossible to predict, sometimes there is simply not enough time to react; it is then that the theory book is rudely grabbed from the helmsman's hand, leaving just his instinctive response and the soundness of his vessel's design to save the day.

KEY SAFETY POINTS

1 Don't ever let the craft go broadside into the standing waves. The combination of strong tidal currents under one side meeting strong winds coming over the top of the wave from the other makes a lethal cocktail of roll-over forces.

2 Have a strong windshield – if it breaks it could kill you. The helmsman should wear goggles as the spray can blind you – a momentary aberration to your sight can spell disaster in this rapidly changing environment.

3 Hold on tight at all times: it's often when you relax in a falsely perceived calm that you are taken by surprise. Most RIB accidents happen in this mode. If you fall onto the decks, or worse, over the side, then not only do you put yourself in peril, but you endanger the whole crew too. Once on the deck you will have to stay there until out of the overfalls, which may be a long time. It is often impossible to get up, and either way you are going to get badly hurt. It is pointless for another crewmember to try to help as that will result in him lying helpless on the deck as well.

4 As mentioned earlier, if someone falls in the water it's too dangerous to come close to effect a rescue. It's best for the crew to watch the MOB constantly – which may have to be for a very long time – until the overfalls peter out and standard rescue drill can kick in. Be warned, in big overfalls it is impossible to see a large RIB at 100 metres, let alone somebody in the water.

5   Wear warm clothing, ideally drysuits, with high-visibility hoods and retro-reflective tape at strategic points. Helmets can prevent serious injury. Use the kind worn by canoeists or, if funds are available, the lightweight helmet type as used by the RNLI.

6   A whistle can dramatically increase your chances of being rescued, as can pinpoint-type red flares.

7   RIBs or FRC with passenger seats behind the helmsman can be dangerous, as persons can be lost overboard unnoticed.

8   Keep all ropes and lines very carefully bound up without any protruding loose ends. They can so easily become wound around your prop, or worse still, if you capsize, ensnare you, with fatal results. Remember, a rope can be your best friend or your worst enemy.

9   Travel with more than one craft whenever possible.

10 If capsized, the safest place is to stay with your upturned RIB if at all possible. RIBs float supremely well upside down. In fact, they are more stable upturned than the right way up. There is one major problem, though: holding on. On most RIBs, all the handles are on the top of the tubes and you are confronted with a 'handleless' smooth hull, except for the transom area from which you must keep clear. I personally always have a tight handline which girdles the RIB at the junction of tube and hull. This is the optimum place to hold on.

11 In my view and experience, in extreme sea states of the type described here, the value of kill cords is debatable. If the helmsman falls overboard you *must* have a spare cord, otherwise you will not be able to restart the engine, but my own inclination is not to attach the kill cord: if the helmsman falls or is thrown overboard, the crewman can smartly step in to seamlessly take control without having to restart the engine. Speed is so essential in overfalls.

12 It is amazing how many people do not secure loose buoyant gear on deck. Outboard fuel tanks are a classic. Make sure they are securely fixed.

13 Self-righting gear, if fitted, should not be deployed until the overfalls are cleared. You are much safer staying with the upturned boat than trying to board what amounts to a sailing boat, with the huge airbag acting as a sail.

14 I have kept the subject of lifejackets until last as they deserve special discussion. We had a very unfortunate incident in Ramsey Sound, South Wales, when one of our passenger RIBs was engaged in a white-water trip over some powerful overfalls in an area known as 'Horse Rock'. At this point there was a towering standing wave just behind an area where huge amounts of tidal water stream up the side of a 50-metre underwater mountain. Caught up in a rare combination of whirlpools, black holes and bad luck, the RIB went broadside over the overfalls and capsized, spilling 14 people into the water. Our golden rule was to always operate in pairs, and as the overfalls were of a relatively short length, the 'Buddy' was able to safely rescue everyone very rapidly.

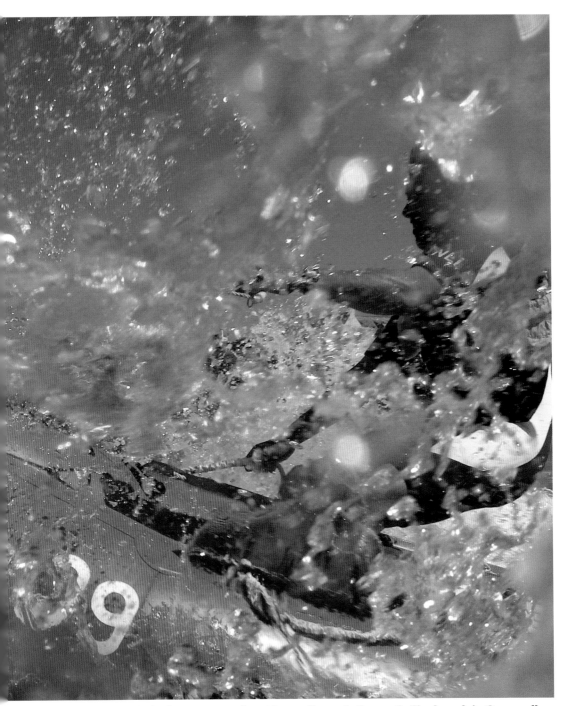

An Arancia inshore reserve boat leaps through the surf off a beach in Cornwall on the way to a casualty. Riding aboard these inflatable boats is a skill of its own.

© *RNLI/Bobby Renaud*

The MAIB (Marine Accident Investigation Branch) investigated and two very significant findings emerged: firstly, the descent into mild hypothermia was very rapid, literally within minutes; secondly, the use and type of lifejacket were key factors in the outcome. It would be tempting to simply say, the higher the Newtons the better the jacket in such disturbed seas, and you would, of course, be right. However,quite the opposite is the effect when trapped under an upturned RIB. Yes, there is an air space or pocket that is of great help, but to clear yourself by way of the tubes requires supreme effort, especially as you are now travelling through the overfalls in a somewhat different manner to that for which you had planned. Our passengers on this day were all wearing half-inflated air/foam lifejackets of 150 Newtons inflated. The ability to adjust the buoyancy and slip under the tubes in this incident undoubtedly saved lives. The downside was the casualties' inability to orally reinflate the jacket when clear of the RIB, due to excessive inhalation of water in the overfalls making the heavier casualties very low in the water. You could argue for manually operated CO_2 jackets – these would be satisfactory in the hands of experienced people, but it takes great presence of mind and experience to operate them in such extreme situations. This is a subject that needs much more debate.

RIB SUITABILITY

Let us now turn to what makes a seaworthy RIB suitable for navigating through overfalls, or any big sea, come to that. RIBs come in all shapes and sizes; most are very good sea boats, as we all know, but some are much better in bad sea states. A RIB that is designed for racing has a long, narrow hull with little buoyancy in the bow. Regrettably these hulls will quickly stuff their noses in the troughs and come to grief amidst the conditions we are focusing on here. What is needed is a high shearing bow with plenty of buoyancy and a 50% overhang of the tubes. Some RIBs have tubes that are so narrow they are virtually ineffective in big seas, and one wonders why they qualify as a true RIB at all.The 50% rule ensures optimum upward pressure from the seas and makes for a vastly more stable boat. On the downside, this extra loading puts additional strain on the tube-fastening system, which has to be very carefully and strongly constructed. We have all heard hair-raising tales of tubes parting company with their hulls. This can lead to catastrophic results, for it is the tube that provides the vessel with its outstanding safety and seakeeping qualities. Well-designed RIBs should have an inboard gunwale or upstand to act as a secondary line of defence should you lose your tubes or, more likely, if they become deflated for any reason. It also provides a much firmer foundation for the tube's anchoring system. Tubes should be of at least 600mm diameter to optimise their true potential, not only for the sake of buoyancy but to minimise the likelihood of people falling overboard; this is calculated from the height of the average knee and the various centres of gravity at play.

On the subject of hull construction materials, while GRP possesses many fine qualities of which we are all fully aware, it is a material that takes very badly to crashing into rocks. While working a RIB in shallow overfalls, my commercial operators would quite regularly strike rocks with our aluminium hulls with a force that would

Rough seas off the west coast of Ireland. With an unhindered fetch of some 3,000 miles, this coastline can be the home of formidable onshore conditions.
© RIB International Magazine

have taken out a GRP hull. On the face of it GRP has immense strength compared to steel and aluminium, but when the material crashes into rocks or any other hard object the gelcoat smashes open with little effort, revealing the soft glass strands which in a millisecond pick up on the rock in a snagging motion. An implosion of forces takes place causing great damage due to the inability of the material to slide over the object. As a result, the damage is always very severe compared with aluminium with its 'slide-over' ability.

Sooner or later in overfalls you will ship a vast amount of water. When we build commercial RIBs for this environment we ensure that the design employed features a transomless stern from which water can be evacuated in seconds. Alternatively, a boat of this type should have very large scuppers. Too many leisure RIBs have inadequate outlets with very high transoms that would retain many tons of water and render the RIB highly dangerous.

In certain calmer situations, of course, you may be able to anchor. But it's no good having a strong anchor and loads of warp if the fastening point is not 'man enough' to take the forces. Our own RIB-building criterion is that the Sampson post should be strong enough for a crane to lift the whole boat out of the water. Handholds should abound at every ergonomically sensible point, the higher up the better in many cases.

ENGINES

Most RIBs are powered by outboards and, alas, are disadvantaged in a very large sea state. In general, most RIBs in big seas will be off the plane, which means we have a planing hull trying to be a displacement hull – not an ideal state of affairs. The LCG (low centre of gravity) is simply all wrong, unless you have weight up forward, which can be impractical. With too much weight aft there is a real chance of you pitchpoling backwards, in extreme conditions, while powering into overfalls against the wind. The other danger is the RIB slipping down the back of a wave at a high angle and burying its transom and outboard into the sea – unless you have an inversion-proofed model it is very likely to stop. Conversely, going with the wind, the aft LCG leads to a lighter, more buoyant bow that is helpful in a broaching situation, but you must be aware of the shortened effective keel length which makes for very sensitive steering.

With inboards/outdrive, the LCG is further forward than with an outboard, so performance into the wind and seas is that much better. If the engine and electrics are afforded a well-designed engine housing they will be better protected from flooding. Power tilt and trim are shared with outboards, but be cautious of this hardware hitting rocks, snagging ropes or, worse, striking casualties in the water.

Perhaps the finest mode of propulsion for these conditions is inboard/waterjet. You do not have to worry about hitting things, and the LCG is even further forward due to the longer transmission train, but the biggest benefit is the controllability when surfing down large waves, for without any appendage immersed in these uncertain waters, control is far more predictable and precise. The helmsman can divert huge amounts of power from forward movement to both steering and reverse via the bucket. He can also

Shaun White's own 10m waterjet-powered craft punching out through heavy surf.
Note the open transom design of this boat, which affords total scuppering ability
in all sea states. © *Ocean Dynamics*

slow down prior to a possible broaching, something that is impossible with a gearbox. Another unique option when travelling into large waves (when you risk that awful free fall before crashing into the trough with the potential for serious damage to both RIB and limb) is to drop the bucket to vertical just before you become airborne, rev up and allow the RIB to see-saw over the wave crest as the stern is lifted up by the jet flow while the bow dives gently into the trough. Remember, also, that you do not risk transmission breakage with a jet due to overspeed while airborne as you do with propellers. Waterjets sometimes have a bad name for cavitations from a standing start in aerated seas: this is invariably due to penny-pinching over the size of the jet. Get a jet of sufficient diameter and the problem is over.

CONCLUSION

Different propulsion systems suit different applications, and though it may sound simplistic, it is absolutely crucial to choose the correct form of power and propulsion system for the task in hand. Professional operators in particular, who invariably demand more of their craft than their private counterparts, can sometimes make errors in this most fundamental area if there hasn't been sufficient research into both the vessel's operating environment and the basic design of craft.

Each different system or combination has its own advantages and disadvantages and like so much related to ship/boat design, a compromise/trade off sometimes has to be made. Good maritime design and construction is all about limiting the latter to a sensible and workable degree and this applies even in the technically/dynamically dependent area of propulsion and power.

In the environment of coastal extremes, there are few margins for error or gear failure. A well-found craft possessing the right components and overall design is essential for operating in dangerous seas close to land.

Hugo Montgomery-Swan

THE OFFSHORE ENVIRONMENT

BRITAIN RECORD HOLDER   31 hrs 22 mins

ENDURANCE RECORD BREAKING

BY MIKE DEACON

Mike Deacon, offshore RIB racer, current holder of the Southern Islands Record and four times holder of the Round Britain World Record, recounts three successful Round Britain record attempts and looks at the logistics, preparation work, forecasting requirements and planning needed on the part of a powerboat team seeking to establish offshore records.

My early interest in 'adventurous ribbing' started with the story of Michael Alexander and Richard Frere who in 1989, when both were in their 60s, circumnavigated Scotland in a 4m RIB powered by two 15hp outboard motors. They were men of a not-so-common breed and their example led to the inauguration of the Round Scotland RIB Race and to the formation of the British Inflatable Boat Owners Association, the RIB club BIBOA.

In the winter of 2000, at the annual dinner of the Rigid Inflatable Boat Expedition Club, I listened to the inspirational Chris Kaye recounting experiences of a voyage from Scotland to Iceland in his RIB *Sabredrive*. After his fascinating speech, I mentioned that I was curious about the Round Britain Records but had been discouraged by suggestions that this would need three or four groups of ground crew, including logistics experts, mechanics, electrical engineers, navigation specialists and other professionals. Large teams, including the Military and the Metropolitan Police, had set previous records, and I asked Chris how he managed to arrange such a large team in support of his extensive RIB expeditions. Chris laughed and said, 'Mike, think of the Round Britain as just a long cruise!' With those few words, Chris established my mindset. It was possible; there would be no ground crew, no mechanics, no support teams, just a few RIB enthusiasts on a long cruise.

I studied the *RYA Rules and Procedure Handbook for Long Distance Offshore Endurance World and National Records* and learnt that the Round Britain Records are divided into various classes dependent upon length of vessel (UIM measurement). The Outright Record was clearly out of reach at 44 hours 3 minutes 30 seconds, set by the famous 2,600hp 50ft Scarab boat *Drambuie Tantalus* in 1992, and I aimed for the record for vessels up to 30ft (9.14m) in length that had stood at 63 hours 32 minutes 25 seconds since 1993.

PAPERWORK

For the 2001 attempt, my list of 50 action points quickly grew to almost 100. As one was removed two more would appear. My head was full of *Procedure Handbook* details and the BIBOA list of cruising equipment. I needed to arrange corrected charts, plotter cartridges, insurance, EPIRB registration, a medical kit, compass correction, Coastguard notification, fuel stops, scrutineering and measurement, as well as submitting our official entry and remembering to pack my annual birthday present of an almanac (28 December!).

In all of this I had to avoid 'looking for flies and tripping over elephants'. Crewmembers Chris Strickland and Jan Falkowski pitched in with their specialist input, and slowly Team *Hot Lemon III* ticked the boxes. For subsequent attempts in 2002 and 2005 I only needed to update all these items, the initial investment of time paying good dividends. I also added simple risk assessments, together with survival and emergency plans.

THE COURSE AND FUEL STOPS

The official distance, as calculated by the RYA/Admiralty, is 1,362.8nm, but our run would be at least 1,450nm to allow for distance off headlands, refuelling stops and a safe offshore course. We would run clockwise for reasons explained later.

There were at least three good choices of routes through the Western Isles, but I chose to run inside Mull and Skye as I was familiar with these waters following several years of wonderful ScotRIB International RIB races; although longer, this inside course would also give shelter from Atlantic swell and keep us within easy reach of many safe havens. We would run inside Stroma Island, just before Duncansby Head, so as to avoid the Merry Men of Mey, which is described in almanacs as being 'the most dangerous and extensive race in the Pentland Firth...should be avoided by yachts at all costs'.

Our time target was approximately 50 hours, needing two night runs. The first night would be in our familiar waters of the south coast and the Irish Sea; the second we would be running in deep water, well offshore down the east coast, having passed Cape Wrath and Duncansby Head in the final hours of daylight, and refuelling in Peterhead – to arrive amongst the gas rigs off Norfolk as dawn broke. We debated whether to run close inshore off Lowestoft or to go offshore to Smith's Knoll, which would lengthen the distance but keep us well clear of a potentially treacherous, unfamiliar area, particularly if conditions turned against us. It was a clear decision: we would run offshore, as boats are designed to float rather than to run over sandbanks and we preferred to have sea room around us.

Each refuelling stop could add an hour to our time and I turned for advice to Jim and Yvonne Mackintosh, a tremendously experienced pair of deep-sea RIB users. I explained my concern that *Hot Lemon III* only had a safe range of some 400nm and sought their views on potential refuelling locations. In his usual direct manner, Jim said: 'Carry more fuel.' I added a deck tank. Three fuel stops would be needed: Bangor (Northern Ireland), Peterhead and Ramsgate.

CLOTHING, PERSONAL EQUIPMENT, SHIP'S GEAR AND RATIONS

No sponsorship was sought for any of our attempts and brand names are included simply because the gear was good.

We wore Musto and Multifabs breathable drysuits with two wicking and insulated underlayers, gloves and beanies or balaclavas, good outer jackets for night running, factor 50 suncream against windburn, and various protective eyewear. To save weight, and being eternally optimistic, we carried no shore wear and would have made an amusing sight in any extended shore stop – a good reason to keep going.

We each carried our own preferred personal equipment such as mini flare packs, knife, whistle, multi-tool, mini torch with red lens, mobile phone and charger, VHF radio and mini EPIRB. For convenience we wore auto-inflate horseshoe-type lifejackets with strobe light and spray hoods rather than our usual permanent buoyancy race jackets; this decision later gave us considerable amusement in the Irish Sea.

On subsequent attempts, we carried lightweight Gecko helmets and McMurdo personal GPS EPIRBs in addition to the ship's main EPIRB; we also positioned towels within easy reach to clear spray from visors and glasses.

SHIP'S GEAR

Warps, repair kit, bellows, pruning saw for fouled lines, throwing quoit and line, boarding ladder, radar reflector, fire extinguishers, foghorn, emergency VHF aerial, hand-held GPS, plenty of in-date flares, duct tape, paddles, spare lifejacket charge canisters, a sturdy bucket and bailer, waterproof flashlight, spare propellers with washers and nuts, wire cutters, anchor and sea anchor, a full set of updated paper charts, a socket outlet for charging, tools, engine spares, filters, belts, lubricants, fuses and rags. We also carried a four person liferaft, a foil thermal protective aid for each crewmember and a good first-aid kit and manual.

Our grab bag was positioned close to the main EPIRB and liferaft and held water, flares, VHF radio, wind-up torch and light sticks, fishing kit, marker dye, first-aid kit, motion sickness tablets, mirror, good carbohydrate food, chocolate, seasickness bags, paper towels, a sponge to dry the liferaft floor, and all this in addition to the usual ocean safety gear in the liferaft.

RATIONS

We knew we would not eat large quantities of food while running fast in an open boat, but that plenty of liquids, long-lasting carbohydrates and some comfort foods would suffice. Our greatest distance from land would only be some 60nm while running down the east coast, and our supplies could easily extend to four days if needed. My wife Maggie supplied our rations at very short notice; she has great skill in selecting roll fillings that are sustaining but not so moist as to turn to mush after some 40 hours in a non-too-friendly environment.

We carried 4 litres of water per person plus a few 'energy drinks' and a supply of comfort-and-sugar-spike chocolate goodies. We also had a fishing line. Jan brought packets of wine gums that were superb and are now standard *Hot Lemon* equipment, although they are a nuisance to remove from bilge pumps. Jan also brought his own special food to spring upon us in the rain off Tobermory.

WEATHER

Weather is fundamental to these runs and we wanted a high-pressure area centred over Manchester to provide a gentle clockwise following wind around our course; for an attempt in winter we would probably run anticlockwise in a low-pressure system. Weather is the Achilles heel of Round Britain attempts, as our latitude and the Atlantic Ocean

Hot Lemon V *running at her optimum in challenging seas.* © ***Chris Davies***

conspire to prevent settled weather extending over the whole of Britain at any one time.

I am indebted to Round the World ribster Alan Priddy who introduced me to Bertie the Weatherman for our first attempt; the naval and meteorological history of Bertie Ramsey merits a chapter by itself, but at 81 years old his study was full of computers, radios and other very techie equipment as he provided highly accurate national and international forecasts to clubs and high-profile sailors worldwide. As Bertie was in failing health for our second attempt in 2002, we enlisted the help of a family friend, student meteorologist Rick Puddifoot, who was studying Ocean Sciences at Plymouth University. For our third run in 2005, Rick had moved away so my son Dave and I monitored the weather ourselves; we used various websites and for several months I recorded forecasts, subsequently matching these to actual conditions. The Met Office site was by far the most reliable; we used their surface pressure charts for an overall view and drilled down for local information. We formed a view using various sites, then weighted the information towards the Met Office; we then stuck a finger in the air and looked at our seaweed.

THE 2001 ATTEMPT ON THE ROUND BRITAIN RECORD (for craft up to 30 feet in length)

HOT LEMON III SPECIFICATION

Hot Lemon III was a standard 8.5m Scorpion RIB built in 1999, but was moulded as an 8.75m hull to give a little more deck space. She had a single Yanmar 315hp diesel of 4.2 litres, driving a Bravo 3X twin-prop outdrive leg. Maximum revs were 3800rpm but we planned to run at 3,500rpm which gave 40 knots at a consumption of 45 litres per hour. She carried 545 litres of diesel in her main tank, theoretically enough for 480nm at 40 knots but reduced to 400nm, allowing a good reserve. An additional deck tank of 270 litres increased our safe range to 640nm.

Seating was two double-person jockey seats plus a bench seat. Electronic equipment comprised an Icom VHF radio, Raytheon radar, a small Lowrance black and white GPS plotter using C-Map cartridges, two depth sounders plus a magnetic compass. The standard propellers were balanced and worked by our local propeller specialist, Thomas Bolton, for maximum fuel efficiency.

Being naive, we imagined sleep would be possible, so we removed the arms and backrest to the bench seat, and a box, nicknamed 'the bunk', was fixed to the bench seat base. The bunk was lined with thin polystyrene and had an air bed held in place by a couple of straps; we rigged an extra long engine kill cord for users.

TEAM *HOT LEMON III*

Having decided to run with a total of three persons I looked around my friends for experienced, knowledgeable, easy-going, 'good in a crisis' sorts who were available at very short notice, and was delighted when Chris Strickland and Dr Jan Falkowski agreed to join the run. Each of these brought considerable boating experience, often in challenging circumstances, and they had each cruised their own RIBs around Britain.

Chris was an electrical engineer with considerable mechanical skills who had raced and cruised his own RIB for many years. Jan brought medical and military skills, had completed a transatlantic crossing by RIB and cruised his own RIB around Ireland. They were each based in London, so we met one evening in The Narrow pub in Limehouse to plot our strategy; we were a pensioner, a grandfather and a psychiatrist – a good team.

THE RECORD ATTEMPT

By late May we were waiting for Bertie's signal, but the days wore on with no sign of the settled pattern we needed. These record attempts have a considerable effect on family life as it is essential the team is available to run at only a few hours' notice – it would be tiresome to leave on a pre-booked holiday just as an ideal weather pattern appears. Availability of officials, dates of sailing regatta in refuelling stops and many other issues can also affect the timing of a run.

Midsummer passed and the days were closing in, more night running. Bertie called on Tuesday 3 July: 'It's looking good to start on Thursday.' I ring the team, our timekeeper, the RYA and the fuel stops; stress builds as I double-check everything. Later that day *Hot Lemon III* is fuelled and we're ready to go.

Bertie called at 1800hrs on Wednesday. The weather pattern had shifted slightly so as to give a northerly 15–18 knots over Scotland; I knew there would be an adverse tide from Kyle to Cape Wrath – we cancelled 24hrs before the planned start time.

By late July we've had two more such early warnings and we're now getting very concerned; we also hear that Sunseeker *XS Racing* are almost ready to start on their own attempt. On Monday 23 July another early warning which, late on Tuesday, becomes Bertie's signal 'go-go-go'. He warns us there will be light rain with mist and a 10 knot head wind in the North Sea.

Team *Hot Lemon III* was timed away from the Solent at 1957hrs on Wednesday 25 July by RYA timekeeper Jonathan Hullock, accompanied by his wife Helen. We ran through the night towards Land's End on the 460nm leg to our first refuelling stop at Bangor and I dozed in the bunk so as to be awake as we approached Land's End. Chris and Jan kept us well clear of fishing boats and overnight sailors and contacted the Coastguard as we passed through each area. We turned Land's End around 0045hrs and settled down for

Every item of Hot Lemon's anatomy has been considered with offshore record breaking in mind. She is, however, essentially of cruising craft design and as such has undertaken many thousands of miles of offshore adventuring. © *Chris Davies*

the run up the Irish Sea, cruising at a comfortable 38 knots. Around 0500hrs we slowed suddenly; I instantly closed the throttle while Chris and Jan flew to the stern to find a lobster pot rope wrapped tightly around the outdrive leg. They quickly cleared the rope, but had we broken the drive or gearbox? Relief as we slowly returned to cruising speed and enjoyed a snack as dawn broke. An engine alarm disturbed our daydreams: the outdrive oil level had fallen low, the rope we previously caught may have damaged the lower shaft seal and this could be terminal. We extracted strands of polypropylene rope from the propeller hub and I balanced on the RIB tube to reach over the hot (stopped) engine to refill the oil reservoir on the transom. Early morning doziness took over and I stepped back off the tube so as to close the engine lid, splosh! When they finished laughing, Chris and Jan retrieved me, complete with glasses. My lifejacket auto inflated three minutes later – not very reassuring.

We spoke with Bangor Marina when we were one hour away, and again ten minutes from arrival as it started to rain. They were fantastic: the young lady attendant was standing on the fuel pontoon in the rain with the fuel hose in her hand as we pulled alongside at 0932hrs having covered the 460nm in 13 hours 35 minutes at an average speed of 34 knots. There was much amusement as one of us ran ashore for a comfort stop, completely forgetting that our drysuits had inaccessible zips across the rear shoulders...

Jan cleared the chandlery of all their outdrive leg oil as the reservoir was now half empty and we had only one bottle of oil remaining. We subsequently stopped every five hours to refill the reservoir and this added 30 minutes to our overall time.

We left Bangor at 1017hrs and were back in familiar waters running past the Mull of Kintyre; we broke into the usual Paul McCartney song and Jan's lifejacket inflated when he caught the pull cord on something. We later discovered that the warning indicator had failed to turn red and was still showing green even though the gas canister was exhausted. Later, the manufacturer told me, 'Yes, we are aware of that problem, but we don't make the indicators and it doesn't seem to cause too much trouble.'

My calculations indicated we were running fast enough to beat the Outright Record of *Drambuie Tantalus* that had stood for nine years. The team checked my figures and although we laughed at the idea there was now a different atmosphere on board, could this really be possible?

As we passed Duart Castle on the south-east corner of Mull we called Scorpion RIBS in Lymington. They couldn't believe we had made such good time and we heard Team Scorpion cheering us on in the background.

In the rain off Tobermory, Jan revealed his secret food supply to be tins of mackerel fillets in tomato sauce; Chris and I will long remember the sight of Jan trying to aim handfuls of sticky red mackerel at his mouth while heading into heavy rain at 40 knots in an open RIB.

We waved to tourists at Kyle of Lochalsh as we passed under the Skye Bridge and there were memories for me at Raasay where I had submarined *Hot Lemon II* with Murray Macleod when running before a gale on an earlier Round Scotland race and then been towed by the RNLI into Portree. Even in July it was cold in 40 knots of wind chill, and after the rainstorm we were pleased with our choice of clothing and extra coats. We stopped just south of Cape Wrath to rig for night running – additional clothing, refill the oil in the leg, check the engine and fuel situation, position more food and liquid to hand and report in to Stornaway Coastguard. On rounding the headland we encountered deep rolling swells; only deft helming by Jan prevented a cold bath for all of us and we were glad it was still daylight. We passed Strathy Point and Scrabster with cheers as we turned south at Duncansby Head – we were heading home.

This was my first time into Peterhead Harbour and I found the entrance daunting in fading light and mist, with its forbidding high and grey concrete walls. Although the entrance is some 200m wide, it faces SSE and our approach from a northerly direction made it difficult to spot. We made the mandatory VHF contact with port control and waited a few moments as a trawler exited, giving us a clear point to head for. We arrived at 2217hrs having run the 480nm in just under 12 hours. Our average speed now increased to 40 knots as we silently had the Outright Record in our minds.

We left Peterhead after a very slick 20 minute fuel stop and headed out into the North Sea. Bertie's forecast was correct: we had mist and a head wind which kicked up a very uncomfortable breaking sea for the next five hours while we ran some 60nm offshore. Helming was a constant job of moving the boat around the sea in response to the size, shape and position of each barely visible advancing wave; throttle use was restrained so as to control consumption. This was a low point: our internal clocks wanted to sleep, it was dark, the sea was very tiresome and we were in a relatively small open boat; the conditions prevented easy conversation and we were each left with our own thoughts as we pushed and shoved through the seas to the next waypoint some 330nm and nine hours away.

The gigantic gas rigs off The Wash were an eerie but very welcome sight in the early morning as we took great care to avoid the sandbanks just before Smith's Knoll, where the depth shoals from 30 metres to 3 metres within a few boat lengths. We panicked as we saw a sandy bottom immediately beneath us just as our two depth sounders decided to take a rest; we slowed slightly as I shredded a chart in the wind to double-check our course and position. We had a very anxious half-hour but subsequently confirmed we were on our correct course and heading, with plenty of depth – we now attribute the concern to clear water and bright sunlight... we think. We had been out of range of mobile phone contact for almost 12 hours but now managed to have intermittent contact with our colleague Kevin Golding who was following our progress; we were desperate for Claire in the Drambuie publicity office and our timekeeper Jonathan to know that our anticipated ETA would be some seven hours ahead of schedule and that we were close to breaking both our Class and the Outright Record. Kevin delivered the goods by contacting Jonathan and Claire, who each leapt into action.

We had intended to refuel at Ramsgate, but frantic calculations showed that if we did so we would miss setting a new Outright Record; we reviewed our fuel situation and all agreed to miss out Ramsgate – it would be all or nothing.

Scorpion base were alarmed not to have heard from us since Peterhead, although we had been maintaining Coastguard contact. Graham at Scorpion had rung the harbourmaster at Dover, only to be told, 'They're passing my window right now. Please

Hot Lemon V: *Note the substantial tie-bar linking the outdrives, plus the hefty air exhausts to the engine housing, to ensure maximum aspiration of the diesel engines.* © *Chris Davies*

ask them to keep clear of the ferries if they do this again.' Apologies to HM.

There was silence as we ran the last 100 miles, scanning the water ahead for lumps of wood, lobster pots or anything else; little was said until at Selsey Bill, some 30 minutes from the finish, we all experienced near death syndrome as *Hot Lemon III* suffered two loud bangs to the hull as we passed over an unseen lump of wood, which we later found to have left green paint down the hull and removed a section of skeg on the outdrive leg; this was certainly the worst moment of the voyage. We were running on diesel fumes and expecting the outdrive leg to fail at any moment, but luck was with us as we were timed in by Jonathan, and Tom Crump, the Chairman of the Powerboat Race Committee, for a total run-time of 42 hours 54 minutes 25 seconds, to set new Class and Outright World Records. Drambuie very kindly arranged a welcome reception in Lymington at only five hours' notice, our names were engraved upon the historic Norman MacKinnon Trophy and we each received a Drambuie quaich (the cup of friendship).

WHAT NEXT?

Peter Dredge and Ian Sanderson in Sunseeker *XS Racing* had met us at the finish. They presented us with a fine bottle of bubbly, and I still treasure the (empty) bottle. Some four weeks after our return, Peter and Ian set to sea and carved three hours from our time in setting a new Outright Record of 39 hours 50 minutes. They also set a new Class Record for vessels 30–50 feet in length, thereby leaving us with our record for vessels up to 30 feet in length. A few weeks after their run, the Outright Record was broken yet again when Hannes Bohinc and Fabio Buzzi set a time of 30 hours 51 minutes 40 seconds in a 6,000 horsepower FB80 called *Record*.

It had been a busy year. The gauntlet had been thrown down, *Hot Lemon III* was sold to a new home in Northern Ireland and *Hot Lemon IV* was conceived.

THE 2002 ROUND BRITAIN RECORD ATTEMPT
(for craft between 30-50 feet in length)

HOT LEMON IV SPECIFICATION

This RIB was a Scorpion 10 metre Sports Cruiser with twin Yanmar 4.2 litre diesel engines, Imco external steering and foot control buttons for the trim, the standard Bravo 1 drives threw 28 pitch propellers that were again blueprinted by Tom Bolton.

At 45 knots cruising speed we used 90 litres per hour. She carried 1,000 litres of fuel which gave a theoretical range of 500nm reduced to 400nm, allowing a reserve. I added a 540-litre deck tank to give a range of +/- 650nm, with a 100nm reserve. With maximum fuel load she weighed over 6,000kg and ran at 48 knots; her maximum speed when lightly loaded was around 54 knots.

Cockpit seating was four superb racing-type bolster seats with electric rise/fall squabs, plus a large bench seat that we used as a passage bunk. Down below she was luxurious with twin berths, a hot/cold shower, a sea toilet, a diesel-powered hob/cabin heater and a marble-effect work surface – not common in a race boat!

My son Dave and I drew full-scale plans for the dashboard and helm arrangements, taking advantage of driver and navigator being side by side without a companionway between them, an essential requirement for safe, fast running. Electronic equipment comprised a colour Raymarine GPS plotter using C-Map charts, a radar plus a Sea-me radar target enhancer, depth sounder, fuel flow meter, large magnetic compass and twin VHF radios, one with DSC, using individual aerials. We had three engine room bilge pumps, the highest of which would illuminate a very loud alarm and red light. The weight of a luxury cabin and fitted bathroom was clearly not ideal for our purpose, although they looked very pleasant. So there we were, ready to have another run, relying once more upon a standard boat with a straightforward but very high-quality engineering installation by Dave Crawford Marine. I had complete confidence in the reliability and ultimate safety of the vessel.

TEAM *HOT LEMON IV*

Fortunately, Chris and Jan were readily available and I was delighted that Dave could also join us. He had now finished university and was very experienced in driving *Hot Lemon*: he is our race driver, Dad is allowed to navigate.

THE RECORD ATTEMPT

By early June we were ready but the weather was not: we repeatedly came within 36 hours of starting, only to cancel. As record times had shortened over the years it was now vital that sea states were as smooth as possible — minutes really counted. At last, Rick gave us the thumbs up but warned of misty conditions. On Tuesday 6 August John Puddifoot, the RYA Power Boat Racing Manager, timed us away from Lymington at 0426hrs.

Conditions were bouncy along the south coast and I was concerned that I had misjudged things; great relief around 0900hrs as the seas smoothed at Land's End, and I was very relieved at our increased speed of 48 knots as the fuel load lightened. Mist set in as we passed Dun Laoghaire with constant radar watch. We entered Bangor Marina at 1515hrs having taken 10 hours 49 minutes to run 460nm, at an average speed of 43 knots. We left at 1545hrs in cold, grey but less misty conditions and ran through wonderful familiar scenery past Oban, Mull, Ardnamurchan and Kyle.

I wanted reasonable tidal conditions at Duncansby Head and had originally set our start time at 0230hrs. However, our previous successful attempt had dulled my decisions and I chose to give us a little more sleep before starting. This seemed the correct decision at the time but, in the event, was wrong.

At 2200hrs we rounded the halfway point at Cape Wrath after 17.5 hours at sea; now running at 50 knots we were on target for our planned 35-hour run. Disaster struck as we approached Duncansby Head in mist and darkness: my start timing was two hours late and we ran into the heavy tidal race I had wanted to avoid. There was no moon or starlight, no shore lights or visible lighthouse, nothing except inky blackness and foaming seas washing over *Hot Lemon* as we slowed to 8 knots. We kept Aberdeen Coastguard informed as we crept away from land, and although *Hot Lemon* would have been well capable of 30 knots in those conditions in daylight, we ran slowly as total darkness hid the pattern of each advancing wave and trough – an extra large one could have been very damaging. This was most frustrating, but incoming foaming water above eye level is character-building stuff. Our GPS could not react quickly enough to the wild conditions and, with not one star to steady our course, we twice turned in a large circle before navigating by our wildly swinging magnetic compass.

At 0344hrs we arrived in a dark and very misty Peterhead, having taken 12 hours to run 480nm, at an average speed of 40 knots. We had lost almost two hours in the heavy conditions and restricted visibility but we calculated we were still in with a chance for the Class Record and were now heading home, spirits lifting as we left at 0415hrs.

Dawn provided some beautiful lighting effects on the banks of mist as conditions calmed, and we ran the 330nm towards the forest of rigs, where we constantly verified our position and course as the seabed shelved repeatedly from 30m to 3m over a few hundred yards. The earlier adverse conditions had used far more fuel than planned, and we ran lightly loaded at 52 knots into Ramsgate to quickly load 250 litres. We left at 1545hrs, only to find very uncomfortable head winds and seas again slowing us; nevertheless, we covered the remaining 120nm to Lymington in under 2.5 hours, at an average speed of 48 knots. The RYA timekeeper, Jonathon Hullock, confirmed our total run of 37 hours 49 minutes 50 seconds, a new record for the 30–50 foot class.

WHAT NEXT?

Hot Lemon IV gave us many more years of race and cruise enjoyment until she was acquired by John and Mary Puddifoot in 2005, renamed *Mystic Dragon*, and taken by sea to the Mediterranean.

Records are set to be broken, and in June 2003 the record we had set in 2001 with *Hot Lemon III* for craft up to 30ft in length was reduced by a superb 10 hours down to 33 hours, 11 minutes and 4 seconds when Tony Jenvey, Neil McGrigor and Simon Rogers had a cracking run in a twin-diesel Revenger RIB. More gauntlets hit the floor! In 2004, Dave and I decided that a realistic challenge was feasible and drew up our wish list for *Hot Lemon V*.

THE 2005 ROUND BRITAIN RECORD ATTEMPT
(for craft up to 30 feet length)

HOT LEMON V SPECIFICATION

The David Marsh designed Scorpion hull had proved itself time and again, giving a fast but comfortable ride in all sea conditions, so I would again use their 10m hull but with an important modification. I turned for advice to Lorne Campbell, a very well-respected race boat designer. My original idea to use larger engines was gently, professionally, but firmly turned down as they could overpower a 10-m boat intended to run fast and safe offshore. Larger engines would also add at least 50% engine weight, needing several more fuel stops.

The specification became obvious: concentrate on power to weight, seakeeping and reliability. Lorne now incorporated twin steps into the hull and we trimmed the nose by a few inches to shorten the measured length. The stepped hull would run faster than a standard hull and I accepted the difficulties of a reduced fuel capacity, a low freeboard at the stern which led to considerable turbo lag, and other minor handling changes. The cabin was completely bare except for storage bins and a sea toilet; foam sandwich was used extensively in the superstructure, but the hull was a standard lay-up except that one layer of GRP was omitted. No fancy materials were used. To save weight there was no windscreen or A frame.

Dave Crawford Marine completed their usual top-quality engineering installation, using a pair of our usual Yanmar 6 LP-STE 315hp diesel engines on Bravo 1 handed drives at 1:1.5 ratio, with Imco external steering. After extensive testing, Steel Developments in London selected a pair of five blade Hydromotive propellers at 28-inch pitch as giving the best results for high-speed running with a heavy fuel load, but when lightly loaded in race trim we used five blade 30-inch pitch propellers.

Seating was four rise/fall bolster seats and a bench seat, but two of the bolsters were removed to accommodate a gigantic 820-litre deck tank which, together with the 900-litre main capacity, gave us a very theoretical range of around 850nm, reduced to a safe 700nm by the stepped hull and a good reserve. With this range we only needed one fuel stop but chose to have two, for safety. Dry weight was some 3,500kg, but fully loaded with gear and fuel she was around 5,800kg, and our speed reduced from 60 knots light to 54 knots heavy. Fully loaded, consumption was 120lph at 54 knots, but this reduced to 100lph on a half fuel load, still running at 54 knots.

Electronic equipment comprised twin Raymarine colour plotters using C-Map charts, two GPS doughnuts for safety and an ST60 repeater showing BTW/COG for fast running, a radar, twin VHF radios (one DSC) on separate aerials, depth sounder, magnetic compass, twin fuel flow meters, the usual engine and trim gauges, floor buttons and the all-important centralised throttle levers.

TEAM *HOT LEMON V*

After installing the large deck tank there were only two seats remaining. That made team selection very easy – it would be Dave and me. As I was approaching the big six-o I needed less sleep, Dave would take the younger person's occasional 'power nap' and we would each have a constant supply of adrenaline and wine gums; we would remain wide awake – and so we did, but for different reasons.

THE RECORD ATTEMPT

The first opportunity in late July was cancelled at five hours' notice due to a sudden change in weather conditions; the weather finally smiled on us a few weeks later and we were timed away by Chris and Helen Strickland at 0300hrs on 11 August. These friends had also kindly volunteered to act as shore contact for communications.

Our engines ran well in the cold night air as we held a steady 54 knots with an 80% fuel load. By sunrise we were well on our way to Land's End and it was a beautiful sight to watch the sun rise over the Lizard behind us. After rounding Land's End we trimmed down into a 1m chop over an underlying swell. Yet again, as in 2002, we ran into banks of mist, and reduced speed to 40 knots for safety. Milford Haven Coastguard reported

Profile of a sea-going projectile. The hard bow of this RIB is designed to reduce the stress loadings on the hypalon buoyancy tubes. © *Chris Davies*

that his colleague at Holyhead had conditions of thick fog; not good. Fortunately, this was to the east, the sky cleared above us, the seas fell away and we enjoyed a real confidence boost as we had a fantastic run 20nm off the Irish coast.

We arrived at Bangor in an impressive 8 hours 48 minutes, having averaged 52 knots over 460nm; at this speed we would finish in some 27 hours and have a chance to claim the Outright Record as well as our Class Record – now there was a challenge.

Bangor Marina is always highly efficient and we cast off after 34 minutes having bunkered 1,300 litres. We then enjoyed wonderful clear skies and calm seas through the Western Isles, although we were a little frustrated as our hull stuck to the glassy surface and kept us down to 50 knots. We generally maintained two hours on and two hours off at the helm, but when Dave took over around 1500hrs he chose to helm for some seven hours as *Hot Lemon* is such fun to drive, particularly when sea conditions deteriorate. After passing under the Skye Bridge, conditions became uncomfortable and we slowed to 49 knots; we passed the halfway point at Cape Wrath having run for 13.5 hours. We were on track for a 27-hour run and the Outright Record.

I'll now confess to a major navigational error. My mind was considering the likely sea conditions around Duncansby Race and we were aiming to pass inside Stromer Island. As we passed Scrabster, I spotted what I took to be Stromer immediately ahead of us. Although the GPS was telling us to turn to port, I was so convinced of our location that I advised Dave to ignore the apparently incorrect GPS and steer to starboard so that we would pass inside Stromer. We pulled to a halt about 0.25nm from Dunnett Beach by which time the alarm bells in my head were ringing loudly enough. I recalled the lesson of flying by instruments: trust them. My vision of Stromer was in fact Dunnet Head, which is joined to the mainland!

We passed Duncansby Head with no serious challenges other than to see the larger of our two GPS screens suddenly go blank with a cheery message 'no input signal.' We hove-to for five minutes while I transferred the input on to our spare GPS, but without success. We continued to run using our small-screen plotter and the magnetic compass, relying upon pre-written course notes. It was impossible to read the screen at speed but I had copied all waypoints into each plotter, and the ST60 repeater screen directly in front of the helmsman saved the day: fast night running would have been almost impossible without this facility.

We exchanged text messages with Maggie and our shore team and updated Aberdeen Coastguard with our position. As we ran towards Peterhead, the following seas increased substantially and we were relieved to arrive at 2200hrs to record an average of almost 50 knots for this leg. Our Peterhead shore support team comprised Jim Clubb on the diesel bowser; on our previous Round Britain attempts, Jim and his colleague Bruce have alternated at the bunkering pier and given us tremendous assistance and enthusiastic encouragement. As we drew alongside the very high pier I looked up to take hold of the fuel line snaking down towards me, only to hear Jim explaining that he wasn't lowering the fuel line, he was lowering a bag of fish and chips and a flask of coffee. Wonderful – thank you, Jim!

After some 30 minutes we were full to the brim, carrying 1,720 litres of diesel, and after obtaining harbourmaster clearance, we moved at displacement speed towards the harbour entrance. We opened the throttles and both engines bogged down at 1,800rpm, some 200rpm short of turbo assistance. The engine intercoolers could not quickly overcome a build up of heat in the engine room during our fuel stop, and almost 1.5 tonnes of fuel had forced our propellers further underwater, a situation exacerbated by the reduced stern flotation of our stepped hull. We thought the game was up; we opened the engine lid, lowered the trim tabs and swung alternately to each side trying to bring either propeller close to the surface for one engine to reach turbo, but no luck. The only alternative was to risk damaging the universal joints in the outdrive legs and raise them beyond their red indicator. As the props came to the surface we played with the throttles and leg trim so as to maintain slight turbo assistance while lowering the legs. We waited for the sound of universal joints breaking, but on this occasion the technique worked. We were soon running at 50 knots in a 2m following sea and Dave handed me the helm so as to catch a 'power nap' as night fell.

Our engines ran very well in the cold night air, but we had a major panic around 0030hrs when a ghostly white shape appeared half a mile off our starboard bow. To this day we have no idea what it was; there was no moonlight shining over clouds, our navigation lights would not give such an effect and nothing showed on the radar. The light slowly closed towards us and we eased away from it. When we were one mile off course I decided to turn and run towards the glow. At this point the apparition accelerated so as to run some 500m ahead of us, and after a few more minutes it sharply accelerated away towards the Humber river.

Rain now set in and we were each silently thinking, 'what are we doing here?' The reduced visibility played tricks on us and at one stage we both thought that we were once again heading for the shore, only to realise that what appeared in the dark, rainy conditions as rolling hills in the mid distance were, in fact, the tops of each successive swell in front of us, which we were approaching at 45 knots.

We passed through the gas rigs around 0400hrs in light rain but slightly smoother sea conditions, and it was bliss to round Smith's Knoll and head SSW towards Ramsgate. Conditions then worsened, as 20–25 knots of westerly breeze funnelled down the Thames Estuary, giving breaking beam seas well in excess of 2 metres. *Hot Lemon* was being picked up and thrown to one side by the heavy seas and we reduced speed to 40 knots. Single V-shaped hulls on a RIB are wonderful in these conditions: we would watch for each incoming sea and adjust our speed so as to allow each wave to run either in front or behind us; alternatively, we would turn and run away to allow the wave to run beneath us. We used a combination of techniques as we had only two choices: continue on our course or run off towards Belgium – we held our course.

We then learnt a good deal about metal fatigue as our aluminium radar mast gave in to the heavy conditions and snapped. Only good fortune and the cables inside the mast prevented the radar dome, VHF aerials and Sea-me radar target enhancer from hitting one of us. I worsened the situation by forgetting to turn off the electricity before severing the cables with bolt croppers while balancing on the cabin roof in the rain and a heavy swell; there were spectacular sparks but the circuit-breaker worked. We secured the debris in the cockpit, rigged a spare VHF aerial and got underway after losing 15 minutes.

We passed Ramsgate, found shelter off Dover and stopped to check fuel and make

Hot Lemon III *returns home to Lymington triumphant.* © *Chris Davies*

contact with our shore support, and this time we remembered to keep the engine lid open to avoid heat build-up. Chris reminded me in plain terms that we had forgotten to make contact over the past ten hours and the Coastguard were minutes away from instigating their procedures. Chris had been awake all night as he awaited our contact, and the Coastguard had told him of the poor conditions. When approaching Ramsgate our mobile phones had leapt into action with his numerous text messages. We now had 120nm to run with an estimated total 160nm of fuel remaining. A quick engine room inspection showed no obvious damage and we decided to run flat out to the finish. The strong westerly wind was reasonably comfortable on our starboard bow until we passed Beachy Head, when we met the seas head-on. Although we were now in 'go for the line mode', discretion prevailed and we ran a slightly longer course close inshore, only to find walls of white surf at Selsey Bill where we put in a number of short tacks to lengthen the waves and momentarily closed throttles to sink into oncoming crests. It was a joy to turn into smooth conditions heading towards Portsmouth, where Dave and I whooped, shouted and congratulated each other as we crossed our line off Lymington at 60 knots, to be timed in by RYA timekeeper Tom Crump for a new Class Record of 31 hours 22 minutes and 46 seconds. Chris and Helen drew alongside in their RIB *Seahound*, together with Team Scorpion in theirs, champagne flowed and we promised Maggie we wouldn't do this again... honest!

CONCLUSION AND LESSONS LEARNT

We achieved our objective in these three record attempts and, so far as I know, did not cause trouble to anyone else.

We also came away from our experiences having learned some key lessons:

1 Weather is all; it overrides the skill of the team, the capabilities of the vessel, the organisation and all other issues. Without appropriate conditions an attempt neither starts nor finishes. Be wary not to rush an attempt under pressure of an advancing year; it could be better to run on a clear, cold, starry spring night than in misty autumnal conditions.
2 Have a small team and use standard gear. Keep it simple: 'It's a long cruise.'
3 Only change your original plans if you are absolutely certain they are flawed. On our 2002 attempt, had I kept to my original planned 0230hrs start time we would have avoided a potentially dangerous situation at Duncansby Head, and would have reduced our overall time by some two hours. All timings must be worked around tides at Duncansby Race; if this is wrong, don't start.
4 Carry more than adequate fuel and don't 'work' the throttles as this dramatically increases fuel used, and it is quite possible to run at a decent speed through choppy conditions using a steady throttle – leg trim and steering will do much of the job.
5 Use a RIB; the stability and reserve buoyancy is a great psychological plus in adverse conditions. They are also fairly easy to board after falling overboard!
6 Keep food and liquid supplies easily available when running at night.
7 Have good clothing; it gets very cold at sea at night and at speed. Wear a drysuit if you're going to fall in – our 2001 attempt would have stopped had I been in ordinary sailing gear.
8 Carry a satellite phone and use it!

SURVIVING OFFSHORE EXTREMES

BY SHAUN WHITE AND HUGO MONTGOMERY-SWAN

The late Shaun White had exceptional experience in all-weather RIBs, and he opens this chapter by looking at the issues relating to the survival of craft and crew in the offshore environment.

14

We have witnessed a rapid rise of interest in extreme sports over the last few years, from parachuting into bottomless canyons in South-East Asia and surfing enormous waves in Hawaii, to experiencing the fastest, deepest, highest extremes that mankind can aspire to against his old foe, Nature. All this is very exciting and admirable, but one could argue the ethics of such sports on the grounds of safety. In their defence, though, they usually involve the lone adventurer who covers his back pretty adequately and gets himself out of trouble, either through his own expertise or with the help of a close-support backup team.

There is, however, one area that's notably devoid of such activities: extreme seas. The very name puts the fear of God into most of us, and the reasons are obvious: of all the extreme experiences we may encounter, being in a small boat in violent seas is one of the most terrifying and lonely situations in which you can find yourself on the planet. In a nutshell, when it comes to facing the full force of Nature and everything that she can throw at us, we are basically cowards...and why not! What's more, culturally, among maritime nations, there has always been a deep social stigma attached to gratuitously setting out with the sole purpose of pitting yourself and your craft against extreme seas, potentially involving expensive rescue operations and risking other people's lives. This is a theatre fit only for the professional mariner with substantial craft and training. Or is it?

Historically, 'last frontiers' have been pushed aside by a combination of man's adventurous spirit and technological advancements. The rapid technical and design evolution of the modern RIB has turned it into a highly seaworthy, capable craft that can safely project itself into sea states hitherto only occupied by creatures with wings, fins and flippers. Now that has to be a clarion wake-up call to all red-blooded

RIB owners, lying awake in bed with a force 11 ripping the slates off the roof and a big macho RIB safely tucked up in the garage. The ultimate challenge haunts you; the demons taunt you. Dare I? Shall I? What if? Would I survive? Common sense and sleep prevail but...you are straight into the most awful nightmare. You and your RIB are no longer safely sleeping, but 3 miles offshore in a force 11 storm. What on earth do you do?

OVERALL SCENARIO

This is a classic storm of oceanic origins, with well-defined waves of up to 7 metres high and some 8 hours to run with nature. Your RIB is an 8m well-found design with an aft console and jockey seating for your crew of four. You are in deep water with no overfalls and little chance of rescue due to your isolated location.

IMMEDIATE ACTION

The first thing you must do is to carefully assess your situation: are you on a lee shore, and if so how far offshore? What is the fuel situation? What is the physical condition of your crew? What lifesaving apparatus (LSA) do you have on board? How long is the storm going to last? Is it going to back or veer?

You must then take positive action to deal with the situation:

1 It is imperative to maintain a 3-mile distance between you and the shore. Apart from fatal contact with the shore, these oceanic waves could be totally unmanageable when they encounter both the shallow seabed and inshore overfalls.
2 Take a GPS bearing or, if you have no navigation aids, a visual bearing on a headland or similar landmark.
3 To hold station you will need to motor ahead at a speed of at least 15 knots to counter the action of the wind and waves.
4 Do not waste fuel: you may be out for a very long time.
5 Try to move portable weight forward to keep the bow down into a head sea situation, and aft for running before, especially in an outboard-powered RIB.
6 Lash down everything that can move, really tightly.
7 Secure everyone with safety lines to strong points on the RIB.
8 Delegate a crewman to monitor the machinery, especially vulnerable fuel lines.
9 Delegate a crewman to eyeball incoming breaking seas (the helmsman's concentration may well be down).
10 Keep morale up: fear, fatigue, injury and hypothermia are all very real dangers and should be prepared for.

11 Have a standby helmsman at the ready: you could easily be knocked down by a wave and injured. You must get the RIB back on course before the next monster hits you.

12 Kill cords are not a good idea in this sort of situation. Not only might the engine fail to restart but you have to keep on course.

13 Secure all loose lines: they can be your best friend or worst enemy.

SCENARIO I

Bad news: it is a lee shore, and only some 3 miles away, with 100m-high cliffs and no safe haven. You have tried to make headway against the waves, which are moving against you at some 15mph and are breaking right over your open RIB. Your crew is terrified. There is the constant screaming of the wind over the breaking seas. Flying spray is becoming a real challenge.

EXECUTION

The main dangers to you in this unenviable situation are obviously events that could capsize your RIB. These are inevitably caused by getting the craft in a broadside attitude, or by being pitchpoled by unmanageable waves. Let's look, therefore, at the main reasons for being broadside. This usually follows the passing of a wave under the craft, leaving you airborne and in freefall for perhaps 7 metres or even more before crashing into the trough that follows, perhaps on the chine if the RIB is laterally unbalanced. You have to pick yourself up within seconds and with great presence of mind in order to avoid the next wave. You might also have injuries to contend with.

As any mariner will tell you, it's the large breaking waves that have to be avoided at all costs: they are perfectly capable of overwhelming the most seaworthy craft. Depending on the sea state, it is usually just the occasional wave that starts to break, but with increasing wind speed most will be encouraged to break given sufficient time and impetus. In any open RIB without a self-righting wheelhouse, you have at this point probably reached the end of the line. There are, however, a few tricks left if some of the waves remain unbroken.

If you see such a monster approaching, get out of the way! How, you may ask? Well, if you have plenty of power at your disposal, dash along the trough ahead of the breaking wave and head up into a more benign section, or make for another sea beyond the length of the immediate monster. The breaking sections of waves are rarely very lengthy. Alternatively, turn through 180 degrees and run in the trough before the breaking wave until you see it break, and then round up to face the next one. On the downside, this manoeuvre could gobble up at least 400 metres of valuable space between you and the coast, and will use a lot of fuel. These manoeuvres are tactically well proven but do require substantial power and 'hair trigger' reaction times.

SCENARIO II

This presents the same situation as scenario I, except that there is a safe haven some 5 miles along the coast and you decide it's the safest option. The problem is moving laterally along the line of the waves, thereby putting your boat in that dreaded broadside attitude.

Extreme conditions for any small craft. Concentration levels need to be high when seeking to avoid dangerous breaking seas such as the one pictured here. Fatigue can set in and mistakes can be made. Fresh turns at the wheel is therefore a wise strategy. © **Safehaven Marine**

Powering on just before meeting the trough will help the bow lift to meet the next sea. © Safehaven Marine

EXECUTION

Your salvation rests once again in those relatively friendly troughs. Consider these your escape routes, even if they can be daunting, transient and unpredictable. As soon as the last crest has passed underneath and you have dipped into the trough, turn smartly through 90 degrees and give it all you have got, to power as far along the trough as possible before you have to head up into the next wave. It is surprising how far you can travel in the seconds allowed, but be warned: you do lose ground to leeward with each cycle.

SCENARIO III

Once again, a similar scenario but with one important omission: there is no lee shore to worry about. There is, however, still a welcome safe haven, 3 miles downwind of your position, which you are going to head for.

EXECUTION

You could be excused for interpreting this heart-stopping ride as exhilarating. Indeed, despite the stature of the waves, on a fine day under azure skies this panorama may look less threatening – even beautiful and exciting. But on a day of gloom, with driving rain and iron-grey seas, this seascape will appear nothing less than ominous, even life-threatening. Again, safe negotiation of these seas will be down to timing and sheer tenacity.

You will need to bring any portable weight aft in order to give the bow as much buoyancy as possible to avoid stuffing and broaching in the troughs. Detail an aft lookout to warn of breaking waves. Pick your moment for the 180° transition from facing the waves to running before them. This will require decisive helming, and it could well be the case that you will immediately be picked up by the next wave and catapulted both upwards and forwards in the most dramatic fashion. If so, you are now power-surfing in the purest sense of the expression, which has to be one of the most exhilarating extreme sports there is, for you are, in effect, falling down the face of the wave from a great height and at breakneck speed.

Things can happen quickly indeed, like stuffing into the back of the wave in front, followed by broaching. So how can you surf the wave for as long as possible and thus keep out of trouble? For one thing, you could try zigzagging down the face like surfers do; this not only allows you to stay with your wave longer, but your entry speed into the back of the wave in front is greatly reduced. Caution: do not slow down too much as you will need all the power you can muster to claw yourself out of the trough. There are tremendous forces trying to hold you down at this point, but you just have to get up and away before being overwhelmed by the following wave. In theory, you can 'ride the trough' of a wave system by tucking yourself in front of a wave and synchronising your speed accordingly, but in reality it seldom works, for things get out of sequence.

In lesser sea states you can afford to let the waves pass underneath you if that is preferable – it is always surprising just how large a wave will pass safely underneath your craft. If your aft lookout warns you that the wave you are surfing is about to break, either steer left or right to clear it, or accelerate in a straight line, but again beware of stuffing.

A confused and dangerous sea in rising conditions well offshore.
© *Hamish McDonald*

ESSENTIAL KIT
Equipment and component listing for craft undertaking offshore passages

Suitable mooring warps for use fore and aft

At least 50 metres of warp and chain coupled to appropriate anchor

1 x sea anchor/parachute-type drogue

Navigation lights plus spare bulbs

1 x all-round white/anchor light plus spare bulb

1 x fixed ship's offshore compass (magnetic)

1 x handheld compass

1 x fixed 25watt radio plus spare/emergency aerial

1 x handheld waterproof VHF

1 x mobile phone in waterproof bag

1 x fixed GPS

1 x EPIRB

A selection of in-date offshore flares in a watertight container

A supply of cotton clothes

1 x bailer/bucket

1 x knife

1 x torch

1 x hand signalling mirror

National ensign

1 x first-aid kit, including seasickness tablets, diarrhoea tablets and lavatory rolls

1 x basic repair kit/selection of items deemed by the skipper to be suited to the practice of effecting running repairs at sea, ie cable ties, string/cord, gaffer tape, spare spark plugs, webbing/ratchet straps, gelcoat repair kit, also emergency tube repair materials in the case of a RIB

1 x spare kill cord

Spare engine oil

Fuel funnel

Spare propeller and spacer nut, split pin etc and prop wrench

Length of plastic tubing/pipe

Selection of bungees

Auxiliary/detachable fuel tanks, complete with 'plug in' fuel lines if extra tankage is deemed necessary

A securely affixed ship's battery, housed with a locker/suitable console (gel-type battery preferred)

Particularly if undertaking offshore passages of a serious nature, the carrying of a fully serviced liferaft (an item that can be either purchased or hired) is sound practice

1 x hand fishing line and one box of matches (latter to be stowed to ensure they remain dry)

Emergency rations of food plus drinking water (minimum 2 litres of water per person)

Charts and marine almanac

Offshore lifejackets with crutch straps

Drysuits to be worn by crew when sea conditions dictate

Suitable head covering – recommend lightweight helmets

Goggles and hat plus gloves

Crew properly clothed and kitted for the conditions.
© *Paul Glatzel*

SCENARIO IV – MAN OVERBOARD

This is a very difficult situation as sometimes fateful decisions have to be made: if you are close to a lee shore, you may have to sacrifice the casualty in preference to saving the majority. If, however, you decide that a rescue is possible, the biggest danger to the casualty is the craft coming down on top of him, which in extreme seas usually results in death or severe injury. Avoid recovery from the stern or the bow at all costs; instead, bring the casualty alongside and, with all possible speed, drag him over the tubes; the RIB's low freeboard is another design asset in such a situation.

SCENARIO V

You have messed up: the boat has capsized and everyone is in the water.

EXECUTION

The first essential is a headcount. Everyone should be fastened on by safety lines, but the lines could be snagged under the RIB. If anyone is missing, minimise the buoyancy in your lifejacket and push yourself under the side of the tubes, never the transom, as there are far too many hazards in this area. Release the victim. If he is unconscious you may have to release some air from his lifejacket too, but remember that it is very difficult to orally reinflate a lifejacket, especially in big seas, once the victim is free. If your lifejacket is fitted with a spray shield, use it: this can be a lifesaver by minimising the ingestion of water. Marshal everyone to the upturned RIB: RIBs are far more stable when upside down and act as a good liferaft provided there are sufficient handholds within reach. All this presupposes that the sea state will allow you to hold on, which is doubtful. Sooner or later, fatigue and hypothermia will probably terminate everything and you will be left wholly in the hands of the elements. In such a situation an EPIRB might be your only hope; along with the time a drysuit, coupled to a lifejacket and appropriate head covering, may just afford you.

In the following chapter, a first-hand account of a successful Atlantic crossing is related, one of at least four such voyages that have been undertaken by a RIB over the last four years. The boat in question featured both outboard power and a sail, with the latter giving the vessel its long-range offshore capability. The fact that a powerboat, especially only 5 metres in length, was able to be modified to take a sail makes this account particularly interesting.

CONCLUSION

In recent years powerboats undertaking offshore voyages have become very much more common. Advance preparation is essential, as is the need to carry the right kit plus all necessary spares and material for effecting basic repairs. Good 'comms' systems and items such as EPIRBs are also regarded as 'must haves' on the offshore boat's inventory. But with good planning and a sound boat, offshore powerboating can be hugely rewarding.

ATLANTIC CROSSING BY RIB

BY AREK PAWELEK

Offshore expeditionary Arek Pawelek relates his own transatlantic survival story and reflects on the key lessons learnt.

The voyage was planned to include two legs, the first from Kandyks to the Canary Islands, a distance of about 700–800 miles, and a sailing of about one month in all; the second leg, from the Canary Islands to Barbados, would cover a distance of approximately 3,000 miles. All this was to be undertaken aboard a 4.4m RIB, powered primarily by sail, on a voyage following in the footsteps of the great Doctor Bombard.

A crazy idea, perhaps, but now I'm glad I've actually done it. On the other hand, if you're thinking of making such a voyage yourself, I hope that my account won't put you off. There is little doubt in my mind that advance preparation is the key. Of course, this applies to any sea voyage, but especially so when you are intending to take on something as vast as the mighty Atlantic Ocean.

PLANNING

'Vast' could also be the word to describe the other necessary side to my undertaking – funding the expedition. For it quickly became apparent that even this project, although involving only a small RIB and a crew of one, would require substantial support. In fact, without the help of sponsors I probably wouldn't have been able to put the project together at all, let alone purchase all the equipment that was necessary for such a voyage. Of course, I would be exaggerating if I said the crossing itself was the 'easy' bit! But the days of 'realistic communism' have long since passed in Poland, so now, like elsewhere, we find ourselves happily enjoying the 'realistic capitalism' everyone hungered for. Therefore, in seeking help, I found each potential sponsor was understandably keen to calculate just how much he would earn on his investment.

The most important piece of equipment was, of course, the craft itself. In my search for the right boat I eventually traced the Polish RIB manufacturer Sportis and established contact with Mr Ludwik Vogt, the chairman of the company. At the factory I was shown around the shop floor, where I was told I could select the most suitable RIB and discuss the various modifications required to convert it from engine power to wind power.

Besides all the specialist kit, the seemingly straightforward matter of food for such a voyage was going to require some very careful thought. But I was under no delusions. Bombard might have crossed the Atlantic on a diet of raw fish but I had decided my menu would be slightly more advanced. For one thing, I've never been much good at catching the fish, and for another, I'm not all that keen on eating them. There was no point in taking canned food as conditions in the boat would simply cause the tins to corrode. To help with my dilemmas, I decided to get in touch with Lyovit Ltd in Kielce who, to my great relief, agreed to take the problem off my hands and sponsor all my food requirements for the duration of the 90 day trip. I soon received from the company a selection of ready-made meals – vegetables, meat and even fruit desserts.

The next area that needed attention was my choice of clothing for the trip. I decided upon breathable thermo-active garments, and these were made to measure by Trango. Little did I know at that time that the Trango gear would be responsible for literally saving my life. Other personal lifesaving equipment and foul-weather gear were acquired from LM Ltd in Konin. LM's jacket and bibs were made from Gore-Tex – a well-proven fabric which would protect me for long periods of time in the worst of conditions. As for the footwear, I selected Haix, model GSG9, the same as is worn by many special-forces units.

The most important instrument that I had on board was the GPS. In the end I decided on a very simple model (also the cheapest, in fact), the Garmin GPS 12. It's worth pointing out that I completed my voyage on a staggering single set of batteries. During the time I was on the Canary Islands I suffered an extreme case of prudence and treated myself to a second Garmin 12 – just in case. Also, prior to my departure from Poland I acquired an Icom M15 VHF and an EPIRB Kannad 406 S. Unfortunately, both pieces of equipment failed on me – the latter during some of my most difficult moments. I also had several short-wave radios, the best of the lot being the simple Grundig Yacht Boy. The more sophisticated model made by Sony, carried in my kit bag, could not withstand the humidity and thus proved quite useless.

From a navigational standpoint, the most valuable amongst my various possessions were the books I acquired. These enabled me to actually *learn* the skill of navigation, as up until then I was still pretty much navigation illiterate! In truth, though, it was not as if I had no idea whatsoever about navigation, but rather it had been limited to finding my way underwater – sub-marine navigation, in other words. (This was a skill I was hoping I wouldn't need to re-employ on the voyage!) The most useful books within my ever growing library were the tautologically named *Navigation: Simple, Easy and Pleasant* by Urbanczyk and *Heavy Weather Sailing* by Adlard Coles. In addition to these books I had a number of charts covering the sea area in which I hoped to remain. In terms of navigational hardware, the compass was an old bit of kit I had prised off a redundant military vehicle some while before. The time was shown by two chronometers, one being my Citizen watch fitted with a diving computer (regretfully this was lost en route), the other being a plastic Casio found many years earlier on a beach on the island of Phi Phi. As luck would have it, the cheaper of the two survived unscathed. To complete the line-up, some friends on the Canary Islands gave me a plastic Ebbco sextant and an almanac, which meant, coupled with pencil, ruler and dividers, I had all I needed to help guide me from one side of the great divide to the other.

The critical matter of water rations played on my mind – preventing me from getting much sleep. From various knowledgeable sources and my own experience I knew that 2 litres per day would suffice. The second leg of my voyage, from the Canary Islands to Barbados, took Bombard some 65 days to traverse. I estimated that it would take me a similar amount of time, so based upon my calculation of 65 days x 2 litres per day, I needed 130 litres of water. Taking into account that there should be some rain en route, especially below N20°, this would mean I could reduce my reserves to about 120 litres. This would form my emergency reserve. Such was the quantity of water, then, to be stored aboard *The Price of Fear*.

In terms of propulsion, the only feasible form of power was the wind. This would be something else I would have to master, for up until my project with *The Price of Fear* I had never sailed a boat before. Ocean Sails Ltd, who took great care to produce just what my little vessel required, made the foresail and mainsail. I carried no spares, for there was barely enough room for a spare handkerchief, let alone a second set of sails. Besides the main rig I carried a spinnaker, which at one point allowed me to make good 106 miles in 24 hours. Being a traditionalist, I also decided upon a pair of oars. These weren't for rowing but solely for beating off any sharks that happened to take a fancy to my little rubber vessel. At 2 metres long and made of solid wood, they were substantial enough to allow me to 'put my oar in'; sharks aren't fussy about what they eat and I thought it possible that they might mistake my RIB for a large Polish sausage! My famous predecessor had himself done battle with these devilish creatures so I thought it only wise to arm myself accordingly. Also important was the self-steering system, which would represent my invisible crewmember or 'right-hand man'. To instruct me in the ways of my mechanical partner, my Dutch friend, Kees van der Staaij, bought me a book on auto-steering. Having read the book I managed to construct an auto-steering system myself out of some pieces of aluminium, plywood, sail, rope, a pulley and a few kilograms of lead. I was truly proud of my construction, especially as it actually worked. (For those interested, it was a system of a horizontal axle connected directly to the tiller handle.)

Safety. This is something a great many people would likely scoff at: 'How can you talk about safety when you're planning to set out across the ocean in a little rubber boat?' Indeed! Add to this the fact that I had absolutely no certificates or qualifications to my name, I suppose to some I could rightly be viewed as little more than a shipping hazard. I, however, viewed the venture in a very different light. Firstly, my RIB already had the natural attributes of a rescue boat, one which had been designed and converted by one of Europe's leading yacht designers, and secondly, I had confidence in my own abilities and the suitability of the equipment I'd chosen to carry. In the words of Alexander the

Great, 'I went forth to conquer'. If not the mighty ocean, at least my own private fears.

Certifications were compulsory in Poland, but in Spain no one even asked. My survival equipment, as already mentioned, included an EPIRB as well as a vast quantity of flares, red and white, plus smokes. A radar reflector was fitted to the top of the mast, and my lifejacket had an ACR light fitted to it. As for documentation, by far the most important was my passport. In fact, it was the only paperwork anyone ever asked to see. Customs formalities? None! The first stamp made in my passport from the time I crossed the Polish-German border (on entry into the EC) was when I arrived in Barbados. (The Polish Customs authorities were, in fact, very much more difficult about me bringing the RIB back to Poland after the voyage.)

Entertainment was supplied by a few radio sets. After sunset I could even receive two Polish language radio stations. I also took with me a number of books, as well as my trusty Walkman and a selection of cassettes. Keeping one's spirits up is central to the whole matter of maintaining good physical health, and in any survival situation the importance of morale should never be overlooked.

THE STORM

The roar of the next wave rearing up astern forces me to react immediately. I instinctively pull on the tiller handle. The sheer force of several tons of water hitting the transom violently throws the boat forward and I'm sent hurtling into space, to land in a heap amidst coils of rope and debris. The boat's acceleration is so great that the sails actually fold back on themselves. A knee-jerk response saves me from being struck by the boom, which flies overhead and skims the edge of my weatherproofs. All about me, spray and tumbling water add to the confusion of the moment, which is intensified by the severity of raw wind power. For the next 100 metres I'm surfing out of control, as if down the face of some giant roller coaster, until the RIB slows and begins lifting once more to tower over the panorama of tumbling crests and deep troughs.

Whilst on the plane I just manage to get a glimpse of the GPS: it shows a speed in excess of 8.6 knots. Not bad for a RIB with a sail reefed hard to the main. Putting her hard about, I am now on my knees, facing the wind with the sea in my nostrils. Though both arms feel like lead, with one hand on the tiller, I endeavour to bail out as much of the shipped sea water I can in the time available.

This is the third day of a storm that has seen winds of force 8–9 blowing relentlessly. Three days of a non-stop battle to survive. Food has become secondary to the intense desire and acute need for sleep. Sleep...how perfect. If only I could slumber for just a moment in order to regain some strength. What an irony, for only a precious few weeks ago I had literally been dreaming of being under sail in mid Atlantic aboard Price of Fear, *attempting to follow in the footsteps of Alan Bombard's successful 1952 crossing...*

Moments like this remain as vivid as ever in my memory, but of course not all the challenges involved high seas and nail-biting drama. Sometimes even the quieter moments proved testing, as in the case of my first few miles at sea.

At the start of my voyage the wind blew steadily from the west, which meant I was being continually pushed towards Gibraltar. However, by evening on the first day it had

A full storm in the mid Atlantic – no place for a small boat. In seas such as these, survival as opposed to headway becomes the priority. © **RIB International** *archives*

eased significantly, until by sunset I found myself sitting in total silence with not even a whisper of wind to ruffle the sails. The problem, too, was the fact that the easterly current, which had now set in, was also playing its part in taking me down towards the Mediterranean. But things rarely remain constant at sea, for soon after this, and without any warning at all, I found myself being jostled by white horses which came slapping boisterously at the sides of my little boat. It was clear two currents were fighting it out and I was 'piggy in the middle'. This lasted for at least half an hour before I was released and allowed to make progress again eastwards.

All around me now an ever-increasing movement of vessels began to show, their lights glinting like tiny stars in the inky blackness. Arming myself with a powerful torch I kept a constant watch so as to avoid being run down by these mighty hulks. Some of them came very close, their wash gently rolling under the RIB's frail hull. As if signalling a final goodbye, the distant lights of the African shore twinkled like a thin jewel necklace before finally vanishing from view as the RIB found her stride in the growing ocean swell. *Price of Fear* and I were now truly on our way towards the great American continent.

Good fortune continued to smile upon us, for after that first night the sails continued to fill, and progress westwards remained good as the gentle winds freshened. That morning, as I enjoyed the solitude of a leisurely breakfast, I spotted two black triangles cutting silently through the water in my direction. I threw everything to the bottom of the RIB and grabbed the boat hook. Suddenly, the black fins separated and began to circle the boat. By now I was kneeling in the bottom of the boat, switching my weapon from hand to hand in an effort to anticipate which one of the attackers would lunge first. Without warning, the bolder of the two spun a fast turn, dived and then surfaced right by the side of the RIB's sponson. My heart was almost beating its way out of my chest before I realised, to my great relief, that these marauding bandits were merely friendly dolphins out for an early morning frolic.

For the next few days the wind continued to build into a steady blow of around force 7 to 8. After reefing the sails and changing the ballast around in the boat, the ride became more acceptable. Now well trimmed, I hardly had to hold the tiller. Once all was secure, I felt relaxed enough to settle down for a few hours' sleep. As I lay in the warm sunshine, within the sanctuary of my trusty vessel, the wind again smiled upon me and veered north-west, then due north. I awoke with optimism: 'At last I am truly heading towards my destination.' Such a naive spirit was quickly quelled, though, when the wind began to grow much stronger. The rising waves could now clearly be seen cross-tracking the currents, and as they did, high seas, steep and white capped, began to advance upon me from all directions. In an effort to respond to the changing conditions, I ran up the storm foresail and put a second reef in the mainsail – but it wasn't easy. Some time earlier, during the course of doing my 'housework', I'd changed things around in the boat again so that I could steer her whilst sitting in the stern. Now she was letting me know she didn't like it and demonstrated this by refusing to point her bow directly into the wind and waves. By changing the trim, I found that with this new set-up, as soon as her speed reduced she had the annoying tendency of ducking broadside to the weather.

This behaviour on the part of *Price of Fear* was dangerous, for in these conditions she could very easily get swamped, even capsize. In fact, during one such episode, just as I stood up to grapple with the rigging, two wave trains met simultaneously, spun the RIB around and nearly sent me flying out the 'side door' legs akimbo! In the general panic and tangled mess I found myself mixed up in on deck, I turned to see several loose items of equipment about to be washed overboard. I lurched to the rescue and at the last moment managed to save the container that held my camera and vital documents. However, to my horror, the orange tin that held the money for the return trip was now merrily making its own way across the ocean waves. But there was no time to vent my rage, for the RIB was in a vulnerable position, slopping half full of water and in a poor state of seaworthiness in the likely event of another wave engulfing us. With seconds to spare I got to the tiller and sails just in time to recover control before the next big wave, several metres high, struck stern on. Then, while steering with just one hand and keeping my eyes peeled for another rogue sea, I frantically set about bailing for all my worth.

I was very aware that I simply had too much sail up. I had no choice, therefore, but to sacrifice speed for safety and put a reef in the main sail. I then put on my waterproof goggles and got to work sorting out the mess. Unfortunately, whilst engrossed in all this a gust of wind tore into the sails. It shot the boom over with such force that it smashed into my head and knocked me flat into the bottom of the boat. Lying there, all I can recall is staring up at the words 'Mountain Shop'. But why, in the middle of the ocean, should I be confronted by such a bizarre image? Had the bang on the head done more damage than I'd first imagined – indeed, was I seeing things? As I awakened, I began to realise that it was actually a tin bobbing around above my head... I was under water! Needless to say, I came to with a start, coughing and spluttering and in shock from the severity of my ordeal. My head thumped with pain. The constant flying sea water, which swept my face as I grappled to recover my boat's increasingly fragile situation, soon got me back on my feet, although I felt dazed and strangely detached from reality. I pulled in the main and set a 240° course. The RIB now lay to the wind steadily and rode the seas less erratically. It was then that I had the opportunity to feel my swollen head, and upon so doing, began to feel very ill.

The next day I streamed the sea anchor. To my annoyance, it refused to hold the boat head to sea, allowing her instead to swing broadside. I decided, therefore, to set it from the stern. This was better, only now the line seemed too short. The waves continuously rolled up the drogue, tangling the line and making it quite useless. Upon extending the line a little more, so as to allow it to reach back to the wave beyond, the drogue's effectiveness increased again. As it steadily took up the slack, a big sea began to rear up astern. I could see the line becoming taut, but the boat's delayed and methodical response in lining itself up to the face of this sea was alarming. She simply wasn't going to make it in time.

The massive wall of green water that collapsed into a boiling cascade over *Price of Fear* was catastrophic. Its impact threw me hard against the tiller handle, straight into my ribs. The realisation that I had yet again suffered a total swamping was sickening. Giving little thought as to whether I had sustained any further injuries, I blindly set to,

Arek's little 'Sportis' boat proved hugely adaptable to virtually all that the sea demanded of her. Well offshore, the sail came into its own.
© *Arek Pawelek*

bailing the half ton or so of water out over the RIB's shallow topsides with all the energy I could muster.

Another massive blow to the transom followed, only this time the drogue line wrenched under the intense load and snapped like a guitar string, flailing its bitter end in a circular motion inches from my face. The sudden release caused the boat to catapult forward, but in spite of this I managed to hold on to the sheet of the mainsail, which saved me on this occasion from being thrown overboard. I promptly pulled in the line, which I found simply dangling, lifeless, over the transom, with just the four pieces of rope at its end where the drogue's chute had been attached. Farewell then to any sleep – back once more to the sails and tiller.

I found, while running in these big ocean swells, that only continuous work with the tiller prevented the boat from being flooded and flipped over. In the gale conditions the wind, too, would blow spume and spray through the air horizontally at head height, which meant both the RIB and I were crusted in salt. My hands were also beginning to suffer from the constant exposure to the conditions and the never-ending wet. No amount of cream or oil seemed to help, for they continued instead to split and become quite badly swollen, despite treatment. From one of my kit bags I pulled the Sony Walkman, and for a while it gave some light relief amidst the chaos, but in working its buttons I found my fingers had begun to lack any feeling. This frightened me.

The storm still refused to abate, and because I continued to be preoccupied with keeping my little ship afloat, I found, to my dismay, I was not drinking nearly enough fresh water. Looking back, I realise now that I was suffering increasingly from dehydration. The logbook entries over the course of this 72 hour period showed I had only drunk about 1.5 litres of liquid – one quarter, in fact, of what I should have consumed.

The next night passed safely, but still the wind strength rarely dropped below force 9. The following morning I treated myself to some instant coffee but without the water. The taste was terrible but somehow it helped all the same. Later, I got knocked out again. It happened when I was checking whether the shackles on the foresail were tight enough. (I had already lost two of them.) A strong gust of wind knocked the boom over when I failed to spot that a knot on the line to which it was fastened had become undone. This time I got it fair and square on the brow. I screamed in agony as well as in rage. As I rose from my crouched position my attention was immediately grabbed by the monstrous form of a curling wave, which I knew instinctively was about to break. The rush of icy water seemed to consume my whole world, and as I held my breath I felt it flooding over my entire body and all that which separated me from the vast depths below. It was intimate; I knew this power now and strangely enough I found myself almost accepting it. Once it had passed I found that it had washed the blood off my goggles. At least that meant I could also see to repeat the then familiar routine of course correction, sail trimming and frantic bailing.

Of course, such dramas are bad enough during the day, but at night the difficulties are even more intense, as is the feeling of disorientation when disaster strikes. I remember clearly, some 2,000 miles into the voyage, when in similar seas I was capsized in a force 11 storm and trapped underneath the deck of the RIB. I managed to get free and haul myself up onto the upturned hull of the capsized boat, but it was a mighty struggle. Of course, I initially tried to right the boat, but with all the equipment secured to the deck it proved quite impossible. I decided, with some reluctance, therefore, to set off the EPIRB, but this required diving under the boat through the chaos of the seas to get the device.

It was clear that the mast had broken during the capsize, so with much effort I devised a way of securing it to the keel which, after many exhausting attempts, finally allowed me to right the RIB, rig a jury sail and get some rest. Nevertheless, I should point out that this entire process took two whole days, during which time I was on the bottom of the boat secured by a single rope amidst the shrieking gale and huge seas. To say that it was both exhausting and at times frightening is probably sufficient for the purpose of this chapter, but my fight to extract myself from this ordeal was not aided by the fact that my only sustenance was the drops of rain that the wind blew into my face from the skies above.

In the blackness of a stormbound night, all too often the only warning one gets of a rogue sea is the sickening roar it gives and the phosphorescent flash exuded by the anger of its tumbling crest. I was lucky to survive such an occurrence: safety line aside, if it hadn't been for my survival clothing, the sail cloth I used to wrap around me, and my ability to urinate warmth inside my suit, I probably would have died of exposure long before dawn.

Fear gives you strength – more strength than you can imagine. My situation was self-induced, but that didn't stop me from being determined to stay alive even in the worst of circumstances. At times I even shouted back at the wind and waves. If this was to degenerate into a fight, then Poseidon should know my little boat and I were prepared to fight with whatever we had, in whatever way we could. But, as crazy as such behaviour may seem, it stirred within me a spirit of survival and gave me psychological strength. Hearing the sound of your own voice can be a great stimulus in a desperate situation. Happily, having survived such near death realities aboard *Price of Fear* over the 54-day crossing, I have since undertaken a RIB voyage around Cape Horn which, as you might expect, presented challenges all of its own.

CONCLUSION

I am, of course, not the first to prove the feasibility of such a venture. Please don't think I wish to discourage anyone from repeating what I did, but I have to say that it was, in all seriousness, very difficult. If the equipment doesn't let you down, remember that your own disposition is vulnerable to weakness or failure – then again, you might just run out of luck. Everybody can find his or her own route to adventure, and this just happened to be mine.

(Translated by Andre Scott and rewritten from the original text by Hugo Montgomery-Swan.)

BOARDING VESSELS
IN ADVERSE
SEA STATES

BY PAUL HOLLANDER

*Paul Hollander, chief engineer and RIB specialist with
the Netherlands Coastguard and principal of Ribtact –
a company that provides craft consultancy and
training – here provides essential knowledge, gained
from his work in the professional arena, on the subject
of boarding vessels in adverse sea conditions.*

For the crews of the Netherlands Coastguard cutters and their rigid inflatables to be able to support the needs of both law-enforcing agencies and local SAR services, a versatile approach is needed. We've been fondly named the 'Pond Police', as we handle all things official in the comparatively shallow and often dangerous confines of the North Sea.

RIBs are key tools in our work. These highly versatile craft are often deployed offshore for transferring personnel to and from a wide variety of vessels, from SAR situations to boarding craft that are potentially hostile in nature. (We have been responsible for transferring SWAT teams onto craft known to be hostile.) In all such scenarios our policy is one of 'risk limitation'. However, in the case of hostile craft, this work ethic can be very difficult to maintain, as risks to both man and machine will inevitably run high.

In this chapter we will discuss some of the challenges faced and techniques employed by these cutter crews in launch-and-recovery situations, as well as the practice of boarding vessels in adverse sea states. The skills required are critical and demand a high degree of understanding of the hydrodynamic interaction between two fast-moving hulls working in close proximity to each other (called pacing). The coxswain's ability to employ these forces to his vessel's advantage is also crucial here.

To be able to pace vessels at higher speeds (sometimes in the region of at least 30 knots) our Coastguard crews have chosen to use davit-launched propeller-driven RIBs. This combination gives our parent vessel the advantage of being able to remain in pursuit or 'under steam' while only having to slow down for the 'unhooking' of the RIB as it comes into contact with the water.

LAUNCH AND RECOVERY

Our launch-and-recovery method is largely performed while steaming just a little faster than the sea in which we are operating. We have found that undertaking these procedures in following seas is preferable to that of a head sea scenario, while heading on a course across the wave direction means that the parent vessel's lateral stability is likely to be reduced. Hence, in a moderate-to-rough sea state, the activation of the ship's stabilisers may well be necessary to prevent a dangerous rolling motion that could jeopardise the auxiliary craft. Skilful and decisive use of the ship's throttles is, of course, paramount, as indeed is the need to position a competent lookout on the deck who can communicate directly with the bridge, either by voice alone or VHF.

When being launched, the RIB, crewed by two persons, is hydraulically swung overboard by means of a deck-mounted crane in little more than a few seconds. Held firmly in a hoisting block, the boat remains stable until lowered to within just a couple of feet above the actual wave tops. Timing and judgement are essential during this part of the procedure. Taking the remaining length of cable, the RIB is duly released from the no-load release hook upon settling in the water. Just before touching down, the engine, with its leg fully trimmed in, is started and then quickly put into gear the moment the hull is immersed. This technique relieves any undue strain on the painter and helps in quickly establishing independent headway.

I recall one occasion when the powering up of the RIB's engine was delayed and for some reason the painter became detached: before we knew it, the vessel had turned some ninety degrees to the mother ship. In an instant we found ourselves being dragged along the side of the ship's hull like a bailing bucket on the end of a lanyard! This failure to establish immediate forward power could have caused the loss of the RIB in question and potentially even the lives of those on board. Quick thinking saved the day, but it's not something I would wish to repeat.

As soon as the RIB's engine is fired and the RIB is making way, the strain/weight is off the painter, with the boat having been freed from the no-load release hook. The RIB now simply stays connected to a painter line while both vessels run side by side. This line is attached to a reinforced bow eye up in the vessel's forepeak, but via runners on a jib system aboard the parent vessel; this line can then be swung neatly in or out.

With an inboard-powered 'duo-propped' craft, or any well-propped RIB for that matter, the propeller's blades should bite quickly and without cavitation or ventilation occurring. Ventilation is where the propeller spins in its own pocket of air, something else that can cause a critical delay during this fast-moving launching procedure. Once the RIB is under power and the painter slackens, the crewman positioned on the RIB's foredeck is able to let the RIB go free by yanking down on the spinnaker hook. (For a well-trained crew, this entire procedure takes some 20 seconds.)

The very last element of this whole procedure is the loading of the boarding party, who jump aboard only when the RIB is under power and all lines are clear. This is for the simple reason that if things were to go wrong during the launch, only two people would be endangered, as opposed to an entire cargo of personnel! In addition, with just two people aboard while the launch procedure is undertaken, the dangers

Ship to ship operations is a skill all of its own, but here in the North Atlantic rendering aid to these offshore sailboarders requires careful timing and delicate but deliberate close quarter manoeuvring.
© Russ Keslake/RIB International archives

associated with poor weight distribution are kept at bay. In fact, a great deal of care and forward planning are given to ensure that the distribution of any weight is optimised for safe hoisting, particularly so when operating amidst difficult sea states.

This practice of launch and recovery is a reasonably calculable and safe affair up to a wind strength of force 8, Beaufort Scale. If carried out in wind strengths above this, other tactics need to be deployed to afford the auxiliary vessel a degree of lee from the prevailing wind and sea. This can be provided by the clever positioning of the mother vessel itself, perhaps a flotilla member, the relative sanctuary of a headland or sometimes even an isolated sand bar.

In the southern part of the North Sea, it is typically just the wind and current that create rough seas. In this sea area, easterly winds in the waters off the British coast whip up vicious seas that are exaggerated by the relatively shallow waters common to the region. Consequently, a

The mechanics of launch and recovery at work as seen from the deck of the mother vessel.
© *Paul Hollander*

high wind from any direction will quickly generate white water which may be made all the more perilous by the many sandbanks that lie off both the British and Continental North Sea coasts. Although they may provide a natural wave break in some circumstances, these infamous navigational hazards have caused the loss of much shipping over the years. Further north, however, towards Norway and the top of Scotland, storm swells issuing out of the Arctic regions may build over a much greater distance or fetch, and in deeper water too. Typically, then, vessels plying these more northerly latitudes are likely to encounter higher seas and larger groundswells than in the southern regions of the North Sea. Despite their size, however, ocean-orientated waves may be no more dangerous than their short, steep and often very confused counterparts. But in terms of undertaking launch-and-recovery procedures, large swells can understandably present increased challenges, requiring crews to call upon even greater skills of judgement and acute timing.

Like many disciplines at sea, successful launch-and-recovery procedures depend on all the elements involved working together in perfect harmony. Harmony in this case means: all vital equipment has been properly maintained and double-checked prior to use; the crew has been thoroughly trained, is fit and the drill has been understood by the helmsman and winchman as well as the actual RIB crew itself; all have to react simultaneously in their roles and, if things do go wrong, it's vital for everyone to understand their task or function; all must remain focused and resist the urge to act outside their discipline or routine. As the seas get rougher the stakes get higher, as does the likelihood of human error or gear failure.

PACING

The need for synergy is never greater than when pacing vessels in rough seas. In this scenario there's hardly time for any eye contact, so short, distinct commands are the order of the day. The cox should only give such commands, though, when he fully knows his intentions. Conversely, his boarding party will make the decision to transfer from the RIB to the intended vessel only when *they* judge the situation to be right.

Driving at higher speeds in adverse conditions also requires the impolite but seamanlike practice of not facing each other to speak. Whilst there is a strong need to remain wholly focused on the sea ahead and the ever-changing behaviour of its waves, it is also imperative to retain a proper perception of the vessel's true speed if a safe approach alongside another craft is to be executed. It's important that members of the boarding crew, who may be loaded with essential kit, remember to work with the rhythm of the boat. To do this, they, like the cox, need to read the sea ahead and anticipate its effect on the motion of the craft. A novice crewmember will be inclined to hold on too tight, brace himself too rigidly, and strain or injure his muscles in the process. 'Go with the flow' is a good motto to live by aboard a fast craft such as a RIB in a heavy seaway. By applying this rule, members of the boarding party will be in a suitable physical state to conduct their tasks effectively on the vessel they are seeking to board.

EXPECTING THE UNEXPECTED

In our line of work, an intended plan may have to change unexpectedly. The sea may become too strong, a hostile situation may be deemed too dangerous, or a breakdown may force an exercise to be aborted. To illustrate further, the plan may have been to collect the boarding team in the usual manner by means of a standard reboarding routine; however, on some occasions, perhaps because those on the vessel boarded have become dangerously hostile, the boarding team may decide that it is safer for them to jump over the side of the ship to be picked up from the water. This is not an altogether unlikely event in our line of work. To simulate this latter situation, it is essential for these teams to be thoroughly practised in swimming at sea in full kit. Such rehearsals should also be made realistic in nature and not simply confined to a summer's day in settled conditions. Rather, each man needs to understand first-hand how to cope with the effects of cold-water shock and the feeling of disorientation, and know how to activate his various life-saving devices with cold hands in a testing sea state. Unless such personnel learn how to be both at ease and orientated within the real environment, their operational abilities will be limited, as will their survival capabilities. This principle of rehearsing even basic procedures aboard a boat is something everyone who goes to sea should take to heart. It can save your life.

High-speed boardings in adverse sea states require the total trust of the crew in their cox and navigator. In turn, the cox and navigator must understand their crew's physical and mental state when operating in heavy weather. The crew's ability to move and think quickly and with split-second timing, not only throughout the passage but also during the boarding process, will be critical. A cox should be able to recognise the telltale signs of a crewmember in trouble, perhaps noting his unease, discomfort or fear. If these problems become apparent within the team, the cox might need to seriously consider

Keeping the shoulder of the craft in, and with positive power applied, the crew are ready to disembark. © Paul Hollander

aborting the operation, or at least getting the crewman in question back on the mother ship without delay before returning to the exercise.

TRAINING

The extent to which a crew can be trained in adverse conditions depends on (a) their personal suitability and capability; (b) the degree of safety cover available; and (c) the limitations of their company's health-and-safety charter. A team member must be inclined towards this line of work. Employers must select crewmembers wisely. In all training instances I recommend role play and the interchanging of duties, for example, letting others take the helm and having the cox undertake a boarding whilst trusting in someone else's driving capabilities. This training routine works wonders for the building of empathy and mutual respect among the team as a whole.

COMING ALONGSIDE

Throughout the boarding process, good technique and an understanding of the forces at play are essential for any coxswain. The task is made difficult by the fact that the weight and speed of a ship underway create energy in the water and, as the laws on the conversion of energy prove, energy cannot be destroyed: it can only be changed from one form to another. In the marine environment, the form this energy takes, of course, is that of waves, and in the case of a large vessel moving through the water at speed, these waves, collectively known as wash, then have to interact with the dominant sea state. The result can be chaos: a very confused sea, as each energy front appears to fight for supremacy with its opposite number. In the midst of this, the approaching RIB has to negotiate its way right into the most dramatic part of the maelstrom in order to offload its human cargo.

In rough conditions, the effect a ship's wash can have on the surrounding sea will require the RIB's cox to constantly recalculate his tactics. To illustrate: imagine you're closing in on a large vessel; whilst reading the waves and choosing your optimum moment, the ship you're coming alongside climbs a rearing wave, only to then smash its full tonnage down into the trough beyond. At that very moment its kinetic energy is passed on, down into the water, thus instantaneously forming additional waves of great energy in the process. If you are sweeping in towards the side of the vessel on a long approach, before coming about to make your final run-in, you might meet such a wave broadside. If, on the other hand, you had the time and were quick enough to respond by turning the RIB's head direct to the wave, you would likely be placing yourself in a much less vulnerable position and on a much safer angle to the breaking wave. However, this temporary change of course would then require a new angle of approach to be established, and quickly too, to ensure the final process of coming alongside does not have to be aborted.

Depending on sea states, these energy-loaded waves can morph into short, steep-sided rogue waves without a moment's notice, and this can make the final run-in, not to mention the actual offloading of personnel, very difficult. In a critical situation this is done by making your approach from the stern away from the propeller wash, before coming alongside the vessel behind its bow wave, ensuring that the two boats maintain a small distance between them.

When a ship's course is upwind, its motion and the boarding craft's vertical movements will often be out of synch with each other. This is when approaches become complicated and dangerous. Weighing the risk is important in such instances before making a commitment in rough seas. I will add, a helicopter's downdraught can be of great assistance in getting the attention of a so-called 'ignorant' ship's crew; this could be used to divert a hostile crew's attention, and allow for a surprise boarding.

BOARDING

As you can imagine, boarding crew have to use acute timing when choosing their moment to jump, particularly in heavy seas when this should be done as the RIB is still rising to a crest. At this point it is important for the cox to keep the RIB even keeled and watch for the right combination of waves and ship movement so as to judge correctly that split second when each person can make their move, one at a time. This could necessitate making several passes, but it is crucial not to consider a jump when the RIB is rising too high alongside the hull of the ship. Once the seas are taking the RIB up to the same height as the ship's guardrails, the boarding craft will be approaching a significant danger zone. Furthermore, if the RIB is lifted higher than the deck of the approached vessel, on its way down the likelihood of its sponson getting damaged on guardrails or gunwales, even snagging or being caught up and rolled over, could be very high.

A common mistake on a transfer approach is to steer at too great an angle towards the ship's hull in an effort to 'comfort' the transfer, but this will only serve to expose the topside of your hull to even greater masses of water that will strike the boat on its beam. Additionally, with forward movement being prevented, in this position the boarding craft will be made extremely vulnerable. On the other hand, when steering parallel to a ship, the craft will not only be better balanced but will also have an escape route open to it. If you have the opportunity to watch the movements of the vessel you're seeking to come alongside, try to figure out the position of its 'pivot point'. This is the area of hull with the least movement. If suction and wake permit you to make your final approach at this point, this is also the safest place to be if the ship veers or rolls unexpectedly. Ideally, when approaching smaller planing craft, and depending on the hull of the ship, the best place to come alongside at speed might be about two-thirds back from the bow (the 'pivot point'), behind its bow wave.

In any event, it's always wise to try to approach on the lee side of a vessel, and with regular boardings we often direct the skipper to alter course to aid our coming alongside. Occasionally, we pull alongside those who do not wish us to board and therefore either ignore us or seek to be evasive. When people need to be rescued, not surprisingly they comply with all our requests unless fear prevents them from doing so. In every situation, even where seconds count in a life-saving scenario, a boarding-craft cox must take care not to rush a manoeuvre. This is where professional training and a cool head pay dividends.

In instances where one is unable to gain the assistance of the ship's skipper, it becomes even more vital for the RIB cox to be knowledgeable of hull types and their various behavioural characteristics. Though I only use prop-driven, Z-drive and outboard craft, different hull forms and propulsion types will necessitate different methods of approach. Similarly, with the RIB itself, however it is powered, all variations will require very different techniques and have their own helming sensitivities and peculiarities. In our line of work, where pressure differences, aerated/foaming water and the effects of suction rule, the stakes are high and the margin for error is very small. Good steerage, therefore, produced by sufficient power, suitable trim and a propeller that is not inclined to cavitate (ie a five-bladed stainless steel prop), as well as an engine that does not suffer from turbo diesel lag, are all essential ingredients for undertaking successful boarding exercises.

With a high-speed planing craft such as a RIB, it can all go wrong, however, if the boat you are seeking to transfer crew onto is travelling too slowly for the RIB to maintain steerage – particularly in a following sea. A flat transom, big tubes/sponsons, shallow draught and steerage that's dependent upon the application of power all make for a vulnerable combination in this situation. This I found to be the case with a beam trawler I was seeking to get crew onto in a force 7 Beaufort. After having negotiated our way around its cables, I came to the stern of the vessel, only to experience a following sea lifting us from the stern, whereupon we lost steerage and shoved the RIB's soft nose section into the stern of the vessel. The nose section had been kept soft on purpose, to maximise its shock-absorbing advantage during a wave-training session prior to the incident.

All appeared well, though, following this minor incident, until later that day when the boat was recovered: I noticed a half-inch crack in the Hypalon reinforcing strip of the RIB's sponson. I thought nothing of it at the time, not until later that same day on another run out into the strengthening conditions, where we stuffed a wave and the sponson peeled off the bow and over the top of the console like the supersprung 'lid' of a cabriolet! I throttled back, and thankfully the boat popped back up again, though the decks were awash. After making headway again with a severely trimmed-up leg, the shipped water quickly drained out over the transom and through the big trunks. Running with the waves, we were able to limp back to the mother vessel with sheepish looks on our bedraggled faces! The lesson learnt here was surely: any impact damage, no matter how small, should be inspected thoroughly before putting to sea again. When it comes to preventative maintenance, leave nothing to chance. (With big RIBs weighing in at several tons or more, some RIB builders add a webbing strop fastened from the bow eye on the vessel's stem to a heavy-duty through-hull mooring cleat up in the forepeak. This can be a useful addition to negate the massive shock loadings imposed upon the bow section of an inflated RIB tube.)

BEYOND NAVIGATION

Being a RIB cox also demands an understanding of navigation, as well as the various sea types that can be encountered offshore, for example, the mouths of estuaries, where the interaction between tides and river flow can cause areas of extreme breaking seas as well as surf lines over sand bars. Other common phenomena, such as overfalls and tide rips that may even move their position off a headland depending on the prevailing wind and tide, must also be understood. Therefore, navigation does not mean simply being able to plot a course on a nautical chart: it means understanding the correlation between chart information and the realities of the environment itself. The latter is derived from experience but, even if you are a professional mariner, truly extreme sea states are pretty rare. So the ability to draw upon previous experiences and apply this knowledge to fresh scenarios, calculating estimated risks and difficulties from all the information sources at your disposal, is fundamental to successful navigation at sea.

In conclusion, no cox should ever allow a love of danger to influence his attitude towards his work and the professional role he performs. He should learn to be at peace with the elements, understanding the make-up of their forces and his functions in relation to them.

Approaching the stern in a heavy sea state. A steady nerve is key to a safe and successful outcome – as is an understanding of the conflicting forces at play in such close proximity to the mother vessel. © Paul Hollander

HIGH-SPEED RACING TECHNIQUES

BY NEIL HOLMES

Neil Holmes, seven times Powerboat Racing World Champion and leading high-speed instructor, discusses in detail the skills and techniques employed by powerboat helmsmen driving craft at speeds in excess of 50 knots.

In my role as a powerboat racing instructor, I have a saying when it comes to driving boats at speed in rough waters: 'If you can see the sky, trim in; if you can see cod, trim out!' What I mean by this, of course, is: if your boat is pointing skywards, trim its nose in; if it's pointing down in the direction of the seabed, trim it out – quickly! It might be simplistic, but getting the angle of attack right, especially in a difficult seaway when the driver is pushing his boat to the limit, is nothing short of critical.

There are many instances where going faster can actually smooth out the ride aboard a planing craft. Nonetheless, to do this you need to be fully conversant with sea types and conditions, as well as what skills are needed to get the best out of the boat and its rig. In terms of high-performance driving, what a helmsman is really seeking to achieve is for his boat to be able to glance off the waves in a rhythmical and consistent fashion – as opposed to running spasmodically, landing in a big ball of spray every tenth trough or so. Understanding such things as trim, therefore, and how it can be achieved, is essential to the process of successful wave negotiation. An erratic or indecisive driving style can result in a boat being brought to a shuddering stop, where injury and damage to crew and boat are likely to be suffered.

Trim and rhythm are two factors we shall explore in some detail within this chapter but while reading, note how different the techniques are to those required on the part of SAR helmsmen, for example, operating raft at relatively slow speeds. Suffice to say, the skill sets required, though needing equal degrees of expertise and understanding, are in truth wholly different. Just to be clear, in this particular chapter at least, when we speak of 'high speed' we mean a typical speed in excess of 50 knots. From here to the top-end racing speed of 130mph, there exists a very different world, a world where, depending on hull types, opposites truly rule.

But to begin this process of understanding, and thus develop the necessary skills required, we first need to analyse whether our boat is really capable of travelling at speed in rough conditions.

HULL SUITABILITY

The size and length of boat, its bow shape, hull design and type all play a big part in the way in which seas can be negotiated at high speed. Monohulls are probably better known for dealing very much more ably with short, sharp seas than their catamaran counterparts. A narrow mono with a fine entry bow should be more efficient in a head sea, due to its ability to slice through the waves and therefore be less likely to go skyward. Though perhaps an unusual example to cite, just consider the semiwave-piercing battleship hulls of the First World War period. Their fine entry profile allowed them to slice through the sea at wholly contemporary big-ship speeds with very little chaotic lift to their forward section of hull. Although they may not have been planing craft, their fine bow design afforded them key attributes in terms of head sea performance and sea-kindly motion. On the other hand, craft with the fuller bow of a beamier monohull design, such as the type employed by the performance-orientated Vosper Thorneycroft semi-displacement Torpedo boats of the 1940s, were not only very efficient speed machines, but were also very good sea boats for their size. Their bows provided impressive recovery in following sea states thanks to the inherent forward buoyancy found in the fuller, often more flared design, of their forward section.

Even in the designing of modern high-speed hulls, certain key attributes pertaining to the historical monohull examples just described remain highly relevant. In simple terms, when it comes to hydrodynamic performance, shape relates to speed, and getting the right shape to generate the optimum result at any single point along the hull is where the elusive art of naval architecture lies. Men like Lorne Cambell, Fabio Buzzi and Ocke Mannefelt are masters of this science.

Catamarans seem to have a reputation for not performing particularly well in rough seas, but as in the case of monohulls there are, of course, differing types of designs and some will perform better than others. My boat *Fina Unleaded*, for example, which I raced during the 1990s, was a 26ft 4-litre offshore 'cat' designed for UK waters, meaning it had to be capable of dealing with the testing and often varying sea states found around our UK coastline. One particular instance of a catamaran dealing better with rough water than its monohull counterpart was during a race off Guernsey in the late 80s. I had the opportunity to go 'head to head' with one of the best monohull racers of the time in very rough conditions amidst the island's tide-ripped waters; in fact, the seas were so rough that curtailment of the championship race was always going to be on the cards that weekend. But after a few persuasive words with the officer of the day, we were assured our long-awaited battle of 'mono versus cat' would not be quashed – despite the weather.

During the first lap both boats ran alongside each other, pretty much like for like. However, it wasn't long before I realised I wouldn't be able to keep this pace up for very much longer: the pain was simply too great. So at the end of the second lap I chose to do the opposite to what my instincts told me. I opened up my throttles and pressed on past my adversary with all due venom.

It became apparent to me that going at my previously slower speed caused my boat to fall into virtually all the 'gaps' or troughs the sea could offer. On the other hand, going faster allowed the vessel to get on top of the sea and glance its way over the crests – one to the other. It took a degree of nerve to get this technique established over the first few peaks and troughs and the slams these afforded me, but the effect of this driving style quickly transformed the craft's performance and the ride in general. The monohull did attempt to keep up but failed in its efforts, either through design or handling, and was consequently outdone by both my catamaran and the day's severe conditions.

After I won the race by some considerable margin, the battered monohull driver walked over, shook me by the hand and said, 'You won, Neil, but how the heck did you do that in a cat...?' Though I didn't consider it appropriate at the time to tell him, the reason why my boat fared so well in the adverse seas was the fact that it had especially good balance in flight. This allowed me to jump much larger 'gaps' or troughs than my adversary aboard his monohull.

As technology has improved over the years, hull shapes and designs have also radically evolved. If someone comes forward with a catamaran design that outperforms a monohull, its vee hull designers will simply go back to their drawing boards and produce a better mono... until today, when technology is so far advanced you can, with a big enough cheque book, get 'cats' to beat 'monos' in the rough, and 'monos' to be faster than 'cats' in the flat! Roles can indeed be reversed...as crazy as that may sound to someone with a traditional nautical knowledge.

Multihulls also have the reputation of being less stable, stem to stern, than their monohull counterparts. But again, I recall one particular rough-water racing season when monohulls turned or flipped over in a whole variety of circumstances – outdoing their supposedly flighty 'cat cousins' by ten to one! Such a result was brought on by the monohulls being pushed beyond their operational limits in an effort to keep pace with their multihull, race-bred alternatives.

There is little advantage in trying to drive fast in rough seas if the boat and its crew are not capable of taking the impacts and shock loadings. When it comes to driving boats beyond the limits of normal leisure use, the craft in question should either be race proven or at least a well-tried, high-performance thoroughbred. In either case, these vessels will be very much more able than a high-powered pleasure boat to cope with the real challenges of speed and adverse sea states. The former type will possess a huge degree of detail throughout its structure, specific to the demands it will be subjected to during a race – where punishment to both man and machine are the order of the day.

One key difference between the standard planing craft and its true racing counterpart is the fact that the race boat is designed to be driven in such a way as to spend most of its time airborne! This fundamental contrast in the way these different planing hulls operate means that the racing driver's techniques will be wholly at odds with the RYA's directives, as contained in its Powerboat Level Two programme, for example. In competitive race driving you want as little of the hull in the water as possible, for a wetted hull constitutes unwanted drag. Another difference that emphasises the contrast between traditional helming and race driving is that at racing speeds, to back the throttle off, perhaps when approaching a ferry wash, would be the very last thing a race driver would think of doing, as decelerating would have the effect of destabilising his hull's dynamics.

Once again, it is opposites at work here, and understanding these forms the very basis of successful high-speed helming. I should also say that unless the throttleman has not only worked out how to literally fly his craft through the seas, and by extension also learnt how to land it safely, his position on the winner's podium will be a rare spectacle.

So, with such thoughts in mind, let us consider the all-important matter of trim devices designed to enable the driver to get the very best out of his waterborne 'flying machine'.

USE OF TRIM AIDS

If you have all the potential required for driving quickly through rough water, but fail to understand how to use the boat and its vital systems to their optimum, then at the very least helming a high-performance craft will prove a frustrating business. Power trim, engine lifter, trim tabs, bow tanks, flood tanks and fuel transfer are all essential aids to driving in adverse conditions. Power trim or engine drive moves the engine trim in and out, making the bow of the boat go up or down, thus altering its angle of attack. The engine lifter will move the engine's thrust line up and down, which will also move the bow up and down and can affect the 'push off' from the crest of the wave. Trim tabs, when used in unison, can help keep the bow down, 'lengthening' the hull, or, used individually, can even lift either side of the boat. Bow tanks, filled or partially filled, will help keep the bow down by adding weight to the boat's forward section and in so doing alter the boat's centre of gravity. (I have known many racing drivers who have complained of loss of speed, blaming the engine's poor power output, only to discover they had 100 litres of water left in the bow tank, thus making the boat 5 miles an hour slower than it should otherwise have been!)

Flood/ballast tanks, filled or partially filled on the centre of gravity, will add to the weight of the boat, enabling more hull to stay in the water, and assist in increasing the boat's stability. Fuel transfer will alter the vessel's centre of gravity by moving the weight of the fuel forward or rearward, but of course won't add any additional weight to the boat, as in the case of flood tanks.

All of the above can be of massive benefit, of course, when used correctly; conversely, when applied incorrectly, such mechanical aids have the ability to make your in-flight entertainment truly terrifying! But in essence, regardless of the aids at your disposal, what you're really trying to achieve is for your boat to travel over the uneven surface of the sea with a level, safe flight projectorary.

Most performance boats are rear trimmed for maximum speed; all the goodies fitted on the boat thereafter are to keep the bow down and achieve more control and handling, particularly in the rough. There is little point in having lots of pretty gauges on your dash if you have no idea what they are for; hence, it's vital that you are able to recognise such things as level trim and your neutral tab setting. Furthermore, the faster you go, the more effect power trim and all the other trimming devices will have on the boat.

SEA CONDITIONS

Reading the sea is one of the most important skills you will need in your driver's skill set. But remember, waves are not just lumps of water in your way; they are moving and changing shape all the time. If you are unable to read the waves you will also find it very difficult to judge how the boat will respond when it hits them at speed. An important element in becoming proficient in driving at speed through rough water is to understand wave types and their patterns, along with what each is going to require from the man at the wheel.

Firstly, wave patterns are very different when encountered at the entrance to, say, an estuary or harbour mouth than those found in open waters or large bays. The former will tend to be confused in form, with little in the way of a predictable pattern to either their make-up or their continuity. Where waves are rebounding off a cliff line, the ride could be likened to driving through a low-level mountain range of pyramid-shaped seas that appear to have no order to their behaviour. Overfalls and tide rips can produce isolated breakers and lines of surf that can make navigation decisions complex. Extraordinary rock features on the seabed can cause whirlpools and 'boiling' water phenomena. All such wave and sea types can be encountered when racing, but for now, let's look at the more fundamental forms and how these should be negotiated.

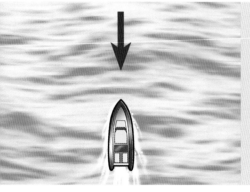

Head Sea (waves coming towards you)

These will throw or lift the bow of the boat skyward, and depending on their frequency and size, you will need to alter your driving techniques accordingly, ie moderating the vessel's speed, trimming its bow down etc.

Following Sea (waves running away from you)

This will make the bow of your boat want to land nose first and thus continue its downward momentum. The latter trend is interrupted by the hull's hydrodynamic lift.

Beam Sea (waves coming side on)

This will make your boat roll from side to side and push you off course accordingly. This is the most difficult sea type to steer in, as it demands constant adjustment and course correction.

Head Quartering Sea (waves coming towards you but at 45 degree angle)

These seas are also inclined to send the bow of the vessel skyward at speed – twisting the boat in the air as she goes.

Following Quartering Sea (waves at 45 degree angle to the boat's stern)

These will make the bow nosedive and can cause a severe twisting in the boat's motion.

These are the most common sea conditions, although there are many more factors to add to the equation when determining your driving techniques: for example, the distance between the waves. If the waves are close enough together and your boat can bridge several of them at one time, their crests will support the boat's hull. Relatively speaking, it wouldn't matter if the waves were 6 inches high or 6 feet high: if there's enough of them underneath you and your forward momentum is sufficient, then flying from crest to crest will be much more advantageous than climbing a crest and surfing down its long side.

It stands to reason that if the waves are distanced a little farther apart, it becomes more difficult to bridge the troughs and therefore maintain a high speed. In addition and further to my comment above, I will point out that size, of course, does matter – in the sense that if you get the crest-to-crest 'flying' technique wrong in a big sea, the repercussions will be much more severe than when undertaking this driving technique in a short, sharp chop. First, a more detailed discussion about how to drive in these various sea types and conditions will be useful.

DRIVING IN A HEAD SEA

Imagine that you are running in calm water at level trim and then start heading into a choppy, short head sea. The sun is shining through the cockpit canopy, your spirits are up and you've just turned the second seaward turn buoy to find yourself at the front of the pack! Now, there are several options available to you as you seek to maintain your lead, depending on what your boat is equipped with. You could trim the engine in, helping to keep the bow down and thus enabling you to keep your speed without the boat becoming too flighty. You could also set both trim tabs to the level setting and thus increase the length of the boat, which will also stop the bow rising. Adding water to the bow tank will hold the nose down, and this is another excellent option at your disposal. But then again, adding water as ballast will increase the weight of your boat and potentially make it slower. Using the trim tabs will also increase the drag, which may again affect your speed, but altering the engine power trim may only add a minimal degree of extra wetted area to the hull's surface – thereby detrimentally affecting your speed to the least extent.

Optimum angle of attack achieved here by this stepped hulled race boat.
*© **Keith Slater***

You're still holding that pole position, maybe by only a small margin, but you're fighting the competition off, despite the flying spray smacking the screen and the sun dazzling your eyes. 'I can't believe it,' you think to yourself. At that moment you quickly glance at the leaping instrumental panel just left of the wheel to note that your speed is now touching a full 60 knots. Sweat is pouring down your cheeks and the sweet scent of high-octane fuel fills your nostrils. As the head sea becomes larger, fiercer still, you now need greater use of the boat's trim tabs and her bow tank if you're to keep her running level.

You are aware, however, that there is a limit to how hard this particular boat likes to be trimmed amidst such conditions. Your single-engine outboard 'charger', with its excessive negative trim angle, tends to list badly on its port side because of the outboard's high prop torque. This makes the whole rig feel unstable, and based upon your experience in the previous race two weeks before, when a wave slapped the flat of your port chine so hard it nearly blew your teeth out, you quickly adjust the leg of the engine back out in order to restore equilibrium.

'Tabs will help keep your boat glued to the water in rough seas.' The words of your mentor and coach ring in your ears. 'If excessive tab is used when you take off from wave to wave, the tabs lose contact with the sea's surface and become ineffective.' 'Shut up!' you rudely tell yourself. 'Any more of this classroom banter entering my headspace and I'll lose the spontaneity that got me in front in the first place!' And at that very moment, a flash of red through the plume of spray off your starboard side confirms that your closest challenger is about to steal your lead.

These conditions are ripe for the classic 'trip and stuff' accident. You've learnt through your practice sessions that the greater the speed the more effect the trim systems have on the craft. In fact, aboard this boat they become surprisingly sensitive, so a moment's heavy-handedness on the trim switch could result in the boat taking an almighty headlong plunge into the foot of an oncoming sea. The thought scares you but heightens your senses at the same time. Your response is to force your nerves further still to do the opposite of what your instincts scream at you: you keep the power firmly applied and grit your teeth!

Back ashore, your coach is hoping that you won't be tempted to fill the bow tank to its maximum – a case of a bit more and a bit more, until it's spewing out of the overflow. This would dramatically alter the boat's centre of gravity, even when travelling through the air between crest tops. He will appreciate that excessive movement of the centre of gravity could cause the boat to clip the top off the next wave, or worse still, cause it to dive on its nose into a wall of green water; he's hoping you remember this pertinent fact too…!

This brief foray into the realm of the cockpit shows the need on the part of the driver to strike a balance between classroom technique, human instinct and 'feel', the latter being something that can only be acquired through hours of practice and having a natural inclination toward the subject matter. Also, the need to understand the controls at your disposal and a certain sensitivity towards their use are vital in order for the boat's systems to be operated to their optimum.

All the techniques I talk about here require practice and experience, so if, for example, you are constantly trying to look over the bow while it points skywards, it means you need to learn how to react faster to the conditions. That means getting out there and practising even more. But if you thought that the foregoing was complicated, now try your hand at doing the same, but from the opposite direction.

DRIVING IN A FOLLOWING SEA

So now you know how to drive in a head sea, what do you need to do differently when driving in a following sea? At speed, this next sea type will make you feel like you're driving down a staircase with the bow dropping away beneath your feet! First make sure your bow tank is empty and your tabs are up, then trim your engine slightly out from level – this should then lift the bow of the boat and curtail its bow-down attitude. How large these waves are, and how fast you're travelling, should ultimately determine how far you should be trimmed out. Excessive trimming out will make the bow rise far too high and increase the potential for a 'trip and stuff'. The boat's flightiness will also cause it to lose its foothold on the surface of the sea. If the top of the wave is spraying your face, or if the bow of the boat drops below your eye line, trim out!

DRIVING IN A BEAM SEA

A beam sea is probably the one most novice boaters dread the most. It can be quite off-putting to see large waves coming towards your vessel sideways on! In big seas, this sea type can make the crew feel quite vulnerable. The knack to driving in these conditions is to have a policy of 'changing lane'. Neutral trim and balance can be achieved if you follow the bottom of the wave trough, although unless you actually want to go in the direction the waves are heading, this tactic is not advisable! Therefore, at some point you will need to jump over to the next 'lane', a technique that can be done in a number of ways.

The preferred method would be to put negative trim on the engine, aim towards the wave (making sure the boat is back on the hull), then, at the top of the wave, flick the wheel and the throttle simultaneously – you should then land neat and tidy in the next trough or lane. Simple! This method can be used to devastating effect in a race, but I would only recommend you try this if you are totally confident of your capabilities. If you're not up to this more advanced helming technique, I would suggest that you just drop your speed and coast over the sea – a much safer option.

DRIVING IN A HEAD QUARTERING SEA

The technique of driving in a head quartering sea is similar to that of a head sea: you need to stop the bow from lifting too greatly, either by trimming the engine in or by filling the bow tank, or a combination of the two. Because this type of sea will want to twist the craft in the air, you will need to hit the wave with the bow as opposed to letting it hit you, thus neutralizing the effect it has on twisting the boat in the process. This is done by turning into the wave at the very last second before quickly straightening the wheel to ensure the boat lands level.

I must point out, however, that if you turn too soon the balance will be affected, and as you start to straighten the wheel, the wave will twist you over. If, on the other hand, you turn too late, the wave will have already twisted you.

Another way to avoid this problem, depending on the size of the waves, is to lower the trim tab on the opposite side to where the wave will be coming from, thus effectively holding that side of the hull up against the same wave that's trying to push the vessel over. This will create more drag and slow your progress by several knots, but it will help the boat hugely to run level.

DRIVING IN FOLLOWING QUARTERING SEAS

In following quartering seas you will need to work at stopping the bow from dropping too greatly. So you'll need to ensure the bow tank is empty, that the engine is trimmed out from level, then just as the boat is about to leave the water, flick the steering wheel

Punching through the crest at speed delivers a dramatic cascade of spray and broken water. If the prop continues to bite, the loss of speed will be temporary and minimal. © Keith Slater

in the direction of the wave you are just about to leave, ie if it's a port quartering sea turn the wheel to port. Make sure, though, that the wheel is straight for landing. You could also use the opposite trim tab, ie when port quartering use starboard tab, but this will depend on wave height.

DRIVING SKILLS

PROP TORQUE

A twin-engine monohull jumping over waves will give you neutral thrust due to the counterrotation of its propellers, but a single-engine installation with only one prop will have a tendency to twist in the air due to its prop torque. You can counteract this by flicking some right-hand down on the helm just as you leave the wave, then straightening the wheel before you land. As with all these techniques, timing is everything, so if the boat doesn't 'jump' in the air, it's you that has upset its balance and direction. If you do it after you've jumped you could make the twisting action even worse. From a timing perspective, then, this rapid correction needs to be applied just as the prop leaves the water. Just how much 'flick' you give the wheel will depend on wind, waves and the speed at which you're travelling.

In perfect flight, just as the author describes in this chapter. © Pascoe International

TRIP AND STUFF

The well-known 'trip and stuff' accident is caused by the bow being trimmed too high. The boat then flies bow up, only to then stall in mid air while still travelling forward. Landing transom first, the boat is next thrown bow forward to have its stern kicked up. This violent action causes the bow to plunge under the water – often with serious consequences. The antidote to this mishap involves applying full power. Again, this will likely be the opposite to what your instincts tell you, but this response will assist in holding up the front section of the boat upon landing, or cause you to actually drive through the wave and emerge the other side – hopefully in one piece!

LARGER WAVES

As the waves get bigger you will have to adjust your degree of trim dramatically, employing, perhaps, more than one trimming device at the same time. This could be your only means of maintaining those winning speeds. And remember, to derive ultimate performance in a rough sea state, the conditions will necessitate that you adjust the trim continuously. The sea's surface inshore will change every half mile or so thanks to coastal tide rips, eddies and overfalls. Travelling at speed means these differing sea conditions will probably come upon you in quick succession. Therefore, the need to adjust to them is likely to become a constant process during the course of a race, and this can become very fatiguing mentally as well as physically. Big seas increase the stakes significantly, and besides the skill of the driver, much will depend upon the nature of the boat's set-up and its actual design suitability to rough water.

SETTING UP THE BOAT FOR LARGER SEAS

As soon as you make the assessment that your boat will not be able to bridge the waves sufficiently for it to be supported, and that jumping from crest to crest is simply not a viable option, it is time to employ a new technique.

With this in mind, you will now have to set your boat up and adjust your driving technique to meet the wave in such a way as to effect a clean jump followed by a smart landing. At speed, getting any one of these wrong can seriously damage your bank balance...not to mention your health! This is driving right on the edge. Therefore, when driving towards a wave at high speed you need to make a judgement as to exactly what speed it can be safely leapt over. This judgement should be made based upon your own experience and capabilities, the length of your boat, its power size and type, and the balance of the craft itself. For example, if you know your boat is not well balanced, don't go hurtling into a wave at full bore expecting the boat alone to look after you. If the crest of the wave is particularly steep, try quickly trimming in to stop the bow going 'moon shot'. When you reach the top of the crest you will need to stop the bow raising any more, so just before take-off, fleetingly snap the throttle back and then reapply. This instantaneous deceleration should keep your flight projectory straight and level, and thus prevent the boat from making a life-threatening ascent.

Conversely, though, backing off too much at this juncture will make you jump over the wave, only to land on the flat face of the next sea or in a heap within its trough. (Better get your head down if you make this error of judgement because it's going to hurt!) But get the timing right and you will land beautifully level with the transom touching just before the rest of the hull makes impact with the water's surface. Feel is a difficult thing to teach when learning an art, and high-speed driving is no less an art than playing an instrument well or riding a horse at competition level.

ENGINE LIFTERS

These can adjust the thrust line of the engine on the boat and, depending on where you move them, can have several different results. Putting the lifter down can give the prop more bite, which in turn can also raise the bow. On the other hand, raising the lifter can give you more speed, as there is reduced drag on the gear case – and it will also help the boat lift further out of the water. Adjustments with this device can raise or lower the bow in the way of fine-tuning the boat's angle of attack. Depending on how high you can get the 'thrust line', it is possible to help hold the bow down if the correct setting is achieved. Be careful, though, because excessive height could affect the engine's cooling system and, if set too high, the prop will also lose its grip. This will result in the nose of the boat dropping and its speed being slowed in the process. In other words, you will have overdone it!

FLOOD TANKS

Positioned on the centre of gravity (when filled), these will increase the vessel's weight and help keep her more stable in confused or choppy waters, where she would normally be thrown around. The effect these tanks can have in steadying the boat's movements help, too, in aiding the helmsman to hold a course amidst such seas.

MOVING FUEL

This is another way of adjusting the trim and balance of a boat, but without adding any more actual weight or ballast. Of course, as fuel is used throughout a race, its use will dramatically shift the boat's centre of gravity. To compensate for this effect and cleverly use the fuel load to maximum advantage, fuel can be pumped around the boat to separate tanks below deck in order to optimise the payload in relation to the performance of the craft.

RULES TO REMEMBER

Prop and flywheel torque will affect the stability of your craft whilst in mid-air between crests. To illustrate: if you open the bonnet of your car and rev the engine in neutral, you can see the engine twist slightly within the engine bay. This, too, is what occurs to your boat's engine when in flight between crests. To avoid the problems associated with prop and flywheel torque, it's important that the throttle is not used in an erratic fashion, as this will cause the boat to twist even more severely, upsetting its balance and its rhythm in the process.

More power lifts the bow, propels the hull forward and increases the length of a jump; less power drops the bow, changes the running angle of the hull and shortens the jump. Either of these can be used to your advantage but, as always, timing is everything. The words 'don't back off' don't mean 'accelerate', they mean 'sustain the throttle

The prop is just 'kissing' the water, but the bow is flying a little high. Trimming in might be the answer here. © Keith Slater

setting you already have'. Many times during training sessions I will tell a client not to back off, perhaps when approaching a large ferry wash, which is a frequent occurrence in our local waters of the Solent. As we mentioned at the outset of this chapter, it's an automatic reaction for most people to want to dump the power just before the critical moment the boat strikes the wave. But doing so in a finely tuned race boat can result in it becoming even more unsettled and out of step. Quickly reducing power alters the balance of the boat and its mechanically maintained stability, which at very high speed is held through the vessel's continual forward momentum. (This situation is different to the heavy-sea scenario described above. Here we are talking about an isolated wave incident.) Sustained speed equals sustained balance as well as surefootedness in the craft, and smooth throttling is the very core of good high-speed technique.

As I said, to drive a performance or race boat fast you need the hull to have as little contact with the water as possible, as opposed to the RYA Powerboat Certificate's requirement to keep it in the water. The reason for this is simple: air is 800 times less dense than water, so the more your hull is in the air, the less drag your boat will suffer. Balancing a monohull on 50% of a 12.5cm diameter gear case, with 15cm of the propeller left in the water and only a 36cm x 18cm cavitation plate, takes a bit of

This race boat appears to have been seriously slowed in its progress by this untimely but dramatic landing. © Keith Slater

practice, and that's before you start leaping over high seas. It's a bit like trying to balance a 7-metre plank on a football!

The faster you go, the more you have to look further ahead. For example, at 70mph you will be travelling at 102 feet per second; it is almost pointless looking at the sea 10 feet in front of the bow, for this will leave you with a reaction time of only one tenth of a second to make any adjustment. A driver new to true high speeds has to learn how to think and judge distance very differently to typical leisure-orientated speeds in the region of 55 miles an hour. If your boat is travelling at 60mph, which is very fast for most boats and an average speed for a performance boat, when you hit the wave you will be flying at 88 feet per second. If you only stay in the air for one and a half seconds you will potentially jump 132 feet before you 'land' or re-enter the water. Even taking into account your loss of propulsion upon leaving the water, you're still going to land 100 feet beyond your take-off point. Now start to go really fast, let's say 135mph. That's a potential jump of an astonishing 198 feet! So when your mate says, 'My dad's performance car is so much faster than your 80mph powerboat,' ask him if he thinks it might be capable of travelling across the equivalent of a roughly ploughed field at full speed, hitting 4ft furrows in its path, that send it leaping 117ft through the air, only to land at full RPM with the engine screaming for mile after gruelling mile. If the answer is 'yes', shake the young man by the hand and do him the honour of offering to witness his final will and testament!

CANOPY ADVICE

Don't think sitting behind a canopy makes the job of driving a fast boat easier. It doesn't. The concept of fitting a canopy is solely to protect the crew from the impact of water in a rapid submerge incident (see 'Trip and Stuff'). Under UIM rules it is compulsory to use a five-point racing harness within a cockpit canopy – a device that prevents the wearer from being thrown around within the cockpit or causing him to have to brace his body. Canopies started to be fitted over 15 years ago to both deep vee and multihulls. The original canopies were almost exactly the same as the original F16 fighter jet canopy, only modified to suit the marine environment. Indeed, the safety offered by a harness and canopy combination is mightily reassuring, but driving skill is still the most important factor in pushing a boat to its limits.

In fact, taking a canopied boat out in the rough presents new challenges. Treating the canopy with Rain-X or a similar water repellent liquid is essential for forward vision to remain clear. When racing, the same rule applies to the visor of a full-face helmet. I was once schooling a client who didn't attend to his water repellent pre-check, and then, while fiddling to lift the visor because he couldn't see ahead clearly, he went into a corner and turned the boat clean over!

In smaller canopied boats in particular, it will be necessary to go sufficiently fast for the water repellent liquid to begin working. This can cause a Catch 22 situation:

Raceboats are not designed for rough sea states but nonetheless are built to withstand mighty forces and a high degree of the unexpected. Such tolerance allows them to cope with impacts of the kind shown here. © Keith Slater

on the one hand your vision is being obscured by the flying spray and rough water that's conspiring to make high-speed driving difficult, but at the same time you need to get up to race speed in order to get the screen clear. Pushing the throttles hard in a canopied boat is what most competitive drivers will naturally desire to do, but misjudging a wave in this type of boat can have serious consequences. In such an instance, the first thing needed is to ascertain which way up you and the vessel are upon re-entering the water. With your helmet on and the harness holding you tightly to your seat you may feel disorientated, but one easy way to find out is to look at the bubbles outside your screen. If they are travelling from your head to your feet you're the right way up. If, though, the bubbles are travelling the opposite way, you're capsized and need to put into effect your escape routine, first locating your oxygen supply. This is now the moment your training, including your pool dunk testing, goes into action to save your life.

It goes against human instinct to sit upside down in the cramped confines of a cockpit canopy to wait for it to fill with water, but this is what you will have to do in order to equalise the pressure that will allow you to open the escape hatch or window. Of course, your air cylinder will allow you to breathe throughout this process – that is if you remembered to check it was in working order before you took the boat out. Once the hatch has been opened to allow the cockpit to fill and the pressures have equalised, you will then be able to escape. Upon opening the hatch, hold the edge of the opening with one hand – this is to orientate yourself with your escape route. Then release the harness with the other hand and pull yourself out through the opening – but before swimming to the surface, remember to remove the air supply from your mouth. Obvious things like this can become anything but obvious when one is in shock, disorientated or even injured.

CONCLUSION

For me personally, the battle is as important as the result. Fighting the elements and pitting my wits against my fellow competitors is what gives me the thrill I love so much in the high-speed arena. I have won races where there was little in the way of a challenge, and have come third in others where I had to fight to keep my place using every fibre of 'know-how'. You can teach people the skills to drive and control the fastest boats known to man, but it's very hard to teach someone the will to win. Driving to win demands an array of skills and abilities. If you're too aggressive you're sure to break the boat you're depending on to carry you over the finishing line. If, on the other hand, you drive with too much finesse, then you won't win and the smell of laurel leaves about your neck will not be yours to savour. Being blessed with the ability to 'feel', coupled to the desire to win, is what makes a champion. That, and a determined dedication to the pursuit of one's art, which comes from a relentless passion for excellence.

MASTERING THE WAVES: IN THEORY AND PRACTICE

BY HAMISH McDONALD OBE

Hamish McDonald is a world authority on the skills associated with the handling of powered craft of all types, particularly Fast Rescue Craft. Advisor to the Maritime Rescue Institute in Stonehaven and Trustee of the International Lifeboat Federation, McDonald's understanding of helming powered craft in extreme sea states is highlighted here as he deals with the interaction between theory and actual practice.

Over the past 30 years not only has there been a significant development in the production of planing powerboats in the size range 7–24 metres but also in the range of environments they are operated in. In order to gain the maximum safe operational potential of these craft it is essential that their coxswains are able to demonstrate both theoretical understanding of, and practical ability in, their boat's performance characteristics and capabilities, seamanship and waterborne operations. I believe that there has been no radical change to these basic skills since people first went to sea in small boats. Modern technology, whether it is in design, construction, navigation or mechanical control of the vehicle being used, is only an aid to the basics of navigation, boat handling and seamanship. Nothing as yet can, or in my opinion will, take the place of sea sense and common sense as the primary prerequisites of any 'small boat' handler.

With the above in mind I make reference to an old coxswain of rowing harpoon boats on one of Scotland's last whaling ships. On his return to Stonehaven in the early 1960s to carry on small-line and creel fishing in his semi-retirement, I spent a lot of time with him and hero worshipped him as a man of the sea. The 'work philosophy' that James Smith knocked into me was: 'Be at peace with nature, be at peace with your place and tools of work, realise your capabilities, work to your limitations.' It took many years to understand the meaning of such simple words, but I now believe that they can be interpreted to form the basis of the structure and methodology for all small-boat operations. The most fundamental aspect of taking a craft to sea is having an understanding of the natural environment that is going to affect you and that craft. This environment, in the case of most boat crews, relates to a fairly localised stretch of coastline and extending sea area. The two natural elements most affecting that

An all-weather Dutch lifeboat in service with KNRM. This is a highly successful modern self-righting waterjet-powered craft originally inspired by the RNLI's Medina Class. © **KNRM/RIB International** *archives*

environment are air and water. If both are inactive then a static boat, floating at their interface, will display only its own inherent buoyancy and stability characteristics. When movement is added to one or any multiple of the three factors, wind, sea or boat, motion will be induced at the interface. If that movement of factors is constant, then generally the resultant induced motion is predictable; however, if the movement is erratic, then the induced motion will be dynamic, less predictable or even non-predictable.

BOAT HANDLING IN THEORY

'BE AT PEACE WITH NATURE' – SEA STATE, WAVES AND CURRENTS

Sea state is the result of weather conditions. Surface friction between the wind and the sea surface slows the wind, and the energy produced becomes a wave. Waves travel in the same general direction as the wind that causes them, although the water itself makes little progress. Waves can be compared to a stretched-out rope that is given an upward flick: a wave travels along the rope which itself does not move forward. As a wave undulates past, each particle of water takes a circular path, the circles diminishing as they descend from the surface.

In deep water the wave's effect is felt to a depth equal to about half the wavelength, so that a wavelength of 20 metres may cause turbulence down to 10 metres. In shallow water the surface wave energy cannot be absorbed in this way, and breakers result. Much of the measurable properties of a wave, such as its length, height, shape and speed, may be changed by its nature and situation. The only relationship that does not change is that of the wave speed being equal to the wavelength divided by the duration. There is a common belief that every seventh wave is larger than the rest. There is no 'law' about this, but it can sometimes happen when two similar wave trains coincide. The pattern arising from several wave trains becomes complex because of the many and varied influences on them. However, considered very generally, some useful predictions may be made.

When a wind of constant velocity blows for a long time across an ocean unaffected by other wave trains, the waves will reach their maximum size. In such conditions, the average wave height (in metres) will be equal to half the wind speed (in knots). The largest waves will attain a height of 2.5 metres for every 10 knots of wind. A strong wind of 50 knots (Beaufort Scale force 9) has been known to produce a storm wave of some 12 metres high.

Sea and swell

For those working at sea, the most important aspect of the weather is likely to be its effect on the sea surface. Apart from tides and currents, all the sea's activities are the results of wind, which affects the sea in three distinct ways: by the speed of the wind, by the length of time that the wind has been blowing, and by the distance that the wind has blown over the water (the fetch). Locally produced disturbances are called 'seas' and are different from remotely produced ones, called 'swells'. Swells may even be the product of a weather system from across an ocean. A cross-swell is caused by a fresh swell being formed from a different direction to the residual swell; the result can produce a most uncomfortable motion which may complicate shallow-water operations.

Waves

Waves are generated as a result of wind moving over the water's surface. As wind velocity increases white caps appear and, if the wind continues, the waves become higher and longer, developing into 'seas'. There are two major types of waves: the broad rounded waves associated with deep water, and the more choppy waves frequently found in shallow water and confined areas of bays and inland lakes.

Breaking waves are the most dangerous kind of waves encountered in any small-boat operations. The ratio of wave height to length determines how dangerous a wave is: the steeper the gradient of a wave, the more dangerous it is. A 20ft breaker will drop 1,500 tons of water on the average 40ft boat caught under it; only specially designed and constructed craft can survive such an impact.

Plunging waves happen when there is a sudden lack of water ahead of the wave, such as is encountered in a steep rise of the ocean floor, which prevents the wave from completing its orbit and causes the water in the crest to be hurled ahead of the front side of the wave and break with tremendous force. Spilling breakers result when waves of low gradient run over gentle slopes. They normally have a small crest of white water spreading evenly down the wave, and they break slowly and without violence.

Deepwater waves are usually defined as wind waves in water where the depth is greater than half the wavelength. A shallow-water wave is a wave that is travelling in water where the depth is less than half the wavelength, ie if the depth of water is small in comparison to the wavelength, the effect of the bottom is sufficient to change the character of the waves. As the waves travel out from their origin they become swells, developing into a series of relatively equidistant waves which track at more or less a constant speed. Consequently, it is possible to time series of breakers.

Wave series within a dominant swell pattern are irregular because of the constant shifting of wind direction and velocity. Storms at sea can create masses of confused waves and build up some groups higher than others. Experienced coxswains know that breakers vary in size, and that there may not be a regular pattern or sequence to their height. But while the space or interval between series of breakers within the dominant swell may vary, the overall sea state remains fairly regular.

When waves move into shallow water they make contact with the bottom, and friction slows them down; those in the shallowest water move the slowest. As different segments of the wave are travelling in different depths of water, the crests bend and the waves change direction constantly. This is why the wave fronts tend to become roughly parallel to the underwater contours of the shoreline, and explains why an observer on the beach always sees the larger waves coming in directly toward him, while offshore they are seen approaching at an angle. The key to the amount of refraction that takes place is the terrain of the ocean bottom. Waves refracted off shoals can produce very dangerous seas. As they pass on each side of the shoal the waves will be refracted from their original line of travel towards each other. The angle where they meet behind the shoal produces a pyramidal-type sea where the wave crests meet.

Surf

The irregular deepwater waves become organised, by the effect of their contact with the bottom in shallower water, into long regular lines of crests moving in the same direction at similar speeds. As the depth of water decreases and becomes very shallow it becomes impossible for the water particles to complete their orbits. When the orbits break, the waves break and the crest tumbles forward, falling into the trough ahead, usually as a mass of foaming white water. The forward momentum carries this broken

Working off a lee shore is a dangerous zone for any vessel, and an option to be considered by skippers of only the most well-found craft. © ***Safewater Marine***

water forward until the waves' last remaining energy becomes a gentle wash rushing up the beach. The zone where the waves give up this energy, and systematic water motions change to produce violent turbulence, is the surf zone.

Sometimes there are two breaks of surf between the beach and the outer surf line. These may be caused by an outer sand bar or reef against which the seas pile up. The movement of water over such outer bars forms the inner surf belt as the water rolls towards the shore. The nature of surf which forms around inlets depends on the size of approaching swells and the bottom contours of inlet floors and reefs. Coxswains can size up the situation by comparing the height and wavelength of oncoming swells with water depth at the inlet. Breakers will normally form when the swells reach water that is a little deeper than their height. But if there is a strong pushing wind, and if the tide is flowing against the swells, waves crest and break at a depth twice their height. The momentum caused by the breaking top of a wave will cause the water to fall ahead or curl because the water mass is not actually going forward; this momentum gives the curl of breakers its tremendous force.

Wind-driven currents

The wind also causes the sea surface to move as a current. The direction of this wind-driven surface current is not the same as that of the wind, but at an angle of 45° to it. In the northern hemisphere it is 45° to the right of the wind direction, while in the southern hemisphere it is 45° to the left. This effect is due to the Earth's rotation and is called the Coriolis effect. The strength of the wind-driven current lessens with increasing depth. The direction of travel also turns progressively away from the direction of the wind. For example, at 11 metres the current direction is 90° to the wind direction. This spiralling change of direction is known as the Ekman spiral. Its effect increases with its distance from the Equator. Except in very shallow water, the surface current speed is equivalent to approximately 3% of wind speed. It decreases, however, at a rate that depends on the stability of the entire water column, the length of time the wind has been blowing, the fetch, and the size of the waves present.

'BE AT PEACE WITH YOUR WORKPLACE AND TOOLS OF WORK'

A major asset to any coxswain is an extensive understanding of the operating environment. This understanding must not only be category specific but must cover the interrelationship of the various categories: traditional localised weather patterns and their effects; coastline and sub sea surface terrain (cliffs, rocks, reefs, shallows and sand bars); tides, tide ranges and directions; currents, eddies in currents at channel bends, near points, and at places where the bottom is uneven; localised types and calendar of indigenous waterborne activity (shipping lanes, ferries, fishing grounds, fishing methods and recreational activities). The coxswain must be familiar with all these vagaries and implications of their potential working environment; in other words, 'water wise'.

YOUR PLACE OF WORK

Traditional localised weather patterns and their effects

Every geographic area has its own mini meteorological environment, and usually the effects of this are very well known and understood by the local farming and fishing communities. The weather forecasting abilities of these sources cannot be taken as a replacement for actual meteorological forecasts, but should be assessed as good supplemental information. However, if the weather-forecasting capabilities of these sources are to be deemed as supplemental, their experience, relative to the ongoing and immediate future effects of weather conditions, should be given primary consideration. Correct analysis of ongoing weather is fundamental to the livelihoods of these sources.

Coastline and sub sea surface terrain: cliffs, rocks, reefs and sand bars

The coastline and sub sea terrain of the operating area act as the shell holding the water that the boat floats on. Every contour and projection of that shell will have an effect on the boat, either by the shell's potential to be in direct contact with the boat, or by the shell's influence on localised wind patterns, water currents, wave structures and patterns. It is therefore essential that a coxswain is aware of all these aspects and their consequent benefits and hazards.

Tides, tide ranges and directions: currents, eddies in currents at channel bends, near points, and at places where the bottom is uneven

Tides, current and surf have a direct effect upon boat operations. All aspects of boat operations are directly influenced by the movements and actions of the sea, regardless of where the boat may be operating. Water motion and surf conditions play a vital part in successful boat operations. Consequently, all crewmembers must have a clear idea of the nature, causes, and effects of tides, current, surf and related forces.

YOUR TOOLS OF WORK

Of utmost importance to any boat coxswain and crew is belief in, and understanding of, the boat itself. If the coxswain and crew do not have faith in their boat, and a total understanding of its characteristics, then the unit that is the boat and crew will never function to its maximum potential.

Planing-hull designs provide new dimensions to a boat's performance and handling characteristics when compared to traditional displacement boats. The traditional displacement hull form meant that the craft was, by definition, in a displacement mode at all times. Planing boats transcend the displacement mode to a planing mode as the water passing its hull increases to a speed of approximately 14 knots. The handling and seakeeping qualities of planing powerboats have totally different sets of characteristics when in displacement and in planing mode and, in fact, demonstrate a third set of characteristics when in the transition between displacement and planing (hump speed).

The additional speed of the planing boat offers many benefits in terms of acceleration, helm response and transit times, but the relative lightness of the boat causes a faster response to, and a greater range of, induced motion. It is often argued that the speed of the planing boat can help its coxswain to get out of a difficult situation, due to the boat's potential for rapid response. This is certainly true; however, this very speed of response can also get the boat into dangerous situations very rapidly. These factors require that a coxswain must have good anticipation, fast reactions and a high level of mental and physical control, and must spend time developing an overall understanding of a boat's characteristics and be comfortable with its overall performance capabilities.

'REALISE YOUR CAPABILITIES'

In general, the basics of sea handling are similar from one boat to another. It is, however, the understanding and ability to implement actions that give due regard to all of the previously described topics, while also taking into consideration the prevailing weather and sea conditions, that defines 'your capabilities'. The confidence and potential success rate of the coxswain will be greatly enhanced by a wide background of theoretical and practical experience. A coxswain must be fully aware and confident of his/her capabilities for decision making and implementation, and be sure of the boat's capability to perform at the levels dictated by their actions.

'WORK TO YOUR LIMITATIONS'

As the spectrum of knowledge and experience of the coxswain increases, so their capability will be enhanced. Alongside this a more precise awareness of limitations should also develop. A coxswain will have begun to have a worthwhile level of sea sense and boat-handling understanding once realising that 'the more you know, the more you know you don't know'.

BOAT HANDLING IN PRACTICE

A boat in the hands of an experienced and proficient coxswain can be shown at its best when handled correctly in adverse sea states. The first aim of the coxswain is to get the boat into the best trim possible for the prevailing conditions and immediate operational role. Once the craft is planing, speed should be increased to the level that provides best overall control, adequate speed over the ground and maximum crew comfort. An experienced coxswain will seldom, if ever, run the boat at maximum speed, as this leaves no reserve capability for unexpected occurrences, which can and do happen and require immediate response. It is seldom that maximum engine revs actually equate to maximum over-the-ground speed; a craft will only produce top speed if the propulsion system maintains the most efficient water flow past the drive system. There is a decrement in speed performance every time the volume of water that transits the drive system is less than the optimum.

While under way, a boat should be driven to achieve maximum speed while providing the greatest possible degree of comfort for all persons on board. To achieve this, the coxswain must be aware of the formation of wave patterns in which they are operating, and then they must drive the craft in the manner that is most likely to overcome any problems.

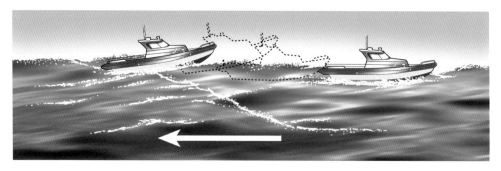

The coxswain should present the boat to oncoming waves at a speed that allows the craft to maintain a slight bow-up angle. This ensures that after passing the crest of the wave, after possibly jumping partially or completely out of the water, the boat will land in a relatively comfortable manner, and also in the best position of readiness for the next wave. The craft should be driven in such a way that it maintains an upright position at all times, with no tendency to land on either of its forward shoulders or its side. It must be stressed that the speed of the craft is critical, and the correct speed required may vary greatly according to the circumstances and sea state.

Most sea swell conditions, except those that are very steep, present few problems to a well-found boat. Best speed can be maintained without the craft's head being thrown up and jumping occurring. In such moderate conditions the coxswain should maintain a speed that allows the craft to keep contact with the water surface and does not induce jumping. In adverse sea state conditions it may be impossible for the helmsman to prevent jumping when travelling at speed, but he should aim for a shallow angle of re-entry.

It is usually high winds with broken sea states that cause most concern. In such conditions the coxswain must ensure that they do not allow the boat's bow to rear up too violently as this may cause a sailing effect, which can be dangerous.

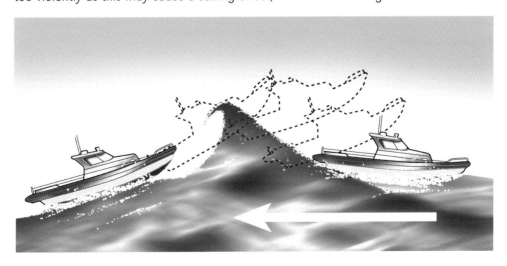

When a boat is presented with a wave that has a curling broken crest, it is essential that the craft is given enough speed and power to break through this wave, but not with so much speed as to cause a very steep angle of re-entry. These are the conditions in which only coxswain experience and boat capability can ensure safe operations. It is also of the greatest importance to accelerate into the crest at the right time to bring the bow up; if the nose is allowed to drop and then accelerated into the sea, it is possible to dig in as the curling water passes over the bow. The boat may easily get caught up in the wave and either be held stationary, or even be dragged along inside the wave for some considerable time.

Track of the boat to avoid the broken curl of the wave

Once the sea state has been well developed a wave may form into a crest, break, and then the broken surf runs down the face of the swell. The coxswain should attempt to take the wave at the point where the crest has not yet broken.

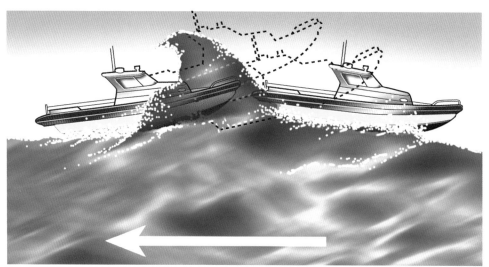

Track of the boat to avoid the broken face of the wave

This type of wave, where the surf runs cleanly down the face, does not present too many problems, even if the boat has to go through the broken water. The broken surf may well pass right over the boat as the craft settles lower in the wave to find the density of water to support its displacement. It is essential in these conditions that the craft is well-found and all personnel and equipment are secured. In such adverse sea states it may well be necessary to throttle right back, only accelerating slightly prior to breasting the crest of the wave to allow safe penetration.

The most dangerous type of wave is a heavy dumping sea, and it is always greatly preferable to dodge such conditions when possible. These waves occur when a large curling unbroken crest forms, then becomes unstable. The crest accelerates and crashes down the face of the still-curling wave. These waves present an almost vertical wall of dense water, with broken surf falling in front. A well-designed and fitted-out boat with a well-trained crew may be capable of withstanding such conditions, but this is dependent on the volume and weight of water landing on the craft, and damage to fittings may well occur. If unable to avoid such a wave, the coxswain must ensure that all personnel aboard the boat are well secured. The coxswain must maintain enough way on the craft to keep its bow into the direction of the wave, approximately 5–10° off a 0° heading to the wave crest. The craft will normally behave in the same manner as a surfboard and pop out the back of the wave. If, however, the coxswain cannot keep the craft's head into the sea and allows it to go beyond 30° off the 0° heading, the possibility of capsize occurring increases significantly.

When a boat has to run broadside to, or diagonally across, the seas in adverse conditions, the helmsman should avoid crossing the path of waves near to the face of their crests. The normal practice is to either run round the back of the bigger waves, or run clear down the face of the wave before altering back onto course. By altering course to avoid the biggest seas, and allowing the craft the easiest passage, best speed can be made.

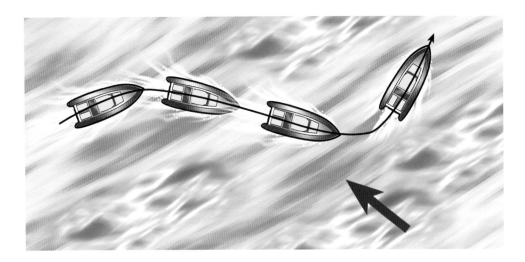

If, on approaching a wave face, the boat starts to take a list away from it, the coxswain should either immediately turn to run directly before the wave, if the craft has the performance to do so, or turn to a 5–10° heading toward it. Under no circumstance must the coxswain allow the boat to maintain a downside list, as the craft will rapidly begin to lift its keel line and can easily dip its downside deck edge and induce a capsize. There may well be times, especially in the dark, when it is impossible to avoid an oncoming wave; in situations like these the coxswain must make every effort to present the craft to the wave in the best manner possible.

Running before in adverse sea conditions can be the most dangerous position for any vessel; however, a well-designed craft with the correct handling and performance capabilities can show off its greatest asset in just such situations when operated proficiently. Detailed oceanographic studies have shown that normal maximum wave speed in adverse sea states is approximately 24 knots. This means that the boat, with speeds in excess of 30 knots, should be able to outrun most normal adverse sea conditions. It must be realized, however, that in certain positions on each wave the boat's speed potential will be reduced, owing to the changes in water density on the surface as the water becomes aerated, and because of the rotational factors of water flow within the wave structure.

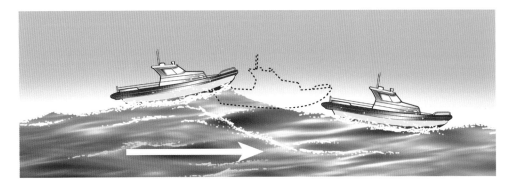

The coxswain must know exactly where to position his or her craft when running before in adverse sea conditions. In slight and moderate sea conditions, the helmsman can maintain almost full speed but must be mindful to ensure that the boat's bow is allowed to rise prior to accelerating up the back of the wave ahead. It should also be noted that, even in moderate sea conditions, if the coxswain decides to jump the wave ahead while running before, the re-entry point into the water may be further away than expected. This is because, almost inevitably in such conditions, the boat will land in the trough and, unless the coxswain has been very careful with the angle of passing over the crest, may be presented with a flat landing.

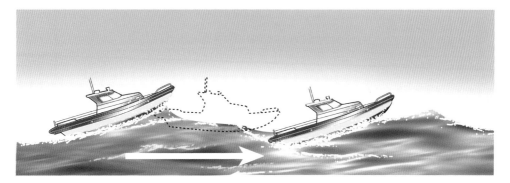

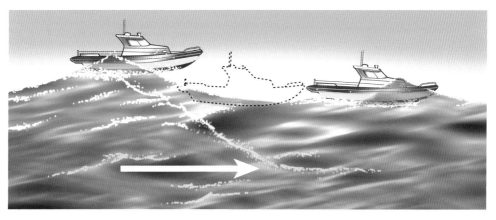

Once the wave size increases, the boat tends only to negotiate the crest and then re-enter the water still on the face of the same wave. It now becomes necessary for the helmsman to allow the boat to regain the correct bow-up attitude before accelerating into the back of the next wave. If this is not achieved the ride becomes unnecessarily uncomfortable, as the bow of the craft is forced into the back of the wave. At this position on a wave, it is totally dependent on the forward section hull form and fairing as to whether the boat and its crew 'stuff' into the back of the wave face. 'Stuffing' a boat can be dangerous to boat and crew. These dangers can be multiplied many times if the 'stuffing' is sufficiently violent to decelerate the boat to the point where the crest of the wave just negotiated catches up with the now stalled craft, and causes it to kedge on its deck edge and subsequently capsize. It is of utmost importance that every effort is made by coxswains to avoid the possibility of 'stuffing' their craft.

When the sea state has increased in size to near gale force wind states, then the wave size may well be such that it becomes too risky to attempt jumping the crest in front or allowing the craft to be positioned close to the following wave crest. The larger the wave height, the greater the problems that exist due to the likely unstable nature of the wave crest. It can be very hazardous to be positioned too close to the back of the preceding wave crest as this area of water is often highly aerated and can drastically affect the performance of the craft. It is also possible that the wave crest and back will collapse vertically down its own face, and if the boat is positioned too near the crest it may well fall below the 'dumping' sea.

It is essential that the boat's speed and acceleration are used to the full when running before in heavy seas. Ideally, the boat should be positioned behind the crest of preceding waves, away from the possible area of aeration, but in front of the base of the trough. This position allows a greater view of the surrounding conditions, and the craft is eased along by the volume of surface water in the wave. The coxswain will vary the craft's engine revs to allow the position to be maintained, and it is often possible to cover a considerable distance on the back of one wave before it is spent. It is also advisable to attempt to run on the waves that appear evenly formed. As each wave begins to spend, the coxswain should manoeuvre the craft diagonally across the sea state to pick up another suitable wave.

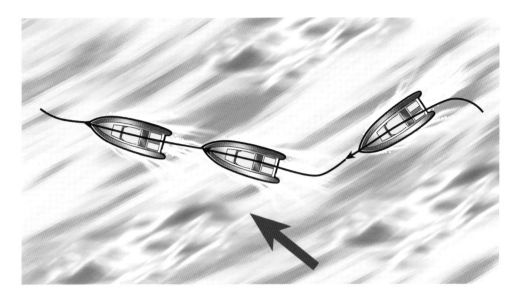

The coxswain must remember that if the boat is made to track diagonally across the front, as opposed to the back, of the waves, it will almost certainly begin to accelerate due to the relative speeds of craft and waves. This situation can be exhilarating but also dangerous, as the handling characteristics of the craft are reduced. In fact, it is possible that the boat will behave like a powered surfboard, and as the acceleration of the water increases, so will the over-the-ground speed of the boat; this reduces the efficiency of the propulsion drive system and the steering, which in turn impacts on the coxswain's control of the boat. The coxswain should always be aware of the possibility of this effect occurring and should drive the craft in a manner most likely to reduce all the known risk factors.

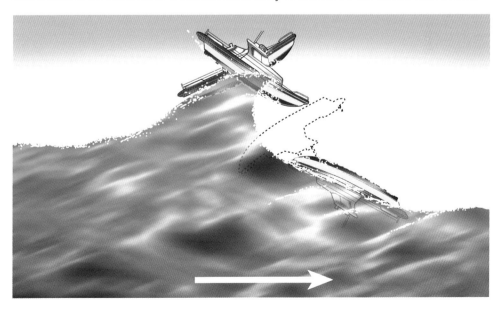

The most hazardous position for the craft while running before is that of being too near the crest of the wave. If the craft does fall down the face of such well-formed waves it can easily be pitchpoled by the sheer speed and weight of the following wave. As the craft accelerates down the face of the crest, the bow will dig into the denser water of the trough because of the extreme angle of descent. This will act as a braking mechanism. The stern of the craft is held in the fast-moving water adjacent to the wave crest and, in extreme circumstances, the force of water on the stern will roll the craft stern over bow. Unlike any other capsize situation where the crewmembers are in the middle of the circle of rotation and therefore experience a deceleration of forces, a pitchpole means that the crew are on the outside of the circle of rotation and are therefore exposed to accelerating forces. A pitchpole event almost invariably results in damage to the craft, with a high potential for injury to personnel on board.

CONCLUSION

In this chapter, then, I hope I have made clear the undeniable and very obvious connection between theory and genuine practice. In just the same way that every detail relating to each wave type will have a direct effect on a vessel's behaviour, so too will every response and decision on the part of the helmsman influence whether a craft succeeds or founders amidst extreme sea states.

INDEX